4-

3/24

FOOD & WINE

Simple Suppers

BY THE EDITORS OF *FOOD & WINE*

SCALLOP GRENOBLOISE (P. 149)

FOOD & WINE
BOOKS

FOOD & WINE® MAGAZINE
EDITOR IN CHIEF Hunter Lewis
VICE PRESIDENT/GENERAL MANAGER Michelle Edelbaum
DEPUTY EDITOR Melanie Hansche
SENIOR EDITORIAL DIRECTOR Sean Flynn
EXECUTIVE EDITOR Karen Shimizu
CREATIVE DIRECTOR Winslow Taft
ASSOCIATE EDITORIAL DIRECTOR, FOOD Chandra Ram
EXECUTIVE WINE EDITOR Ray Isle
MANAGING EDITOR Caitlin Murphree Miller
PHOTO DIRECTOR Tori Katherman

FOOD & EDITORIAL
RESTAURANT EDITOR Khushbu Shah
SENIOR FOOD EDITOR Cheryl Slocum
FOOD EDITOR Paige Grandjean
ASSOCIATE EDITOR Amelia Schwartz
ASSISTANT FOOD EDITOR Andee McKenzie
ASSISTANT EDITOR Lucy Simon
BUSINESS MANAGER Alice Eldridge Summerville

COPY, RESEARCH & PRODUCTION
PRODUCTION DIRECTOR Liz Rhoades
COPY EDITORS Erin Clyburn, Wynn Duvall

DESIGN & PHOTOGRAPHY
ART DIRECTOR James Slocum
PHOTO EDITOR Dan Bailey
ASSISTANT DESIGNER Ann Martin Fole

CULINARY DIRECTOR AT LARGE Justin Chapple
EXECUTIVE PRODUCER Kwame Onwuachi

DIGITAL
EXECUTIVE FEATURES EDITOR Kat Kinsman
SENIOR EDITOR Maria Yagoda
SENIOR DRINKS EDITOR Oset Babür-Winter
SENIOR EDITOR, NEWS AND TRENDING Adam Campbell-Schmitt
SENIOR EDITOR, OPERATIONS Ashley Day
SENIOR SOCIAL MEDIA EDITOR Sam Gutierrez
SOCIAL MEDIA EDITOR Merlyn Miller
SENIOR DIGITAL PRODUCER Elsa Säätelä
PHOTO EDITORS Alexis Camarena-Anderson, Matt Taylor-Gross
NEWS WRITER Stacey Leasca

DOTDASH MEREDITH CONSUMER MARKETING
DIRECTOR OF DIRECT MARKETING-BOOKS Daniel Fagan
MARKETING OPERATIONS MANAGER Max Daily
MARKETING MANAGER Kylie Dazzo
CONTENT MANAGER Julie Doll
SENIOR MARKETING COORDINATOR Elizabeth Moore
SENIOR PRODUCTION MANAGER Liza Ward

WATERBURY PUBLICATIONS, INC.
EDITORIAL DIRECTOR Lisa Kingsley
CREATIVE DIRECTOR Ken Carlson
ASSOCIATE DESIGN DIRECTOR Doug Samuelson
CONTRIBUTING COPY EDITOR Russell Santana, E4 Editorial Services
CONTRIBUTING PROOFREADER Carrie Truesdell
CONTRIBUTING INDEXER Alberto Sancho, E4 Editorial Services

CONTENTS

THE JOYS OF SUPPER

THERE ARE OCCASIONS THAT CALL FOR a fancy multicourse dinner—an elaborate appetizer, an elegant starter soup, a main dish that wows, a sophisticated and fussy dessert. But most days—and especially on weeknights—you want to come home and make something that satisfies your hunger and smooths away the stresses of the day without a long list of ingredients and a lot of effort. In other words, a simple supper.

The word "supper" implies simplicity, ease, and comfort. This book celebrates the concept of supper with a wide array of pasta and grain dishes, simple roasted and grilled meats, poultry, and seafood, fresh vegetable salads and sides, meatless dishes, and even dessert. On a cool fall or cold winter night, warm up with Pork Loin Braised with Mushrooms and Wine (p. 57) or piquant Pulling-from-the-Pantry Puttanesca (p. 156). When the weather warms, turn to a simple grilled fish dish such as Grilled Mahi-Mahi with Lemongrass-Lime Aïoli (p. 130), with chile-spiked Red, Hot, and Cool Strawberries (p. 252) for dessert. For weeknight entertaining, start with Baked Cheese and Herbs and Crudités (p. 10) followed by a main dish of make-ahead chilled Spice-Crusted Beef Tenderloin with Caper Vinaigrette (p. 38) or Cold Roasted Leg of Lamb with Cilantro-Jalapeño Yogurt (p. 66). And for those truly exhausting days, when the world has got you down and you can't fathom making a meal but need something that nurtures you in multiple ways, sit down to the simplest of suppers—a creamy Boursin Omelet (p. 178) for one, accompanied by some crusty baguette, a crisp green salad, and a glass of chilled sparkling wine.

Supper—it's that simple.

THE EDITORS OF FOOD & WINE

CHARRED FOCACCIA AND
STEAK SALAD (P. 186)

APPETIZERS & COCKTAILS

When hosting a dinner party, you want to keep each course as uncomplicated as possible. These simple starters can be part of a multicourse menu, or a few can constitute a spread of nibbles for more casual entertaining—enjoyed while sipping a drink that fits the season and occasion.

SPICY TUNA SUSHI "BISCOTTI" (P. 8)
AVOCADO SUSHI "BISCOTTI" (P. 9)
NASU MISO SUSHI "BISCOTTI" (P. 8)

SPICY TUNA SUSHI "BISCOTTI"

PHOTO P. 7

At Sushi Note in Sherman Oaks, California, chef Kiminobu Saito offers wine-friendly bites like sushi biscotti, crispy thin cakes of fried sushi rice with toppings like spicy tuna or miso-basted eggplant that play well with wines selected by co-owner Dave Gibbs. For pairing with sushi, Gibbs says he thinks about both the texture of the fish—whether it's firm, chewy, or delicate—and any sauces or garnishes. Although sometimes, he doesn't have to think too hard about what to open next: "At the moment," he says, "we're fairly obsessed with just how fantastically well old [2008] Stony Hill Gewürztraminer pairs with everything."

TOTAL 25 MIN; MAKES 20

- 7 oz. sushi-grade fresh tuna, cut into small cubes (about 1 cup)
- 2 Tbsp. thinly sliced scallions
- 2 Tbsp. masago (orange salt-cured smelt roe) (such as Sushikko)
- 2 Tbsp. Kewpie mayonnaise
- 1½ Tbsp. ponzu
- ¾ tsp. la-yu (Japanese chile oil)
- ¼ tsp. kosher salt
- 20 Crispy Rice Cakes (recipe opposite)
- 1 serrano chile, seeded and thinly sliced

Stir together tuna, scallions, masago, mayonnaise, ponzu, la-yu, and salt in a medium bowl. Top each Crispy Rice Cake with about 1 teaspoon tuna mixture and 2 or 3 serrano slices, and serve immediately. —KIMINOBU SAITO

WINE Pair with a Ovum Base Line Riesling or Stony Hill Gewürztraminer

NASU MISO SUSHI "BISCOTTI"

PHOTO P. 7

TOTAL 40 MIN; MAKES 18

- 1 (10-oz.) Japanese eggplant, cut into ½-inch cubes (about 3 cups)
- 3 Tbsp. canola oil
  Cooking spray
- ¼ cup white miso
- 3 Tbsp. granulated sugar
- 18 Crispy Rice Cakes (recipe opposite)
  Pinch of kosher salt

1 Preheat oven to 425°F. Toss together eggplant and oil in a medium bowl. Spread in an even layer on an aluminum foil–lined baking sheet coated with cooking spray. Bake until tender, about 20 minutes, stirring halfway through.

2 Meanwhile, bring a small saucepan of water to a simmer over low. Place miso and sugar in a small heatproof bowl large enough to cover top of saucepan. Set bowl on top of saucepan, creating a double boiler. Cook, stirring occasionally, until smooth, about 20 minutes. Remove from heat; stir in roasted eggplant. Top each Crispy Rice Cake with about 1 teaspoon warm miso topping, and sprinkle with salt. —KIMINOBU SAITO

WINE Mount Eden Chardonnay or Saget La Perrière Marie de Beauregard Vouvray

AVOCADO SUSHI "BISCOTTI"

PHOTO P. 7

TOTAL 15 MIN; MAKES 18

1 medium (5 oz.) ripe avocado
18 Crispy Rice Cakes (recipe follows)
Flaky sea salt (such as Maldon)

Cut avocado in half lengthwise. Cut each half crosswise into 2 pieces; cut each piece into 14 thin slices. Shingle 3 or 4 avocado slices over each Crispy Rice Cake. Sprinkle with salt to taste. Serve immediately. —KIMINOBU SAITO

WINE Pour a Lail Blueprint Sauvignon Blanc or a iLauri Tavo Pinot Grigio

CRISPY RICE CAKES

ACTIVE 30 MIN; TOTAL 8 HR 55 MIN; MAKES 56

6 cups cooked sushi rice, cooled
3 Tbsp. rice vinegar
2 Tbsp. granulated sugar
1 Tbsp. plus 1/8 tsp. kosher salt
Cooking spray
3 Tbsp. canola oil

1 Line a rimmed quarter sheet pan with plastic wrap, leaving 2 inches of overhang on all sides. Place rice in a large bowl. Stir together rice vinegar, sugar, and salt in a small bowl until salt is dissolved. Drizzle over rice; gently fold together. Lightly pack rice into a 1-cup dry measuring cup; invert onto prepared pan. Repeat with remaining rice, creating 2 rows of 3. Moisten hands slightly; gently press rice into an even layer. Place another piece of plastic wrap directly on surface of rice; press firmly into a compact, even layer (1/2 inch to 5/8 inch thick). Fold overhanging plastic wrap over top, gently pressing on top and smoothing outer edges. Chill 8 hours or overnight.

2 Preheat oven to 475°F with oven racks in middle and lower third of oven. Remove baking sheet from refrigerator. Unwrap plastic wrap, and remove top piece on rice; invert rice onto a work surface. Remove plastic wrap from back. Cut into 56 (1½- × 1-inch) pieces. Lightly coat top of rice pieces with cooking spray. Brush 2 rimmed baking sheets with oil. Place 28 rice pieces, cooking spray–coated sides down, on each oiled baking sheet. Bake until crisp and lightly golden, 14 to 20 minutes. Flip and top immediately. —KIMINOBU SAITO

MANGO-AND-HALLOUMI FRITTO MISTO

Seafood and vegetables are often the stars of fritto misto (mixed fry). In this version, F&W's Justin Chapple swaps in ripe but firm mangoes and sturdy Halloumi cheese, showcasing their incredible versatility. A batter of fizzy club soda, flour, and cornstarch forms a crust that is light but dippable.

ACTIVE 30 MIN; TOTAL 35 MIN; SERVES 6

Neutral oil (such as grapeseed), for frying

2 cups all-purpose flour (about 8½ oz.)

½ cup cornstarch (about 2¼ oz.)

1 tsp. baking powder

2 tsp. kosher salt, divided

2½ cups club soda

2 ripe but firm medium mangoes, peeled and cut into ¾-inch wedges

8 oz. Halloumi cheese, cut into 1-inch pieces

6 medium scallions, cut into 4-inch pieces

1 medium lemon, thinly sliced and seeded

Chile oil, for serving

1 Heat 2 inches of neutral oil in a large Dutch oven over medium-high to 360°F. Whisk together flour, cornstarch, baking powder, and 1 teaspoon salt in a large bowl. Whisk in club soda until mixture is smooth and the consistency of thin pancake batter. Let batter stand 5 minutes.

2 Working in batches, dip mango wedges, Halloumi pieces, scallion pieces, and lemon slices in batter, letting excess drip off; add to hot oil. Fry, turning occasionally, until golden and crispy, 1 to 3 minutes depending on size. Transfer to a wire rack set over a baking sheet. Sprinkle fritto misto with remaining 1 teaspoon salt. Serve with chile oil for dipping. —JUSTIN CHAPPLE

WINE Melony, bright Loire white: Domaine Champalou Vouvray Sec

BAKED CHEESE WITH HERBS AND CRUDITÉS

French etiquette may relegate cheese to its own course between dinner and dessert, but it's easy to rationalize adding cheese to the table when it's warm and dippable and surrounded by fresh vegetables. A splash of vermouth helps cut through the richness of the cheese and allows the herbs and garlic to permeate.

ACTIVE 10 MIN; TOTAL 25 MIN; SERVES 6 TO 8

2 (8- to 9-oz.) rounds Camembert or Brie cheese

1 to 2 garlic cloves, peeled and thinly sliced

2 to 3 Tbsp. (1 to 1½ oz.) dry vermouth, fino sherry, or dry white wine

1 bunch (½ oz.) fresh rosemary

1 bunch (½ oz.) fresh thyme

1 Tbsp. extra virgin olive oil

Assorted crudités, for serving

1 Preheat oven to 350°F. Remove and discard paper wrapping from cheese rounds. If cheese is packaged in thin wooden boxes, return round to bottom of box. Discard wooden lid. Using butcher's twine, tie twine around outside of bottom of box to ensure it doesn't open during baking.

2 Using a sharp paring knife, make 6 to 8 (½-inch-deep) slices in top of each cheese round. Press garlic slices into slits. Drizzle each cheese round with vermouth. Toss together rosemary and thyme with olive oil. Arrange herbs in an even layer, just large enough to use as a bed for cheese rounds, on a parchment paper–lined baking sheet. Place cheese rounds on herb bed. (Unwrapped cheese rounds can also be baked in small, ovenproof ramekins on herbs.)

3 Bake until cheese is soft and melty, 15 to 20 minutes. Serve immediately with crudités. —REBEKAH PEPPLER

MANGO-AND-HALLOUMI
FRITTO MISTO

CRISPY HEN-OF-THE-WOODS
MUSHROOMS WITH MARINARA
AND PARMIGIANO-REGGIANO

CRISPY HEN-OF-THE-WOODS MUSHROOMS
WITH MARINARA AND PARMIGIANO-REGGIANO

Feathery and dramatic, hen-of-the-woods mushrooms (also known as maitake) become delightfully crispy when fried. You know they are nearly ready when the sizzling oil starts to subside. Here, prepared marinara and freshly grated Parmigiano-Reggiano cheese give these crispy mushrooms Italian-American flair.

TOTAL 25 MIN; SERVES 4

2 cups marinara sauce

Canola oil

1¼ lb. fresh whole hen-of-the-woods (maitake) mushroom heads (about 4 heads)

Kosher salt, to taste

Freshly grated Parmigiano-Reggiano cheese, for serving

Finely chopped fresh flat-leaf parsley, for garnish

Lemon wedges, for serving

1 Heat marinara in a medium saucepan over medium, stirring occasionally, until hot, about 5 minutes. Cover and keep warm over very low.

2 Pour oil to a depth of 3 inches in a large, heavy saucepan or Dutch oven; heat over medium-high until oil reaches 350°F. Working in batches if needed, fry mushrooms in hot oil, carefully turning occasionally, until just crisp, about 5 minutes. Transfer to a plate lined with paper towels to drain. Trim off tough ends; season with salt to taste.

3 Spoon marinara onto plates or a platter, and top with mushrooms. Generously sprinkle with freshly grated Parmigiano-Reggiano cheese, and garnish with parsley. Serve with lemon wedges. —JUSTIN CHAPPLE

WINE Earthy, berry-forward Chianti: Castello di Volpaia Chianti Classico

NOTE Find hen-of-the-woods mushrooms at specialty and Asian grocery stores or online at dartagnan.com.

SHERRY-SCENTED MUSHROOM DUXELLES

Named for the 17th-century French marquis d'Uxelles, duxelles is a mixture of minced mushrooms cooked down in butter with shallots and deglazed with wine. It's delicious spread on small toasts as an appetizer—or folded into omelets as a filling or tossed with hot cooked pasta as a sauce.

ACTIVE 35 MIN; TOTAL 45 MIN; SERVES 6

1½ lb. fresh cremini mushrooms

6 Tbsp. unsalted butter (3 oz.)

3 small shallots, finely chopped (about ¾ cup)

½ tsp. plus a pinch of kosher salt, divided, plus more to taste

¼ tsp. black pepper, plus more to taste

3 Tbsp. (1½ oz.) dry sherry

1½ tsp. chopped fresh thyme

Pinch of freshly grated nutmeg

1 Working in about 4 batches, pulse mushrooms in a food processor until very finely chopped, about 8 pulses per batch. Transfer chopped mushrooms to a bowl; set aside.

2 Melt butter in a large skillet over medium. Add shallots and a pinch of salt, and cook, stirring often, until shallots are softened, about 3 minutes. Add finely chopped mushrooms, pepper, and remaining ½ teaspoon salt. Increase heat to medium-high, and cook, stirring occasionally, until mushrooms start to release their liquid, about 6 minutes. Reduce heat to low; cook, stirring occasionally, until liquid has evaporated and mushrooms look dry, about 20 minutes. Stir in sherry, thyme, and nutmeg, and cook, stirring occasionally, until sherry has evaporated, about 2 minutes. Remove pan from heat. Season duxelles with salt and pepper to taste. Let cool slightly, about 10 minutes. —JUSTIN CHAPPLE

MAKE AHEAD Store in an airtight container in refrigerator up to 1 week, or freeze up to 1 month.

MUHAMMARA (ROASTED RED PEPPER AND WALNUT DIP)

This recipe comes to F&W from Jeanette Chawki, an instructor in Lebanese cooking through The League of Kitchens in New York City. Smooth, thick, and layered with flavor, this mildly spicy dip of roasted red bell peppers and toasted walnuts is thickened with finely ground crispy breadsticks. Pomegranate molasses adds a piquancy that plays off the sweetness of the juicy roasted bell peppers, and spicy pepper paste brings just a touch of heat. This dip is delicious on pitas, or serve it with fresh vegetables for dunking.

ACTIVE 25 MIN; TOTAL 45 MIN; SERVES 4 TO 6

2 medium-size red bell peppers

½ cup plus 1 Tbsp. olive oil, divided, plus more for drizzling

4 oz. plain breadsticks (about 8 pieces)

1 cup toasted walnut halves, plus 11 toasted walnut halves, divided

¾ cup minced white onion

1 garlic clove, minced

2 Tbsp. spicy pepper paste

2 Tbsp. tomato paste

2 Tbsp. pomegranate molasses or 1 Tbsp. fresh lemon juice

1 tsp. ground cumin

1 tsp. paprika

½ tsp. Aleppo pepper

3 Tbsp. tahini

½ tsp. kosher salt

1 Preheat oven to 400°F. Line a rimmed baking sheet with parchment paper; set aside. Trim and discard tops and bottoms from bell peppers. Cut each trimmed bell pepper lengthwise into 4 equal pieces; remove and discard ribs and seeds. Toss together bell pepper pieces and 1 tablespoon oil in a medium bowl. Arrange pepper pieces, skin side up, in a single layer on prepared baking sheet. Roast in preheated oven until tender, 15 to 20 minutes. Transfer roasted bell peppers to a medium bowl, and cover with plastic wrap. Let stand at room temperature to steam until completely tender and cool enough to handle, about 10 minutes. Remove and discard skins from bell peppers; set bell peppers aside. Reserve any juices in bowl.

2 Process breadsticks in a food processor until finely ground. Pass finely ground breadsticks through a fine wire-mesh strainer into a medium bowl. Set aside ½ cup fine breadcrumbs in a small bowl; reserve any remaining breadcrumbs and large unsifted crumbs for another use. Process 1 cup walnuts in food processor until finely ground, about 30 seconds. Place ground walnuts in a separate small bowl; set aside. Pulse onion and garlic in food processor until well combined and finely minced, stopping to scrape down sides as needed, 3 to 5 pulses. Add roasted bell peppers and reserved juices to food processor; process until smooth, stopping to scrape down sides as needed, about 1 minute. Add ground walnuts, reserved ½ cup breadcrumbs, spicy pepper paste, tomato paste, pomegranate molasses, cumin, paprika, and Aleppo pepper; process until smooth, about 1 minute. Add tahini, salt, and remaining ½ cup oil; process until smooth and thick, stopping to scrape down sides as needed, about 30 seconds.

3 Scoop muhammara onto a plate, and smooth out into an even circle. Using the back of a large spoon, swirl just inside the border to create a shallow moat, keeping the middle slightly mounded. Arrange 10 walnut halves around border, and place remaining 1 walnut half in the middle. Garnish with a drizzle of oil.
—JEANETTE CHAWKI

MAKE AHEAD Muhammara may be stored in an airtight container in refrigerator up to 3 days.

NOTE Find spicy pepper paste, pomegranate molasses, and Aleppo pepper at Middle Eastern grocery stores or online at kalustyans.com.

CROSTINI WITH GRILLED SWEET ONIONS AND BLUE CHEESE

PHOTO P. 266

Classically trained chef Andrae Bopp has worked at Michelin-starred restaurants and is currently chef-owner of AK's Mercado in Walla Walla, Washington. He's also a white water rafting guide on the Snake River on the Idaho-Oregon border. On the river, Bopp wraps whole sweet Walla Walla onions in foil and tosses them into the coals of the campfire to roast and caramelize; here, we've adapted his recipe for your home grill. Don't skip the zippy honey-vinegar drizzle—it coaxes out even more flavor from the sweet onions and balances the blue cheese.

ACTIVE 5 MIN; TOTAL 45 MIN; SERVES 12

- 2 large Walla Walla or sweet onions, each cut into 4 wedges (root end left intact)
- 2 Tbsp. plus 2 tsp. aged sherry vinegar, divided
- 4 tsp. extra virgin olive oil
- 1 tsp. fine sea salt
- ½ tsp. black pepper
- 10 oz. blue cheese, softened (about 2½ cups)
- 1 baguette, sliced and grilled or toasted
- ¼ cup honey
- ½ cup toasted pine nuts
- Fresh thyme leaves, for garnish

1 Place onion wedges, cut sides up, on a rimmed baking sheet. Drizzle evenly with 2 tablespoons vinegar and the oil; sprinkle evenly with salt and pepper.

2 Preheat a gas grill to medium (350°F to 400°F) on one side, or push hot coals to one side of a charcoal grill. Place onion wedges, cut sides up, on oiled grates over unlit side of grill. Grill, covered, 20 minutes. Turn onions onto one cut side; grill, covered, until grill marks form, about 10 minutes. Turn onions onto remaining cut side; grill, covered, until tender, about 10 minutes. Remove from heat.

3 Let onions cool slightly; discard any outer charred pieces. Finely chop 2 onion wedges; stir together with softened blue cheese in a medium bowl until combined. Cut remaining onion wedges lengthwise into thinner wedges, and separate into petals. Spread blue cheese mixture evenly over baguette slices; top with onion petals. Whisk together honey and remaining 2 teaspoons vinegar; drizzle over crostini. Sprinkle with pine nuts; garnish with thyme leaves.
—ANDRAE BOPP

WINE Tangy Washington state Riesling: Sleight of Hand Cellars The Magician

CORN HUSK-GRILLED GOAT CHEESE
WITH CORN RELISH AND HONEY

These grilled packets of cheese are tangy, sweet, and smoky—the perfect appetizer on a summer night.

TOTAL 35 MIN; SERVES 4

- 2 large ears fresh yellow corn
- 1 (8-oz.) goat cheese log, cut in half crosswise, at room temperature
- 2 scallions, white and light green parts only, thinly sliced
- 1 red Fresno chile or red jalapeño, stemmed, seeded, and finely chopped
- 4 tsp. extra virgin olive oil
- 1 Tbsp. fresh lime juice
- 1 tsp. kosher salt
- Pinch of black pepper
- 3 Tbsp. torn fresh basil
- 3 Tbsp. coarsely chopped fresh cilantro
- 2 Tbsp. honey
- Grilled crostini, for serving

1 Open vents of a charcoal grill completely. Light a charcoal chimney starter filled with briquettes. When briquettes are covered with gray ash, pour onto bottom grate of grill, and push to one side. Adjust vents as needed to maintain an internal temperature of about 500°F. (If using a gas grill, preheat to very high [about 500°F] on one side.)

2 Working with 1 ear of corn at a time, carefully remove husk, making sure not to tear husk. Remove and discard silk from corn, and set corn aside. Overlap a few of the long edges of husk pieces on a work surface; place 1 goat cheese half lengthwise down center. Continue overlapping remaining husk pieces, cupping them around goat cheese to completely enclose log. (You are essentially replacing the corn cob with the cheese log.) Gather excess husk pieces at each end, and tie with kitchen twine or a piece of corn husk, securing cheese in a cylindrical packet. Repeat with remaining ear of corn and remaining half of goat cheese.

3 Stir together scallions, chile, olive oil, lime juice, salt, and black pepper in a medium bowl; set aside.

4 Place goat cheese packets and corn on oiled grates over lit side of grill. Grill, covered, turning goat cheese packets and corn often, until packets are charred and cheese is softened, about 4 minutes. Transfer goat cheese packets to unlit side of grill to keep warm. Continue grilling corn, covered, turning often, until charred in spots and tender, 10 to 12 minutes.

5 Place grilled corn on a cutting board. Using a clean kitchen towel or pair of tongs to stand corn upright, cut kernels from cobs. Add corn kernels, basil, and cilantro to scallion mixture, and toss to combine.

6 Place cheese packets on a serving platter. Cut a slit lengthwise through top layer of charred husks to expose goat cheese. Drizzle cheese with honey, and spoon corn relish over top. Serve hot with grilled crostini. —ANDREA SLONECKER

MAKE AHEAD Recipe may be prepared through Step 3, covered, and chilled until ready to grill, up to 1 day.

WINE Strawberry-scented sparkling rosé: NV J Vineyards Brut

GOAT CHEESE AND QUAIL EGG CANAPÉS

Winemakers Mireia Taribó and Tara Gomez served these canapés of airy whipped goat cheese and tender quail eggs on crisp crackers as a first course at a feast at their winery, Camins 2 Dreams, in Santa Barbara County, California.

ACTIVE 25 MIN; TOTAL 30 MIN; SERVES 8

12 quail eggs

3 Tbsp. chia seeds

2 oz. goat cheese (about ½ cup), chilled

½ cup heavy cream

Kosher salt, to taste

24 cornmeal or polenta crackers (such as Farmer's Pantry Original Cornbread Crisps)

Thinly sliced fresh white sage leaves and lemon peel strips, for garnish

1 Place quail eggs in a small saucepan, and add cold water to cover by 1 inch. Bring to a boil, uncovered, over medium-high. Boil 3 minutes. Using a slotted spoon, transfer eggs to a bowl of ice water. Let stand 5 minutes. Peel eggs; set aside.

2 Toast chia seeds in a small skillet over medium, stirring often, until fragrant and glistening, 3 to 4 minutes. Transfer seeds to a bowl; set aside.

3 Combine goat cheese and heavy cream in bowl of a stand mixer fitted with the whisk attachment. Start beating on low speed, and gradually increase speed to medium-high, beating until mixture forms stiff peaks, 45 seconds to 1 minute total. Season with salt to taste.

4 Spread about 2 teaspoons goat cheese mixture on each cracker. Working with 1 quail egg at a time, roll egg in toasted chia seeds to coat. Discard any excess chia seeds. Cut eggs in half lengthwise, and place 1 egg half on each cracker. Garnish with white sage leaves and lemon peel strips. —MIREIA TARIBÓ, TARA GOMEZ, AND CARMEN SANDOVAL

MAKE AHEAD Quail eggs and chia seeds may be prepared up to 1 day ahead. Store peeled quail eggs in an airtight container in refrigerator. Store toasted chia seeds in an airtight container at room temperature.

DEVILED EGGS

These silky deviled eggs are enriched with mayonnaise, Dijon mustard, and dill. This is a perfect recipe for snacking or your next gathering. A heavy dose of mayonnaise gives the filling of these deviled eggs an extra-silky texture and rich flavor, while sharp Dijon mustard and fresh dill add acidity and brightness to the classic appetizer. Granulated garlic and white pepper impart a subtle complexity without affecting the creamy texture of the yolk filling, and a light dusting of paprika to finish adds a decorative touch and a mildly sweet flavor to balance the richness.

TOTAL 10 MIN; SERVES 14

14 hard-cooked eggs

1½ cups mayonnaise

1 tsp. chopped fresh dill, plus more for garnish

1 tsp. Dijon mustard

⅛ tsp. white pepper

⅛ tsp. granulated garlic

Paprika, for garnish

Peel eggs, and cut in half lengthwise. Scoop yolks into a medium bowl. Place egg whites on a platter, and set aside. Add mayonnaise, dill, Dijon mustard, white pepper, and granulated garlic to bowl with egg yolks, and whisk until mostly smooth, about 1 minute. Transfer mayonnaise mixture to a piping bag or a resealable plastic freezer bag with a ½-inch hole cut in 1 corner. Pipe evenly into egg white halves. Garnish deviled eggs with paprika and additional dill. —GENOVA DELICATESSEN

MAKE AHEAD Deviled eggs can be prepared up to 1 day in advance and stored in an airtight container in refrigerator.

NOTE Shock hard-boiled eggs in a large bowl of ice water to quickly stop the cooking process.

DEVILED CRAB-STUFFED MINI CORNBREAD MUFFINS

At his dinner parties in Harlem, chef and cookbook author Alexander Smalls pairs creamy, slightly spicy, fresh deviled crab with tender corn muffins, barely sweetened with brown sugar and studded with corn kernels, for a quick one-bite appetizer. Choose fresh crab over pasteurized for the best flavor.

ACTIVE 20 MIN; TOTAL 35 MIN; SERVES 12

DEVILED CRAB

- 4 oz. fresh lump crabmeat (about ¾ cup), drained and picked
- ¼ cup panko
- 2 scallions, finely chopped
- 3 Tbsp. mayonnaise
- 2 Tbsp. finely chopped jalapeño
- ¾ tsp. paprika
- ¾ tsp. kosher salt
- ¼ tsp. celery seeds
- ¼ tsp. cayenne pepper, or more to taste

MUFFINS

- ⅓ cup fine yellow or white cornmeal (about 1¼ oz.)
- ⅓ cup all-purpose flour (about 1½ oz.)
- 1 Tbsp. light brown sugar
- ¾ tsp. ground coriander
- ¾ tsp. kosher salt
- ½ tsp. baking powder
- ½ cup buttermilk
- 2 large eggs, beaten
- 2 Tbsp. vegetable oil
- ½ cup fresh or thawed frozen yellow corn kernels (about 2¼ oz.)
- Cooking spray
- Finely chopped fresh cilantro, for garnish

1 **Make the deviled crab:** Preheat oven to 400°F. Stir together crabmeat, panko, scallions, mayonnaise, jalapeño, paprika, salt, celery seeds, and cayenne in a small bowl until crabmeat breaks apart into shreds and mixture is evenly combined. Set aside.

2 **Make the muffins:** Whisk together cornmeal, flour, brown sugar, coriander, salt, and baking powder in a medium bowl. Whisk together buttermilk, eggs, and oil in a small bowl. Add buttermilk mixture to cornmeal mixture; whisk until smooth. Stir in corn kernels. Lightly grease (with cooking spray) a 24-cup miniature muffin pan. Divide cornmeal mixture evenly among muffin cups (about 1 tablespoon each). Spoon about 1¼ teaspoons deviled crab in center of batter in each cup. Bake in preheated oven until lightly browned and a toothpick inserted in center comes out clean, 12 to 15 minutes.

3 Carefully remove muffins from pan, and place on a serving platter. Sprinkle with chopped cilantro, and serve warm. *—ALEXANDER SMALLS*

MAKE AHEAD Deviled crab mixture can be made up to 1 day ahead and stored in an airtight container in refrigerator. Muffins can be baked up to 2 hours ahead and reheated in a 200°F oven until just warm, 3 to 5 minutes.

WINE Lively, lemony white: Sun Goddess Sauvignon Blanc

CHILLED LOBSTER TAILS WITH GREEN GODDESS AÏOLI

Steamed lobster tails are served with an herb-packed mayonnaise-based dip in this chilled appetizer.

ACTIVE 15 MIN; TOTAL 35 MIN; SERVES 12

½ cup plus 2 Tbsp. mayonnaise

½ cup loosely packed fresh parsley leaves

½ cup loosely packed fresh basil leaves

1 large scallion, chopped (about 3 Tbsp.)

2 Tbsp. fresh lemon juice (from 1 lemon)

4 oil-packed anchovy fillets (from 1 [2-oz.] can) (see Note)

1 small garlic clove, finely grated (about 1½ tsp.)

Kosher salt, to taste

Black pepper, to taste

6 (4- to 6-oz.) fresh Maine lobster tails, halved lengthwise

1 Process mayonnaise, parsley, basil, scallion, lemon juice, anchovies, and garlic in a food processor or blender until smooth, about 1 minute and 30 seconds. Season with salt and pepper to taste. Refrigerate aïoli until well chilled, about 20 minutes.

2 Meanwhile, fill a large bowl with ice and water; set aside. Fill a large saucepan with water to a depth of 2 inches; place a steamer basket over saucepan, and bring water in saucepan to a boil over high. Add split lobster tails to steamer basket, flesh side up; cover and steam until lobster shells are bright red and meat is barely firm to the touch, 4 to 6 minutes. Transfer lobster tails to ice bath using tongs, and let cool 5 minutes. Drain well.

3 Working with 1 lobster tail at a time, carefully remove meat from shell; cut meat crosswise into 3 equal pieces. Arrange meat back in shell so it resembles the tail. Serve with aïoli. —JUSTIN CHAPPLE

MAKE AHEAD Green goddess aïoli can be made up to 1 day in advance and stored in an airtight container in refrigerator.

NOTE Store leftover anchovies in a small glass jar in refrigerator up to 1 month.

CRAB SALAD

This quick and easy salad combines bright and acidic lime juice with cilantro, mint, and succulent crabmeat.

TOTAL 10 MIN; SERVES 4

3 Tbsp. Kewpie mayonnaise

3 Tbsp. minced red onion (from 1 onion)

½ tsp. finely grated lime zest plus 1 Tbsp. fresh lime juice (from 1 lime)

1 Tbsp. minced fresh cilantro

1 Tbsp. minced fresh mint

1½ tsp. minced serrano chile (from 1 stemmed and seeded chile), plus more to taste

Kosher salt, to taste

Black pepper, to taste

8 oz. fresh Jonah, stone, Dungeness, or other local lump crabmeat, picked over

Toasts, crackers, or endive spears, for serving

Stir together mayonnaise, onion, lime zest and juice, cilantro, mint, and chile in a medium bowl until combined. Season lightly with salt and black pepper to taste. Gently fold in crabmeat until evenly coated. Season with additional minced chile, salt, and black pepper to taste. Serve with toasts, crackers, or endive spears. —JUSTIN CHAPPLE

MAKE AHEAD Crab salad can be made up to 1 day in advance and stored in an airtight container in refrigerator.

NOTE Kewpie mayonnaise is more eggy and sweet than American-made mayonnaise. Find it in the international aisle of most grocery stores.

CHILLED LOBSTER TAILS
WITH GREEN GODDESS AÏOLI

OYSTERS WITH YUZU
KOSHO MIGNONETTE

OYSTERS WITH YUZU KOSHO MIGNONETTE

This simple chilled appetizer combines citrusy and slightly spicy yuzu kosho with briny oysters on the half shell.

ACTIVE 5 MIN; TOTAL 20 MIN; SERVES 12

¼ cup rice vinegar

2 Tbsp. minced shallots (from 2 shallots)

1½ tsp. yuzu kosho (from 1 [3-oz.] jar)

1 tsp. extra virgin olive oil

2 dozen oysters on the half shell

Stir together vinegar, shallots, yuzu kosho, and oil in a small bowl until combined. Let stand at room temperature to allow flavors to meld, at least 15 minutes, or in refrigerator up to 24 hours. Serve with oysters over ice. —JUSTIN CHAPPLE

MAKE AHEAD Yuzu kosho mignonette can be made up to 1 day in advance. Store in an airtight container in refrigerator.

NOTE Yuzu kosho is available at most Asian grocery stores or online at mtckitchen.com.

ICED OYSTERS WITH BITTER LEMON VINAIGRETTE

Baltimore-based chef Spike Gjerde insists on buying fresh produce from local growers and products from small-scale makers. Here, he uses Keepwell's bitter lemon vinegar to create a tart, clean accompaniment to oysters. Spicebush berries, also called Appalachian allspice, have a lemony, piney flavor. Order from integrationacres.com. Use any extra to muddle in the bottom of a gin and tonic.

TOTAL 20 MIN; SERVES 4

¼ cup bitter lemon vinegar (such as Keepwell)

1 Tbsp. finely chopped shallot

¼ tsp. dried spicebush berries or black peppercorns, finely crushed

12 oysters, freshly shucked on the half shell

Stir together vinegar, shallot, and crushed spicebush berries in a small bowl. Serve oysters over ice with vinaigrette. —SPIKE GJERDE

WINE Crisp, minerally Muscadet: Pierre Luneau-Papin Clos des Allées

MISO MARY LIBERTINE

An ode to Japanese ingredients, this Bloody Mary gets a satiating and savory punch from shiro dashi and white miso.

TOTAL 10 MIN; SERVES 1

MISO MARY MIX

- ¾ cup shiro dashi
- ¾ cup Chinese black vinegar
- ¼ cup plus 1 Tbsp. shichimi togarashi
- ¼ cup white miso
- 1 Tbsp. sriracha
- 1½ tsp. kombu bouillon powder
- ¾ tsp. kona wasabi powder

ADDITIONAL INGREDIENTS

- ¼ cup tomato juice
- 3 Tbsp. (1½ oz.) vodka or mezcal (such as Tito's Handmade Vodka or Encantado Mezcal Artesanal)
- Nori (dried seaweed) sheet, for garnish

1 **Make the miso:** Mary mix: Process shiro dashi, vinegar, togarashi, miso, sriracha, kombu powder, and wasabi powder in a blender until smooth, about 30 seconds. Transfer to a resealable container, and refrigerate until ready to use.

2 **Make the cocktail:** Combine tomato juice, vodka or mezcal, and 3 tablespoons miso Mary mix in a cocktail shaker filled with ice. Cover with lid, and shake until well chilled, about 15 seconds. Place a large, long ice cube in a highball glass. Strain cocktail over ice, and garnish with a nori sheet. Serve immediately.
—LIBERTINE COCKTAIL BAR AT CASA BONAY, BARCELONA, SPAIN

MAKE AHEAD Miso Mary mix can be stored in a resealable container in refrigerator up to 1 week.

NOTE Shiro dashi, shichimi togarashi, kombu powder, wasabi powder, and white miso paste can be found at most Asian markets or online at japanesetaste.com. Chinese black vinegar can be found at most Asian markets or online at bokksumarket.com.

POMEGRANATE-GINGER SPRITZ

Pomegranate is winter's most stunning fruit; here, it provides both a sweet, wine-color base and a jewel-like garnish. The baking-spice notes of Angostura bitters soften the juice's tartness with cozy flavor.

TOTAL 5 MIN; SERVES 1

- 1 Tbsp. pomegranate arils
- 2 dashes Angostura bitters
- 2 Tbsp. refrigerated pomegranate juice
- 1½ Tbsp. (¾ oz.) brandy (or amber rum)
- 1 Tbsp. (½ oz.) ginger liqueur (such as Domaine de Canton)
- 4 to 6 Tbsp. (2 to 3 oz.) chilled dry sparkling white wine
- Splash of club soda (optional)
- Thin lemon slices

Fill a large wine glass halfway with ice, adding pomegranate arils as you add ice. Add bitters, pomegranate juice, brandy, and ginger liqueur. Top with sparkling wine and, if desired, club soda, and stir gently. Add lemon slices. —FOOD & WINE

GIN TOASTY

A gin and tonic takes on the comforting vibe of a hot toddy in this ingeniously simple riff, perfect for a snowy winter day.

TOTAL 5 MIN; SERVES 1

¼ cup plus 3 Tbsp. hot water (3½ oz.)

3½ Tbsp. (1¾ oz.) gin

1½ Tbsp. tonic syrup (¾ oz.) (preferably Jack Rudy Cocktail Co. Classic)

Orange peel twist

Stir together the hot water, gin, and tonic syrup in a mug until combined. Garnish with orange peel twist. —BROOKS REITZ, JACK RUDY COCKTAIL CO., CHARLESTON, SOUTH CAROLINA

GINGERBREAD MARGARITA

This cozy margarita has a warm, wintry, cake-spice panache that wouldn't be out of place at a holiday party. The spiced syrup is key: It intensifies the orange flavors of the cocktail while adding a seasonal spice hit that brings much-needed warmth during the winter months.

TOTAL 5 MIN; SERVES 1

¼ cup (2 oz.) añejo tequila

1½ Tbsp. fresh lime juice (¾ oz.)

1½ Tbsp. Spiced Orange Syrup (¾ oz.) (recipe follows)

½ oz. orange liqueur (such as Gran Gala)

Orange peel twist

Cinnamon stick

Fill a mixing glass halfway with ice. Add añejo tequila, lime juice, Spiced Orange Syrup, and orange liqueur; stir until chilled, about 20 seconds. Strain tequila mixture into a coupe glass. Wrap orange peel twist around cinnamon stick, and lay across coupe glass to garnish. —DAVID MARZORATI JR., BALDAMAR, ROSEVILLE, MINNESOTA

SPICED ORANGE SYRUP

Layers of oranges and sugar spiced with cloves, cinnamon, allspice, and nutmeg macerate to yield this versatile syrup.

TOTAL 15 MIN, PLUS 12 HR MACERATION; MAKES ABOUT 1⅔ CUPS

1½ cups granulated sugar

¼ tsp. ground cloves

¼ tsp. ground cinnamon

¼ tsp. ground allspice

¼ tsp. ground nutmeg

2 large navel oranges, sliced ¼ inch thick (about 3 cups)

⅓ cup classic simple syrup

Stir together sugar, cloves, cinnamon, allspice, and nutmeg in a medium bowl. Layer oranges and sugar mixture in a large lidded container. Seal; let stand at room temperature 12 hours. During final hour, shake vigorously every 15 minutes until sugar is mostly dissolved. Pour through a fine wire-mesh strainer into a 2-cup glass jar. Press oranges with the back of a spoon; discard solids. Stir until sugar is dissolved. Stir in simple syrup. Cover and refrigerate up to 2 weeks. —DAVID MARZORATI JR., BALDAMAR, ROSEVILLE, MINNESOTA

MIAMI VICE

This summery cocktail swirls frozen strawberry daiquiri and piña colada in one glass for a creamy, sweet, and frothy fruity drink. Instead of using ice, strawberries and pineapple are frozen prior to blending to achieve a plush frozen consistency without watering down the drink.

TOTAL 30 MIN, PLUS 4 HR FREEZING; SERVES 4

BITTERS-SOAKED FROZEN STRAWBERRIES

- 3 **cups halved fresh strawberries (from 1 qt. strawberries)**
- ¼ **cup (2 oz.) Regans' Orange Bitters**

PIÑA COLADA

- 2 **cups drained canned crushed pineapple in juice (from 2 [20-oz.] cans)**
- 1 **cup well-shaken and stirred cream of coconut (such as Coco López) (from 1 [15-oz.] can) (see Note)**
- ½ **cup (4 oz.) Don Q Piña rum**
- 4 **dashes Angostura bitters**

STRAWBERRY DAIQUIRI

- ½ **cup (4 oz.) Don Q Añejo rum**
- ¼ **cup turbinado sugar**

ADDITIONAL INGREDIENTS

- 4 **fresh strawberries, hulled**
- 4 **pineapple leaves (from 1 pineapple)**

1 **Make the bitters-soaked frozen strawberries:** Stir together strawberries and bitters in a medium bowl. Let stand at room temperature until strawberries have absorbed bitters flavor, about 10 minutes, stirring once after 5 minutes. Drain and transfer soaked strawberries to a gallon-size resealable plastic freezer bag. Seal bag, and freeze until strawberries are frozen, at least 4 hours or up to 3 months.

2 **Meanwhile, make the piña colada:** Place crushed pineapple in a gallon-size resealable plastic freezer bag. Seal bag; spread pineapple in an even layer. Freeze until pineapple is frozen, at least 4 hours or up to 3 months.

3 Remove frozen pineapple from freezer; remove from bag. Using your hands or a knife, break pineapple into small (about 1-inch) pieces. Combine cream of coconut, rum, bitters, and pineapple pieces in a blender, adding pineapple last. Process until smooth, about 1 minute. Pour piña colada into a small pitcher; place in freezer until ready to use.

4 **Make the strawberry daiquiri:** Remove bitters-soaked frozen strawberries from freezer. Combine rum, sugar, and frozen strawberries in a blender, adding frozen strawberries last. Process until smooth, about 1 minute, stopping to scrape down sides as needed. (The room-temperature alcohol will begin melting the strawberries.)

5 Pour piña colada evenly into 4 glasses (about ½ cup each); top evenly with strawberry daiquiri (about ½ cup each), and stir mixtures in each glass until swirled together. Spear each hulled strawberry with 1 pineapple leaf; place 1 speared strawberry in each glass for garnish. —THOMAS HOUSTON, SUPERIOR SEAFOOD AND OYSTER BAR, NEW ORLEANS

NOTE Cream of coconut is a thick, syrupy sweetened coconut cream and may not be substituted with coconut cream.

BEEF, PORK & LAMB

When the craving for something hearty hits—a perfectly charred steak, toothsome burger, crispy cutlet, or juicy pork chop—look no further than these simply delicious meats prepared in a world of styles and flavor profiles.

STEAK, POTATOES, AND TOMATOES
WITH QUICK CHIMICHURRI (P. 34)

DOUBLE-CUT RIB EYE WITH SWEET GORGONZOLA BUTTER

At her modern chophouse, Jar, in Los Angeles, 2002 Best New Chef Suzanne Tracht's menu changes with the seasons. To celebrate summer, she says, "this juicy, sweet combo of Gorgonzola and beef alongside fresh heirloom tomatoes is how I kick off the outdoor months." A two-rib prime rib eye mini-roast makes it easy to light up the grill. Tracht offers good reason to source your steak from a trusted butcher: "You want your guests passing around the bones at the end." Serve the grilled beef with Sweet Gorgonzola Butter.

ACTIVE 50 MIN; TOTAL 1 HR 35 MIN; SERVES 4

1 (3- to 3½-lb.) 2-rib prime rib eye roast, frenched

2 Tbsp. extra virgin olive oil or vegetable oil

1 Tbsp. kosher salt

1 tsp. black pepper

2 Tbsp. coarsely chopped fresh flat-leaf parsley

Pinch of fleur de sel, or to taste

Sweet Gorgonzola Butter (recipe follows)

1 Preheat grill to very high (500°F and up). Drizzle rib eye with oil, and sprinkle with kosher salt and pepper. Let stand at room temperature 30 minutes.

2 Place rib eye on oiled grates; grill, covered, turning often, until seared on all sides, about 10 minutes. Reduce heat to medium-high (400°F to 450°F), and continue to grill, covered, turning occasionally, until a thermometer inserted in thickest portion of rib eye registers 115°F, about 30 minutes for medium-rare.

3 Remove from heat, and let rest at least 15 minutes or up to 30 minutes. To serve, cut rib eye between bones into 2 steaks. Thinly slice each steak against the grain; sprinkle with parsley and fleur de sel. Serve with Sweet Gorgonzola Butter. —SUZANNE TRACHT

NOTE A double-cut prime rib eye, a rib eye roast that is 2 bones thick, maximizes the ratio of charred crust to juicy meat. Frenching the bone isn't essential but makes the meat easier to carve. The keys to grilling a thick cut are to turn it often so it cooks evenly and to remove it from the grill at a lower internal temperature than usual (115°F for medium-rare). Letting it rest 15 to 30 minutes allows for carryover cooking off the grill; during this time, the internal temperature will rise to perfect medium-rare (around 125°F).

WINE Powerful Super-Tuscan red: Tenuta San Guido Guidalberto

SWEET GORGONZOLA BUTTER

Chef Suzanne Tracht makes this rich, indulgent compound butter with Gorgonzola dolce, the milder, sweeter, less acidic form of Gorgonzola piccante. Letting the mixture firm up in the fridge allows you to cut clean rounds.

ACTIVE 15 MIN; TOTAL 1 HR 15 MIN; MAKES ¾ CUP

4 oz. Gorgonzola dolce, crumbled (about 1 cup)

¼ cup unsalted butter (2 oz.), softened

Gently fold Gorgonzola into butter until just combined. Place mixture on a piece of plastic wrap or parchment paper, and roll into a 6-inch log; twist ends to seal. Chill 1 hour. Remove log from plastic wrap or parchment; cut into ½-inch-thick slices. —SUZANNE TRACHT

CHARRED CUCUMBER PANZANELLA
WITH GRILLED STEAK

A crusty, high-quality sourdough will stand up to the seeded salsa verde and keep the bread from disintegrating in this recipe from 2019 F&W Best New Chef Caroline Glover of Annette in Denver.

ACTIVE 45 MIN; TOTAL 1 HR 20 MIN; SERVES 4 TO 6

2 (1-lb.) Wagyu or well-marbled New York strip steaks

5 Tbsp. olive oil, divided, plus more for drizzling

4½ tsp. kosher salt, divided

1¾ tsp. black pepper, divided

12 oz. Persian cucumbers (about 5), halved lengthwise

1 lb. day-old sourdough bread, cut into ¾-inch-thick slices

¼ cup unseasoned rice vinegar

1 tsp. Dijon mustard

1 tsp. honey

1 garlic clove, smashed

¼ cup neutral oil (such as rice bran oil)

2 lb. heirloom tomatoes, cut into 1-inch pieces (about 5 cups)

1 cup thinly sliced English or Persian cucumber

1 cup thinly sliced red onion, rinsed under cold water

1 Tbsp. sweet sherry vinegar

Flaky sea salt (such as Maldon)

Fresh basil leaves

Salsa Verde (recipe follows)

1 Preheat grill to high (450°F to 500°F). Rub steaks with 1 tablespoon olive oil, and sprinkle with 2 teaspoons kosher salt and 1 teaspoon pepper. Let stand at room temperature 30 minutes.

2 Meanwhile, place cucumber halves, cut sides down, on oiled grates. Grill, uncovered and without turning, until cut sides are blackened, 10 to 15 minutes. Remove from grill, and set aside to cool completely, about 30 minutes.

3 Drizzle both sides of bread slices with remaining ¼ cup olive oil, and sprinkle with ¾ teaspoon kosher salt and ¼ teaspoon pepper. Place on grates, and grill, uncovered, turning occasionally, until charred but still chewy, 3 to 4 minutes. Remove from grill, and let cool slightly, about 5 minutes. Tear bread into 1-inch pieces, and toss with ½ teaspoon kosher salt and ¼ teaspoon pepper. Set aside.

4 Place steaks on oiled grates. Grill, uncovered, until medium-rare, 4 to 5 minutes on each side, or to desired degree of doneness. Transfer steaks to a cutting board, and let rest 10 minutes before thinly slicing against the grain.

5 Combine cooled cucumber halves, rice vinegar, Dijon, honey, garlic, and ¾ teaspoon kosher salt in a blender. Process until smooth, about 20 seconds. Add neutral oil; process until just incorporated, about 8 seconds. Transfer mixture to a large bowl; add bread pieces, and toss to coat. Let stand until slightly softened, about 3 minutes. Add tomatoes, cucumber slices, onion slices, sherry vinegar, remaining ½ teaspoon kosher salt, and remaining ¼ teaspoon pepper; gently fold to combine. Finish with a drizzle of olive oil, and garnish with additional pepper, flaky sea salt, and basil leaves. Serve panzanella with steak and Salsa Verde. — CAROLINE GLOVER

WINE Medium-bodied, plummy Merlot: Frog's Leap Rutherford

SALSA VERDE

TOTAL 10 MIN; MAKES 1¼ CUPS

1 Tbsp. fennel seeds, toasted

1 tsp. cumin seeds, toasted

1 tsp. coriander seeds, toasted

1 bunch fresh cilantro (about 3 oz.), bottom 2 inches of stems trimmed

2 cups loosely packed fresh basil leaves (about 1 oz.)

1 garlic clove

1 cup rice bran oil or other neutral oil

2 Tbsp. white wine vinegar

1 tsp. kosher salt

1 Finely grind fennel seeds, cumin seeds, and coriander seeds in a mortar and pestle or spice grinder; set ground spices aside.

2 Combine cilantro, basil, garlic, and oil in a blender; process until smooth, about 30 seconds. Transfer to a bowl, and stir in vinegar, salt, and ground spices. Cover and chill immediately to keep the vibrant green color. If making a day ahead, wait to add the vinegar until ready to serve. —CAROLINE GLOVER

STEAK, POTATOES, AND TOMATOES
WITH QUICK CHIMICHURRI

PHOTO P. 29

Juicy late-summer tomatoes, verdant fresh herbs, and golden potatoes pair with simply seared and sliced steaks. This recipe works well with boneless strip and hanger steaks, two cuts that render juicy, exceptionally tender meat that are countered with the chimichurri. This recipe can easily be doubled for a crowd. The dish is inspired by Matthew Conway, sommelier and owner of The Tippling House in Charleston, who encourages you to level up this easy steak dinner with a chilled bottle of red wine. "The most overlooked aspect of food and wine pairing is temperature," he notes. "Steak and Syrah isn't revolutionary, but try that red wine cold with hot, fatty steak. The combination of flavor and temperature variation will leave you wanting another bite."

ACTIVE 25 MIN; TOTAL 35 MIN; SERVES 4

- 1 cup loosely packed fresh flat-leaf parsley leaves, roughly chopped (about ½ cup)
- ½ cup plus 3 Tbsp. extra virgin olive oil, divided
- 3 Tbsp. fresh oregano leaves, roughly chopped (about 2 Tbsp.)
- 2 Tbsp. red wine vinegar
- 4 tsp. kosher salt, divided
- 2 large garlic cloves, grated with a Microplane grater (about ½ tsp.)
- ¼ tsp. crushed red pepper
- 1½ lb. small golden potatoes, halved lengthwise (about 4 cups)
- ¾ tsp. black pepper, divided
- 2 (1-lb.) boneless strip steaks or 2 lb. hanger steaks
- 3 Tbsp. canola oil
- 2 large (11-oz.) heirloom tomatoes or beefsteak tomatoes, cut into ½-inch-thick slices

Flaky sea salt, for garnish

1 Preheat oven to 450°F. Stir together parsley, ½ cup olive oil, oregano, vinegar, 1 teaspoon kosher salt, garlic, and crushed red pepper in a small bowl until combined; set chimichurri aside.

2 Toss together potatoes, ¼ teaspoon black pepper, 1 teaspoon kosher salt, and remaining 3 tablespoons olive oil on a large rimmed baking sheet until evenly coated. Roast potatoes in preheated oven until crispy and fork tender, about 20 minutes, stirring once during final 5 minutes of roasting time. Remove from oven.

3 While potatoes roast, sprinkle steaks evenly with remaining 2 teaspoons salt and ½ teaspoon black pepper. Heat canola oil in a large cast-iron skillet over high until oil smokes. Add steaks to skillet; reduce heat to medium-high, and cook, undisturbed, until steaks are evenly browned on bottoms, about 5 minutes. Flip steaks, and cook, undisturbed, until browned on other side, about 5 minutes. Place steaks upright on their sides in skillet; cook, rotating occasionally on their sides and holding upright, until a thermometer inserted in thickest portion of steak registers 130°F for medium-rare, or to desired degree of doneness, 5 to 10 minutes for strip steaks or about 2 minutes for hanger steaks. Transfer steaks to a cutting board, and let rest 5 minutes.

4 Cut steaks into ½-inch-thick slices, and divide evenly among 4 plates. Arrange potatoes and tomatoes evenly on plates. Drizzle evenly with reserved chimichurri, and garnish with flaky sea salt. —ANNA THEOKTISTO

MAKE AHEAD Chimichurri can be made up to 2 days in advance and stored in an airtight container in refrigerator.

WINE Pax North Coast Syrah

HANGER STEAK WITH KIMCHI GLAZE AND MISO BUTTER-GRILLED VEGETABLES

This summer-cookout showstopper by 2016 Best New Chef member Ravi Kapur, owner of Liholiho Yacht Club in San Francisco, is your umami-packed, Hawaiian-inspired answer to grilling monotony. The glaze comes together quickly and layers tart pineapple and tangy kimchi onto juicy hanger steak as it grills. It's thinner and runnier than traditional barbecue sauces, so be sure to baste the meat several times while it grills to caramelize the sugars and develop grill marks. Leftover miso compound butter will keep for five days in your fridge and is a transformative addition to seafood, tossed with pasta, or brushed on grilled vegetables.

ACTIVE 30 MIN; TOTAL 1 HR 10 MIN; SERVES 4

½ cup unsalted butter (4 oz.), softened

2½ Tbsp. white miso

1 cup pineapple juice

½ cup drained kimchi (such as Wildbrine Korean Kimchi)

¼ cup packed light brown sugar

¼ cup ketchup

1 (1½-lb.) hanger steak (about 1½ inches thick)

2 tsp. kosher salt

White sesame seeds and thinly diagonally sliced scallions, for garnish

2 lb. mixed grilled vegetables (such as squash, zucchini, baby bell peppers, and/or scallions)

1 Stir together butter and miso in a small bowl until well blended. Chill miso butter in an airtight container until ready to serve, up to 5 days.

2 Process pineapple juice, ½ cup water, kimchi, brown sugar, and ketchup in a blender until very smooth, about 25 seconds. Transfer to a large saucepan. Bring to a simmer over medium. Simmer, stirring occasionally, until thickened and reduced to about 1 cup, about 15 minutes (glaze will be grainy). Set kimchi glaze aside at room temperature.

3 Season steak all over with salt. Let stand at room temperature 30 minutes. Meanwhile, preheat grill to high (450°F to 500°F). Brush one side of steak with kimchi glaze; place steak, glazed-side down, on oiled grates, and brush top with some of the kimchi glaze. Grill, uncovered, until glaze is caramelized in spots, about 12 minutes for medium-rare, turning and basting often with kimchi glaze. Transfer steak to a cutting board, and let rest 10 minutes. Cut steak against the grain into slices, and divide among 4 plates. Garnish steak with sesame seeds and scallions, and serve with your favorite grilled vegetables tossed in miso butter to taste. —RAVI KAPUR

MAKE AHEAD Miso butter can be kept in an airtight container in refrigerator up to 5 days. Cooled kimchi glaze can be kept in an airtight container in refrigerator up to 5 days.

WINE Taut, curranty Cabernet Franc: Lang & Reed North Coast

ENTRECÔTE WITH GREEN OLIVE TAPENADE BUTTER

This recipe offers a simple technique for both a perfectly cooked rib eye and a flavorful compound butter packed with pungent anchovies, piquant Dijon mustard, and salty capers that packs a briny punch when melted onto the juicy grilled steaks. Look for small and nutty picholine olives, sweet and buttery Castelvetrano olives, or large and tart Cerignola olives in the olive bar or at specialty grocery stores. For a classic bistro-inspired meal, serve the steak alongside a pile of french fries and a mesclun salad. You can keep the butter in the freezer for up to three months to quickly upgrade grilled steaks, pork chops, or fish fillets.

ACTIVE 20 MIN; TOTAL 35 MIN; SERVES 2 TO 4

¾ cup pitted green olives (such as picholine, Castelvetrano, or Cerignola)

½ cup loosely packed fresh flat-leaf parsley leaves

2 Tbsp. capers, drained

1 tsp. Dijon mustard

2 drained anchovy fillets (from 1 [2-oz.] can)

1 large garlic clove, smashed

4 oz. unsalted butter, at room temperature

2¼ tsp. kosher salt, divided

1¼ tsp. black pepper, divided

2 (12-oz.) rib eye steaks (1 inch thick)

2 tsp. olive oil

1 Pulse olives, parsley, capers, mustard, anchovies, and garlic in a food processor until a coarse paste forms, 7 to 9 pulses. Transfer mixture to a medium bowl. Add butter, ¼ teaspoon salt, and ¼ teaspoon pepper; stir together using a fork or spatula until well combined. Set aside at room temperature until ready to use.

2 Preheat grill to medium-high (400°F to 450°F). Brush steaks evenly with oil; sprinkle evenly with remaining 2 teaspoons salt and 1 teaspoon pepper. Place steaks on oiled grates; grill, uncovered, until steaks are well seared and lightly charred and a thermometer inserted in thickest portion of meat registers 130°F (for medium-rare), 4 to 5 minutes per side. Transfer steaks to a carving board, and generously spread each with 2 tablespoons tapenade butter. Reserve remaining ¾ cup tapenade butter for another use. Let steaks rest 5 minutes. (Butter will melt and coat steaks.) Cut steaks against the grain into ½-inch-thick slices, and serve. —JUSTIN CHAPPLE

WINE Earthy, spicy Rhône red: Château de Rouanne Vinsobres

SPICE-CRUSTED BEEF TENDERLOIN
WITH CAPER VINAIGRETTE

Intense and fruity spices like coriander and caraway wake up the flavor of roasted and chilled beef tenderloin from cookbook author Maria Helm Sinskey. Caper vinaigrette dresses both meat and greens for a gorgeous main.

ACTIVE 30 MIN; TOTAL 4 HR 5 MIN; SERVES 8

- 2 tsp. coriander seeds, crushed
- 2 tsp. caraway seeds, crushed
- 2 tsp. fennel seeds, crushed
- 2 tsp. smoked paprika
- 1½ Tbsp. plus 1¼ tsp. kosher salt, divided
- 2¼ tsp. black pepper, divided
- 1 (3½-lb.) center-cut beef tenderloin, tied
- ⅓ cup plus 2 Tbsp. extra virgin olive oil, divided
- ¼ cup Champagne vinegar
- 2 Tbsp. Dijon mustard
- 2 Tbsp. drained nonpareil capers, chopped
- 2 Tbsp. finely chopped fresh flat-leaf parsley
- 4 oz. fresh arugula, for serving

1 Stir together coriander seeds, caraway seeds, fennel seeds, paprika, 1½ tablespoons salt, and 2 teaspoons pepper in a small bowl. Rub mixture all over beef; place on a wire rack set inside a large rimmed baking sheet. Let stand at room temperature 1 hour.

2 Preheat oven to 450°F with oven rack in top third of oven. Rub beef with 2 tablespoons olive oil. Roast until an instant-read thermometer inserted in thickest portion registers 120°F, 35 to 40 minutes. Remove beef; let rest until completely cool, about 1 hour. Wrap tightly in plastic wrap; refrigerate until chilled, 2 hours.

3 Whisk together vinegar, mustard, capers, parsley, remaining ⅓ cup oil, remaining 1¼ teaspoons salt, and remaining ¼ teaspoon pepper in a small bowl. Untie beef; cut into ¼-inch-thick slices. Serve chilled or at room temperature with arugula and vinaigrette. —MARIA HELM SINSKEY

WINE Peppery Italian red: Arnaldo-Caprai Montefalco Ross

SKIRT STEAK AND ASPARAGUS
WITH SALSA DE SEMILLAS

Loaded with pumpkin seed kernels, cashews, and sesame seeds, salsa de semillas is a lesser-known but beloved Mexican nut-based salsa.

TOTAL 50 MIN; SERVES 4

½ cup plus 1 Tbsp. olive oil, divided

½ cup cashews, coarsely chopped

¼ cup raw pepitas

1 Tbsp. black sesame seeds

2 tsp. finely chopped garlic

½ tsp. dried Mexican oregano

1 Tbsp. plus 2 tsp. finely chopped unseeded dried chipotle chile, divided

2 tsp. kosher salt, divided, plus more to taste

1 (1½-lb.) skirt steak

2 lb. fresh asparagus, trimmed and cut into 1-inch pieces

Lime wedges, fresh cilantro leaves, and cooked long-grain rice, for serving

1 Heat 6 tablespoons oil in a medium saucepan over medium-low until fragrant. Add cashews, pepitas, sesame seeds, garlic, and oregano; cook, stirring often, until cashews are light golden and toasted, 5 to 7 minutes. Remove from heat; stir in 1 tablespoon chipotle and ½ teaspoon salt. Transfer to a small bowl.

2 Slice steak with the grain into 3-inch-wide strips; slice strips against the grain into ⅜-inch-wide strips.

3 Heat 1 tablespoon oil in a large cast-iron skillet over high. Add half of the steak; sprinkle with ¾ teaspoon salt. Cook, undisturbed, until a crust forms, 5 to 7 minutes. Flip and cook just until no longer pink, about 15 seconds. Transfer steak to a medium bowl, and wipe skillet clean. Repeat process using 1 tablespoon oil, remaining steak, and remaining ¾ teaspoon salt. Wipe skillet clean.

4 Add remaining 1 tablespoon oil to skillet; heat over high. Add asparagus; cook, stirring often, until crisp-tender, about 5 minutes. Return steak and accumulated juices to skillet. Stir in remaining 2 teaspoons chipotle; season with salt, if desired.

5 Transfer steak mixture to a serving plate; top with ¼ cup salsa. Squeeze limes over steak mixture; garnish with cilantro, and serve with rice and remaining salsa. —PAOLA BRISEÑO GONZÁLEZ

WINE Light, spicy Grenache: Folded Hills Grant

GRILLED BONELESS SHORT RIBS
WITH SCALLION-SUMAC GREMOLATA

Typically cooked low and slow, these boneless short ribs get perfectly tender on the grill. A quick brush with fish sauce adds a layer of umami, while the brown sugar rub provides a shortcut to charred flavor. Thinly sliced and topped with a charred scallion gremolata, they're right at home on your late-summer plate.

TOTAL 45 MIN; SERVES 4

1½ Tbsp. fish sauce

4 (8-oz.) boneless beef short ribs

3 garlic cloves, divided

2 Tbsp. light brown sugar

6 scallions

2 tsp. canola oil, plus more for grill grates

⅓ cup finely chopped fresh flat-leaf parsley

2 tsp. grated orange zest

1½ tsp. sumac

½ tsp. kosher salt

¼ tsp. black pepper

½ tsp. flaky sea salt

1 Brush fish sauce on all sides of short ribs. Grate 2 garlic cloves using a Microplane; place in a small bowl. Add brown sugar to garlic, and stir to combine. Rub garlic mixture on all sides of short ribs. Let stand at room temperature while preparing grill.

2 Open bottom vent of grill completely. Light charcoal chimney starter filled with briquettes. When briquettes are covered with gray ash, pour them evenly onto bottom grate of grill. Drizzle scallions with oil; toss to coat. Coat top grill grate with oil. Cover and heat grill to medium-high (400°F to 450°F). Place scallions on oiled grate. Grill, uncovered, turning often, until medium-charred, 1 to 2 minutes. Transfer to a cutting board; let cool slightly.

3 Arrange short ribs on oiled grate. Grill, covered, flipping every 2 minutes, until a thermometer inserted in thickest portion registers 125°F to 130°F, 10 to 12 minutes. Remove short ribs from grill; let stand 5 minutes.

4 Mince remaining garlic clove; place in a small bowl. Add parsley, orange zest, sumac, kosher salt, and pepper. Rub together with fingers to combine.

5 Thinly slice grilled scallions. Add to parsley mixture; toss gently to combine. Cut short ribs against the grain into thin slices; sprinkle with flaky sea salt. Serve with gremolata. —ANN TAYLOR PITTMAN

WINE Aromatic, peppery Syrah: Melville Estate

NOTE If boneless are not available, ask your butcher to slice English-cut short ribs off the bone into rectangular steaks.

COSTILLAS (ARGENTINEAN GRILLED BEEF SHORT RIBS)

The League of Kitchens cooking instructor Mirta Rinaldi shared this recipe for Tira de Asado, Argentinean-style grilled beef short ribs. The meaty short ribs are a favorite asado recipe, and to go with them, Rinaldi makes a balsamic chimichurri. You can make a meal out of the ribs or cut them into thirds for sharing. While three-bone ribs are traditional, four-bone short ribs work, too. Find three-bone ribs at wildforkfoods.com or four-bone ribs at Asian markets. Note that sal parrillera has larger crystals than kosher salt, so it dissolves more slowly into the meat and imparts a pleasantly salty, mineral taste.

ACTIVE 20 MIN; TOTAL 35 MIN; SERVES 6

3½ lb. flanken-cut 3-bone beef short ribs, at room temperature (about 6 short ribs, 1¼ inches thick)

1½ Tbsp. coarse sea salt or sal parrillera (such as Dos Anclas)

Mirta's Chimichurri (recipe follows)

1 Preheat grill (preferably a wood fire) to medium-high (400°F to 450°F). Meanwhile, pat ribs dry with paper towels. Sprinkle all sides of ribs evenly with salt, pressing salt into meat and rubbing it on bones.

2 Arrange ribs diagonally and spaced 1 inch apart on lightly oiled grill grates. Grill, uncovered and undisturbed, until bottoms of ribs are browned and release from grates, 4 to 6 minutes. Flip ribs; grill, uncovered, until browned and a thermometer inserted near the bone but not touching it registers 130°F, 2 to 4 minutes. Remove from grill, and let rest 5 to 10 minutes.

3 Serve ribs whole, or, if serving with an assortment of meats for a larger group, cut each rib into thirds on the diagonal. Serve with chimichurri. —MIRTA RINALDI

WINE Smoky, full-bodied Argentinean Malbec: El Enemigo Malbec

NOTE Find sal parrillera at Latin American markets or online.

MIRTA'S CHIMICHURRI

In Argentina, where there is grilled meat, there is chimichurri. Traditional recipes for the country's most popular condiment call for red wine vinegar, but Mirta Rinaldi and her family prefer the sweeter flavor of balsamic. Rinaldi always keeps a jar in the refrigerator; as it ages, the vibrant color mellows, but the sharpness remains. It's the perfect partner for ribs or grilled chicken, steak, or pork.

TOTAL 10 MIN; SERVES 6 TO 8

1 cup finely chopped fresh flat-leaf parsley (from about 2 bunches)

1 Tbsp. dried oregano

1½ tsp. crushed red pepper, or more to taste

1 tsp. paprika

1 tsp. kosher salt

1 tsp. black pepper

4 small garlic cloves, grated with a Microplane (about ¾ tsp.)

1 cup extra virgin olive oil

2 Tbsp. balsamic vinegar

Combine parsley, oregano, crushed red pepper, paprika, salt, black pepper, and garlic in a medium (1-pint) lidded jar or a medium bowl. Stir together; add oil and vinegar. Seal jar, and shake (or stir mixture in bowl) until well combined. —MIRTA RINALDI

MAKE AHEAD Chimichurri can be stored in an airtight container in refrigerator up to 2 weeks.

SALPICÓN TACOS

Chef Juan Pablo Loza of Rosewood Mayakoba in Playa del Carmen, Mexico, makes this refreshing salpicón, a basic salsa made here with cucumber, radishes, habanero, red onion, and tomatoes. "This is a classic way to serve different leftovers, which you have to reheat and add in to the salsa so all the spice and citrus will soak the meat, making this a warm and cold filling in a hot tortilla," he says. "You don't need to add anything else. It's so simple and perfect just like that."

ACTIVE 20 MIN; TOTAL 25 MIN; SERVES 4

- 3 medium plum tomatoes, diced
- 3 medium radishes, finely diced
- ½ cup finely diced red onion
- ½ cup peeled, seeded, and diced cucumber
- 2 tsp. fine sea salt, plus more to taste
- 2 medium habanero chiles, halved
- 3 Tbsp. fresh orange juice
- 3 Tbsp. fresh lime juice
- 1 lb. cooked skirt steak, flank steak, or pork shoulder, cut into ¾-inch cubes
- 2 Tbsp. chopped fresh cilantro
- 1 medium avocado, diced
- 8 (6-inch) white corn tortillas, warmed

Stir together tomatoes, radishes, onion, cucumber, and salt in a medium bowl; let stand until juicy, about 5 minutes. Stir in chiles, orange juice, and lime juice. Stir in meat and cilantro. Gently fold in avocado. Add salt to taste. Serve with corn tortillas. —JUAN PABLO LOZA

BEER An ice-cold Tecate with a lime (or chilled silver tequila, such as Milagro)

CAMBODIAN BLACK PEPPER BEEF (LOK LAK)

Wok cooking happens quickly, so prepare each ingredient beforehand. Nite Yun, 2019 Best New Chef, has an intensely flavorful marinade that not only tenderizes flank steak but also adds punchy flavor in just a few minutes of cooking. Golden Mountain seasoning sauce is slightly saltier than soy sauce, with a hint of sweetness. Find it online and at Asian markets. Kampot peppercorns are available at oaktownspiceshop.com.

TOTAL 20 MIN, PLUS 8 HR MARINATION; SERVES 4

⅓ cup oyster sauce

¼ cup crushed garlic (about 8 garlic cloves)

3 Tbsp. cooking rice wine

2¾ Tbsp. raw sugar

2 Tbsp. soy seasoning sauce (such as Golden Mountain)

2 Tbsp. dark soy sauce

2½ tsp. crushed plus 1 tsp. coarsely ground Kampot or other black peppercorns, divided

2 Tbsp. cornstarch

2 Tbsp. water

2 lb. flank steak, cut into ¾-inch cubes

2 Tbsp. olive oil

2 cups thinly sliced red onion (from 1 medium onion)

2 Tbsp. fresh lime juice (from 1 lime)

1 tsp. coarse sea salt

8 butter lettuce leaves

1 unripe red tomato, cut into 8 wedges

1 Stir together oyster sauce, garlic, rice wine, sugar, soy seasoning sauce, dark soy sauce, and crushed Kampot peppercorns in a small bowl.

2 Stir together cornstarch and 2 tablespoons water in a medium bowl until cornstarch is dissolved; add beef, and toss to coat. Add ¼ cup of the oyster sauce mixture; cover and refrigerate 8 hours or overnight. Cover remaining oyster sauce mixture, and set aside.

3 Heat oil in a wok over high. Carefully add beef mixture to wok, and cook, shaking wok often, until beef has a brown sear, 4 to 5 minutes. Add red onion and remaining oyster sauce mixture, and cook, shaking wok often, 2 minutes more.

4 Stir together lime juice, sea salt, and coarsely ground Kampot peppercorns. Place beef, lettuce leaves, and tomatoes on a platter, and serve with lime sauce.
—NITE YUN

WINE Light-bodied, spicy Loire Cabernet Franc: Bernard Baudry Les Granges Chinon

BRISKET MEATBALLS IN TOMATO PASSATA

At Vic's, her New York City restaurant, chef Hillary Sterling does a special Italian-influenced Passover menu that includes this riff on the requisite brisket, which appears as brisket meatballs. "Everyone makes brisket [for Passover], and the Italians make polpette, so why not bring them together?" says Sterling. The meatballs are sauced in Sterling's riff on traditionally uncooked passata, which gets a quick simmer and a flavor update with orange, oregano, and chile flakes.

ACTIVE 25 MIN; TOTAL 45 MIN; SERVES 8

MEATBALLS

Cooking spray

3 cups crumbled unsalted matzo (about 5 [7-inch] sheets)

⅓ cup water

2½ lb. ground brisket

2 large eggs

2 Tbsp. olive oil

4¼ tsp. kosher salt

1 Tbsp. ground fennel seeds (optional)

1 tsp. crushed red pepper

¼ tsp. black pepper

TOMATO PASSATA

½ cup sliced garlic (about 18 garlic cloves)

3 Tbsp. olive oil

2 (28-oz.) cans whole peeled San Marzano plum tomatoes, drained and crushed

¼ cup fresh marjoram leaves (from 1 bunch)

5 (4×1-inch) orange peel strips

1 Tbsp. kosher salt

1 tsp. crushed red pepper

GARNISHES

Crumbled matzo

Fresh marjoram leaves

Chile oil (such as Roland)

1 **Make the meatballs:** Preheat oven to 425°F. Set a wire rack inside a large baking sheet; coat with cooking spray. Combine crumbled matzo and ⅓ cup water in a large bowl. Add brisket, eggs, oil, salt, ground fennel (if using), crushed red pepper, and black pepper. Mix with hands until combined. Shape mixture into 16 balls (about ⅓ cup or 3¼ ounces each). Arrange meatballs on prepared wire rack. Bake until browned and a meat thermometer registers 150°F, about 22 minutes.

2 **Meanwhile, make the tomato passata:** Cook garlic and oil in a large skillet over medium-high, stirring often, until garlic is soft but not brown, about 1 minute and 30 seconds. Add crushed tomatoes, marjoram leaves, orange peel strips, salt, and crushed red pepper. Bring to a boil over medium-high; remove from heat.

3 Transfer meatballs to tomato passata in skillet. Serve warm, garnished with crumbled matzo, marjoram, and chile oil. —HILLARY STERLING

WINE Dark-fruited kosher California Cabernet: Baron Herzog

SPICY POT ROAST WITH ORANGES, SWEET POTATOES, AND CALABRIAN CHILE GREMOLATA

Whole orange segments and freshly squeezed orange juice and zest give this hearty winter braise from Justin Smillie, chef and author of Slow Fires: Mastering New Ways to Braise, Roast, and Grill, *a burst of fresh citrus flavor. Creamy sweet potatoes and celery root along with tender beef chuck fill out this satisfyingly hearty meal.*

ACTIVE 40 MIN; TOTAL 3 HR 10 MIN; SERVES 8

½ cup olive oil, divided

1 (4-lb.) boneless chuck roast, trimmed

4 tsp. kosher salt, plus more to taste

1 tsp. black pepper, plus more to taste

2 oranges, divided

1 medium yellow onion, thinly sliced

2 cups unsalted beef stock or water

1 (28-oz.) can whole peeled San Marzano plum tomatoes, crushed

3 whole Calabrian chiles in oil, divided

1 large sweet potato, peeled and cut into 1-inch pieces

1 lb. celery root, turnips, or rutabagas, peeled and cut into 1-inch pieces

½ cup packed chopped fresh flat-leaf parsley

Crusty bread, for serving

1 Preheat oven to 300°F. Heat ¼ cup oil in a large Dutch oven over medium-high. Season chuck roast with salt and pepper. Add chuck roast to Dutch oven, and sear, turning occasionally, until browned on all sides, 15 to 20 minutes. Transfer to a plate, and set aside.

2 Scrub 1 orange, and cut into 8 wedges; discard seeds and core, and set aside. Add onion to Dutch oven; cook over medium, stirring and scraping bottom of pan often with a wooden spoon, until onion is soft and translucent, about 8 minutes. (Add ¼ cup water while cooking onion if too many browned bits accumulate.) Add beef stock, tomatoes, 1 chile, and orange wedges; bring to a boil. Return chuck roast and any accumulated juices to pan; bring to a simmer over high.

3 Cover and transfer to preheated oven; braise 1 hour and 30 minutes. Uncover and stir in sweet potato and celery root. Return to oven, and braise, uncovered, until meat and vegetables are tender but not falling apart, 1 hour to 1 hour and 30 minutes. Remove from oven, and let rest 15 minutes. Transfer chuck roast to a work surface; shred into large pieces. Skim off fat from Dutch oven, and discard. Return shredded beef to Dutch oven.

4 While meat rests, zest remaining orange to equal 1 tablespoon zest and squeeze to yield 3 tablespoons juice. Finely chop remaining 2 chiles to equal 1 tablespoon. Stir together parsley, orange zest and juice, chopped chiles, and remaining ¼ cup oil; season with salt and pepper to taste. Divide roast mixture evenly among bowls; top with parsley mixture. Serve with crusty bread.
—JUSTIN SMILLIE

MAKE AHEAD After roast is shredded and returned to Dutch oven, let cool to room temperature. Cover and refrigerate up to 2 days. Gently reheat over low.

WINE Earthy Calabrian red: Librandi Duca Sanfelice Cirò Rosso Riserva

NOTE We like the Tutto Calabria brand of Calabrian chiles.

BLACKENED SKILLET PORK CHOPS
WITH BEANS AND SPINACH

A stellar spice blend is one of the easiest ways to amp up the flavors of a dish, taking a simple seared pork chop or baked chicken thigh to the next level.

TOTAL 25 MIN; SERVES 4

4 (10-oz.) bone-in rib-cut pork chops

2 Tbsp. plus 2 tsp. Blackening Spice Blend (recipe follows)

2 Tbsp. canola oil

1 (15-oz.) can cannellini beans, drained and rinsed

¾ cup chicken stock

1 small shallot, minced

4 cups fresh baby spinach

1 tsp. kosher salt

Lemon wedges, for serving

1 Rub each pork chop all over with 2 teaspoons Blackening Spice Blend.

2 Heat oil in a large cast-iron skillet over medium. Working in batches, add pork chops to skillet, and cook until blackened and an instant-read thermometer inserted in thickest portion of pork registers 135°F, about 5 minutes per side. Transfer to a plate, and set aside.

3 Add beans, stock, and shallot to skillet. Cook over medium-low, stirring often, until hot, about 2 minutes. Add spinach in large handfuls, and stir until just wilted, about 2 minutes. Season with salt, and serve with pork chops and lemon wedges. —KELSEY YOUNGMAN

WINE Smoky, dark-fruited Malbec: Kaiken Ultra

BLACKENING SPICE BLEND

TOTAL 10 MIN; MAKES ⅓ CUP

4 garlic cloves, grated

1 Tbsp. garlic powder

1 Tbsp. smoked paprika

1 Tbsp. kosher salt

1 Tbsp. grated fresh ginger

1 tsp. cumin seeds, toasted and ground

1 tsp. coriander seeds, toasted and ground

1 tsp. freshly ground black pepper

1 tsp. cayenne pepper

½ tsp. ground turmeric

½ tsp. packed light brown sugar

½ lime

In a small bowl, combine grated garlic, garlic powder, smoked paprika, salt, fresh ginger, ground cumin seeds, ground coriander seeds, black pepper, cayenne pepper, turmeric, and brown sugar. Squeeze juice from lime over spice mixture, and stir until well combined. — KELSEY YOUNGMAN

PORK CHOPS WITH THREE-APPLE SLAW

For his zippy version of coleslaw, F&W's Justin Chapple swaps the cabbage for a mix of sweet and tart apples—Gala, Honeycrisp, and Granny Smith—and then tosses them with a creamy, Tabasco-laced dressing.

TOTAL 30 MIN; SERVES 4

4 (10-oz.) bone-in rib-cut pork chops (about 1 inch thick)

1½ tsp. kosher salt, divided

¾ tsp. black pepper, divided

1 Tbsp. canola oil

1 Honeycrisp apple

1 Gala apple

1 Granny Smith apple

¼ cup mayonnaise

4 tsp. apple cider vinegar

1 tsp. poppy seeds

¼ tsp. hot sauce (such as Tabasco)

4 inner celery stalks, thinly diagonally sliced, plus ¼ cup celery leaves

1 cup chopped fresh flat-leaf parsley

⅓ cup snipped fresh chives

1 Season pork chops with 1 teaspoon salt and ½ teaspoon pepper. Heat oil in a large cast-iron skillet over medium-high. Add pork chops to skillet; cook, turning occasionally, until browned and an instant-read thermometer inserted in thickest part of chop registers 135°F, 5 to 6 minutes per side. Set aside.

2 Cut each apple lengthwise into quarters, and discard cores. Thinly slice apple quarters lengthwise; stack slices, and cut lengthwise again into thin sticks.

3 Whisk together mayonnaise, vinegar, poppy seeds, and hot sauce in a large bowl; season with remaining ½ teaspoon salt and remaining ¼ teaspoon pepper. Add apple sticks, celery, celery leaves, parsley, and chives; toss to combine. Serve immediately with pork chops. —JUSTIN CHAPPLE

WINE Apple-citrusy Alsace Riesling: Lucien Albrecht Réserve

PORK LOIN WITH TONNATO SAUCE AND SUMMER SALAD

PHOTO P. 263

In this riff on the classic Italian dish vitello tonnato, pork loin replaces veal, and prepared mayonnaise makes the tuna-based sauce fast and simple. The pork, sauce, and vegetables may be prepared a day ahead for effortless summer entertaining.

ACTIVE 30 MIN; TOTAL 4 HR 40 MIN; SERVES 8

1 (1½-lb.) center-cut pork loin, tied

3½ tsp. kosher salt, divided

1½ tsp. black pepper, divided

1 cup mayonnaise

1 (5-oz.) can tuna in olive oil, drained

2 Tbsp. fresh lemon juice

8 cups mixed torn baby lettuces

12 oz. mixed heirloom tomatoes, halved or cut into chunks

4 multicolor carrots, shaved into ribbons

4 Persian cucumbers, sliced

8 Easter Egg radishes, quartered

1 Season pork with 1½ teaspoons salt and ¾ teaspoon pepper. Place pork, fat side up, on a rimmed baking sheet; let stand at room temperature 30 minutes.

2 Preheat oven to 450°F. Roast pork until fat is lightly browned, about 15 minutes. Reduce oven temperature to 375°F without opening oven door. Continue cooking until an instant-read thermometer inserted in thickest portion registers 135°F, 25 to 30 minutes. Transfer pork to a platter, and let cool completely, about 1 hour. Cover with aluminum foil, and refrigerate until chilled, about 2 hours.

3 Process mayonnaise, tuna, lemon juice, 1 teaspoon salt, and ½ teaspoon pepper in a food processor until very smooth, about 30 seconds.

4 Toss together lettuces, tomatoes, carrots, cucumbers, and radishes in a large bowl; season with remaining 1 teaspoon salt and ¼ teaspoon pepper. Untie pork, and cut against the grain into ⅛-inch-thick slices. Serve pork and salad with tonnato sauce. —JUSTIN CHAPPLE

WINE Light northern Italian red: Fratelli Alessandria Speziale Pelaverga

**PORK CHOPS WITH
THREE-APPLE SLAW**

PORK LOIN BRAISED WITH MUSHROOMS AND WINE

Fistfuls of fresh herbs, fragrant strips of orange peel, and plenty of garlic perfume the wine-infused braising liquid that penetrates this essential Corsican comfort food. The resulting jus is vibrant and richly seasoned; ladle extra over the polenta on each plate.

ACTIVE 50 MIN; TOTAL 1 HR 20 MIN; SERVES 4

- 1 (2-lb.) boneless center-cut pork loin, tied with kitchen twine
- 1½ tsp. coarse sea salt
- ½ tsp. black pepper
- 3 Tbsp. olive oil
- 1 lb. white button mushrooms, quartered
- 8 small white spring onions (about 10 oz.), trimmed, white parts only
- 3 large garlic cloves, smashed
- ½ cup (4 oz.) Corsican Muscat wine
- 1 cup lower-sodium chicken stock
- 3 fresh rosemary sprigs
- 6 fresh thyme sprigs
- 8 (3-inch) orange peel strips
- Cooked polenta, for serving

1 Preheat oven to 400°F. Sprinkle salt and pepper evenly over pork. Heat oil in a large ovenproof skillet or Dutch oven over medium-high.

2 Add pork to pan; cook over medium-high, undisturbed, until golden brown on one side, about 3 minutes. Turn pork. Repeat until each side is browned, about 12 minutes. Remove pork from skillet.

3 Add mushrooms, onions, and garlic to pan; cook over medium-high, stirring often, until liquid from mushrooms has released and evaporated, about 8 minutes. Add wine; cook, scraping up browned bits from bottom of pan, until wine is reduced by half, about 5 minutes. Add stock, rosemary, and thyme; cook, undisturbed, 3 minutes. Return pork to pan. Cover, transfer to preheated oven, and roast until a thermometer inserted in thickest portion of meat registers 130°F, about 30 minutes.

4 Remove pan from oven. Transfer pork to a cutting board; let rest 5 minutes. Meanwhile, add orange peel strips to mushroom mixture in pan. Bring to a boil over medium-high; boil until sauce has slightly thickened, about 3 minutes. Discard orange peel strips, rosemary, and thyme.

5 Remove and discard twine from pork. Slice pork against the grain. Serve over polenta with mushroom mixture. —FOOD & WINE

WINE Aromatic Corsican white: Antoine Arena Carco Patrimonio Blanc

NOTE If you can't find Corsican Muscat, you can substitute Moscato d'Asti.

GREEN CHORIZO AND POTATO TACOS

A punchy green chorizo is the star of these petite tacos, but the hidden heroes are the tiny cubes of fried potato—they're salty, crispy, and absolutely irresistible.

ACTIVE 25 MIN; TOTAL 30 MIN; SERVES 6

⅓ cup canola oil

2 cups finely diced russet potatoes (from 2 medium potatoes)

2¼ tsp. kosher salt, divided

Green Chorizo (recipe follows)

⅓ cup lower-sodium chicken broth

¾ cup finely diced white onion, rinsed in cold water

½ cup chopped fresh cilantro

18 (4-inch) corn tortillas, warmed

Lime wedges, for serving

1 Heat oil in a large nonstick skillet over medium. Add potatoes in a single layer, and cook, stirring occasionally, until golden brown and crisp, 12 to 15 minutes. Transfer to a paper towel–lined bowl, and toss with ¾ teaspoon salt. Do not wipe out skillet, and return skillet to heat over medium-high; add Green Chorizo, and cook, stirring often, until crumbled and cooked through, about 5 minutes. Stir in chicken broth and 1 teaspoon salt. Cook, stirring occasionally, until liquid is mostly absorbed, about 30 seconds to 1 minute.

2 Stir together onion, cilantro, and remaining ½ teaspoon salt. Top each tortilla evenly with about 2 tablespoons chorizo, about 1 tablespoon potatoes, and about 1 teaspoon onion mixture. Serve tacos with lime wedges.
—PAIGE GRANDJEAN AND LIZ MERVOSH

BEER Hoppy craft beer: Green Flash Brewing Co. West Coast IPA

GREEN CHORIZO

Look for ground pork with plenty of fat, or ask the butcher at your meat counter to grind pork shoulder for you. Don't let the chorizo rest longer than 30 minutes or the acid will impact the texture of the pork. Cooking slightly dulls the color of the herbs; use a dash of spinach powder to amp up the green.

ACTIVE 20 MIN; TOTAL 1 HR 25 MIN; MAKES ABOUT 1½ LB.

1 medium serrano chile (about ½ oz.)

1 large poblano chile (about 6 oz.)

2 unpeeled garlic cloves

1 tsp. coriander seeds

1 tsp. cumin seeds

1 cup packed fresh cilantro leaves (from 2 bunches)

¼ cup apple cider vinegar

2 Tbsp. spinach powder (such as Koyah) (optional)

1 Tbsp. fresh Mexican oregano leaves

1½ tsp. kosher salt

1 lb. 80/20 or 70/30 ground pork

1 Roast chiles over the open flame of a gas burner or under the broiler in a preheated oven, turning occasionally, until charred all over, about 2 minutes for serrano and 6 minutes for poblano. Transfer to a bowl, and cover tightly with plastic wrap. Let stand 15 minutes. Stem, peel, and seed poblano. Stem and peel serrano, reserving seeds. Pat chiles dry, and set aside.

2 Heat a medium cast-iron skillet over medium. Add garlic cloves, and cook, turning occasionally, until charred and softened, about 12 minutes. Let garlic cool, and peel cloves. Add coriander seeds and cumin seeds to skillet; cook, stirring constantly, until fragrant, about 20 seconds. Finely grind seeds in a spice grinder or mortar and pestle.

3 Combine chiles, garlic, ground spices, cilantro, vinegar, spinach powder (if using), oregano, and salt in a food processor. Process until a coarse paste forms, about 1 minute, stopping to scrape down sides of bowl as needed. Cover and chill until cold, about 30 minutes.

4 Using hands, gently break up pork into small pieces in a large bowl. Add chile mixture, and gently combine until pork is well coated and mixture is thoroughly combined. Cover and chill 30 minutes. —PAIGE GRANJEAN AND LIZ MERVOSH

BRAISED SAUSAGE AND FENNEL
WITH TOASTED SPICES

BRAISED SAUSAGE AND FENNEL WITH TOASTED SPICES

With whole pink peppercorns and fennel seeds, this simple braise is gently perfumed and aromatic with fresh spring flavors inspired by the braised fennel at Red Hook Tavern in Brooklyn, New York, from chef Allison Plumer. Use a fresh, spicy sausage here to complement the creamy bean puree and sweet fennel.

ACTIVE 25 MIN; TOTAL 55 MIN; SERVES 4

¼ cup extra virgin olive oil, divided

6 hot Italian sausage links, pricked with a fork

2 large (13-oz.) fennel bulbs, cut in half lengthwise, cores removed, bulbs cut into 1-inch wedges, fronds reserved

2 Tbsp. fennel seeds

4 tsp. pink peppercorns

2 cups chicken stock or lower-sodium chicken broth

¼ tsp. kosher salt

1 cup hummus

Lemon zest and lemon wedges, for garnish

1 Heat 2 tablespoons oil in a straight-sided 14-inch skillet over medium-high. Add sausages; cook, turning occasionally, until browned on all sides, about 5 minutes. Transfer sausages to a plate. Add fennel wedges, cut sides down, to skillet; cook until browned on both sides, about 2 minutes and 30 seconds per side. Transfer to plate with sausages.

2 Add fennel seeds, peppercorns, and remaining 2 tablespoons oil to skillet; cook over medium-high, stirring constantly, until toasted and fragrant, 30 seconds to 1 minute. Remove half the spice mixture from skillet, and reserve for garnish.

3 Add stock to skillet, stirring and scraping bottom of skillet to loosen browned bits. Bring to a simmer over medium-high. Return sausages and fennel wedges to skillet; cover and reduce heat to low. Cook until fennel wedges are tender, about 30 minutes. Sprinkle with salt.

4 Spread hummus smoothly on a platter. Top with sausages and fennel wedges; spoon sauce from skillet over platter. Garnish with lemon zest, lemon wedges, reserved fennel fronds, and reserved spice mixture. —KELSEY YOUNGMAN

WINE Earthy Mediterranean red: Cosimo Taurino Notarpanaro

ROASTED MERGUEZ SAUSAGE
WITH APPLES AND ONIONS

For this sheet pan dinner, use Honeycrisp or Pink Lady apples, which hold their shape better during roasting than other varieties. Plus, their pleasant sweetness balances the intensely spiced merguez sausage.

ACTIVE 15 MIN; TOTAL 40 MIN; SERVES 4 TO 6

1½ lb. thin merguez sausage coil or links

3 (10-oz.) Honeycrisp or Pink Lady apples, cut into 1½-inch wedges

3 (6-oz.) red onions, cut into ¾-inch wedges

6 fresh thyme sprigs

¼ cup extra virgin olive oil

8 medium garlic cloves, coarsely chopped

1 tsp. lemon zest

1½ tsp. kosher salt

1 tsp. black pepper

½ cup chopped fresh flat-leaf parsley

1 Preheat oven to 425°F. Insert 2 skewers into sausage coil in an X shape. Place sausage coil in middle of a large rimmed baking sheet. (If using links, arrange in a single layer on baking sheet.)

2 Toss together apples, onions, thyme, olive oil, garlic, and lemon zest in a large bowl; season with salt and pepper. Scatter apple mixture around sausage on baking sheet. Roast until sausage is cooked through and apples are tender but not falling apart, about 25 minutes. Remove skewers, and cut sausage into large pieces. Sprinkle with parsley. —JUSTIN CHAPPLE

WINE Rich Lebanese red: Massaya Cap Est

ROASTED "REBLOCHON"

In the French Alps, Reblochon, a bloomy-rind cow's milk cheese, is melted in a special brazier for reblochonnade—a meal of the melted cheese served with roasted sausages, boiled potatoes, and other bites. While unpasteurized Reblochon isn't imported to the United States, there are many American farmhouse cheeses (such as Jasper Hill Farm Little Hosmer or Sweet Grass Dairy Green Hill) that make wonderful substitutes in this reblochonnade, adapted by Food & Wine *Senior Food Editor Mary-Frances Heck for home ovens.*

TOTAL 10 MIN; SERVES 2

1 (about 8-oz.) chilled wheel bloomy-rind, soft cow-milk cheese, such as Jasper Hill Farm Little Hosmer, Sweet Grass Dairy Green Hill, or Marin French Cheese Camembert

1 lb. small yellow potatoes, boiled until skins split

¼ lb. assorted ham and charcuterie

½ lb. fresh grilled sausages or sautéed mushrooms

Baguette, cornichons, mustard, and green salad, for serving

1 Arrange a rack in top of oven or toaster oven, and preheat broiler to high. Unwrap cheese; use a thin, sharp knife to cut wheel in half lengthwise, creating 2 half-moons. Turn 1 half-moon onto its cut side; cut lengthwise through the side of cheese to create 2 identical halves. Arrange cheese cut side up to form a round in a small 4- to 6-inch skillet. Repeat with remaining half-moon. Keep skillets with cheese chilled until ready to serve.

2 Just before serving, divide potatoes, charcuterie, sausages, baguette, cornichons, mustard, and salad among plates. Place skillets directly under broiler; roast cheese until top is lightly crisped and golden in spots and cheese is just pourable, 3 to 5 minutes. Working quickly, pour cheese from 1 pan over each plate. Serve immediately. —MARY-FRANCES HECK

WINE Crisp, lemony Savoie white: Domaine Labbé Abymes

CRISPY PORK CUTLETS WITH TONNATO SAUCE

Thinly sliced pork cutlets stand in for veal in this quick-and-easy weeknight version of 2020 Best New Chef Daisy Ryan's Vitello Tonnato. While the crispy pork is irresistible, it's Ryan's take on tonnato, a tuna-based sauce, that steals the show. "The lemon is the key component, bringing contrasting brightness," Ryan says of the sauce. "It instantly makes any dish more impressive, and the buttery texture is almost luxurious." Creamy and rich tonnato sauce, thickened and flavored with oil-packed tuna fillets, gets a balancing lift from fresh lemon and pickled caperberries. Reserve the oil from the tuna and whisk it together with lemon juice, salt, and pepper for a quick and easy salad dressing, if desired.

TOTAL 40 MIN; SERVES 4

1¼ cups extra virgin olive oil, divided

¼ cup jarred caperberries, plus more for garnish

3 drained anchovy fillets

1½ tsp. grated lemon zest plus 1 Tbsp. fresh lemon juice

½ tsp. black pepper, divided, plus more for garnish

2 (6.7-oz.) jars oil-packed tuna fillets (such as Tonnino), drained

½ cup water

4 (6-oz.) boneless pork loin chops, pounded to ¼-inch thickness

1½ tsp. kosher salt, plus more to taste

½ cup all-purpose flour (about 2⅛ oz.)

2 large eggs, beaten

2 cups panko

2 cups loosely packed fresh flat-leaf parsley leaves

¼ cup thinly sliced red onion, rinsed under cold water and patted dry

Lemon wedges, for serving

1 Preheat oven to 200°F. Process ½ cup oil, caperberries, anchovies, lemon zest and juice, and ¼ teaspoon pepper in a food processor until almost smooth, about 1 minute. Add tuna; process until smooth and thick, about 2 minutes, scraping down sides as needed. Transfer to a bowl; stir in ½ cup water until smooth. Cover and refrigerate until ready to use.

2 Evenly sprinkle salt and remaining ¼ teaspoon pepper on both sides of pork. Place flour, eggs, and panko in 3 separate wide, shallow bowls. Working with 1 cutlet at a time, dredge in flour, and shake off excess. Dip in eggs; let excess drip off. Dredge in panko to coat. Place on a plate.

3 Heat ½ cup oil in a 12-inch skillet over medium. Working with 1 or 2 cutlets at a time, cook in hot oil until golden brown, crisp, and cooked through, 2 to 3 minutes per side. Transfer to a baking sheet lined with paper towels; sprinkle lightly with salt to taste, and place in preheated oven to keep warm. Repeat with remaining cutlets, adding remaining ¼ cup oil to skillet after cooking 2 cutlets.

4 Divide cutlets among 4 plates; spoon about ⅓ cup tonnato sauce over each cutlet. Top evenly with parsley and onion. Garnish with additional caperberries and pepper. Serve with lemon wedges and remaining tonnato sauce.
—ANNA THEOKTISTO

MAKE AHEAD Tonnato sauce can be made up to 1 day ahead and stored in an airtight container in refrigerator.

WINE Lively, nectarine-scented Italian white: Pieropan Soave Classico

COLD ROASTED LEG OF LAMB
WITH CILANTRO-JALAPEÑO YOGURT

Cold slices of lamb are a fail-safe dinner party main. A tangy yogurt sauce laced with lime and cilantro takes it to the next level.

ACTIVE 35 MIN; TOTAL 3 HR 55 MIN; SERVES 8 TO 10

3 garlic cloves

¼ cup chopped shallot

2 Tbsp. extra virgin olive oil

1 tsp. cumin seeds

1½ Tbsp. plus 1 tsp. kosher salt, divided

2¼ tsp. black pepper, divided

1 (3¾-lb.) well-trimmed boneless leg of lamb (4½ lb. before trimming)

1 cup plain whole-milk Greek yogurt

1½ cups loosely packed fresh cilantro leaves, plus more for garnish

3 Tbsp. fresh lime juice

3 jalapeños, seeded and chopped

1 scallion, chopped (about 2 Tbsp.)

4 anchovy fillets (¼ oz.)

½ tsp. flaky sea salt

Pita bread, for serving

1 Preheat oven to 325°F. Place garlic, shallot, oil, cumin seeds, 1½ tablespoons kosher salt, and 2 teaspoons pepper in a mini food processor; process until mostly smooth. Rub spice paste over lamb. Tie with kitchen twine, securing at 1-inch intervals. Transfer to a wire rack set in a large rimmed baking sheet.

2 Roast lamb until an instant-read thermometer inserted in thickest portion registers 135°F, 1 hour and 20 minutes to 1 hour and 30 minutes. Transfer lamb to a platter, and let cool to room temperature, about 1 hour. Cover with aluminum foil, and refrigerate until chilled, about 1 hour.

3 Place yogurt, cilantro, lime juice, jalapeños, scallion, anchovies, remaining 1 teaspoon kosher salt, and remaining ¼ teaspoon pepper in a mini food processor; process until smooth, about 45 seconds.

4 Remove and discard twine from lamb. Cut lamb into thin slices, and sprinkle with flaky sea salt. Garnish with additional cilantro. Serve with sauce and pita bread.
—JUSTIN CHAPPLE

WINE Juicy, complex Côtes du Rhône: Coudoulet de Beaucastel

LAMB CHOPS WITH MANGO HONEY

This rack of lamb from St. Louis–based chef Gerard Craft benefits from a long marination; go overnight if you can for the deepest flavor. Be sure to finish with a sprinkling of flaky sea salt and plenty of mango honey.

ACTIVE 20 MIN; TOTAL 50 MIN, PLUS 6 HR REFRIGERATION; SERVES 8

- 4 scallions, thinly sliced
- ⅓ cup soy sauce
- ⅓ cup finely chopped peeled fresh ginger
- ¼ cup fresh lime juice (from 2 limes)
- ½ jalapeño, seeded and finely chopped (about 4 tsp.)
- 1 (2½-lb.) rack of lamb
- ¾ tsp. green peppercorns
- ¾ tsp. coriander seeds
- ¾ tsp. anise seeds
- 1 cup mango nectar
- ½ cup honey
- 4 fresh rosemary sprigs, tied together with butcher's twine
- Flaky sea salt

1 Stir together scallions, soy sauce, ginger, lime juice, and jalapeño in a large resealable plastic freezer bag. Add lamb to bag, and seal, squeezing out air. Refrigerate lamb 6 hours or up to overnight.

2 Heat a skillet over medium-high; add green peppercorns, coriander, and anise. Cook, stirring often, until toasted, about 1 minute. Stir in mango nectar, and cook, without stirring, until liquid is reduced by half, about 8 minutes. Remove from heat, and pour through a fine wire-mesh strainer into a bowl; discard solids. Stir in honey.

3 Preheat a gas grill to very high (500°F and up) on 1 side, or push hot coals to 1 side of a charcoal grill. Remove lamb from marinade; discard marinade. Place lamb on oiled grates over lit side of grill. Grill, covered, turning often, until seared on all sides, about 6 minutes. Transfer lamb to unlit side of grill, fat side up. Grill, covered, until a meat thermometer inserted into thickest portion registers 130°F, about 25 minutes. Using rosemary as a brush, glaze lamb with mango honey. Transfer lamb to lit side of grill, and grill, turning often, to create a lightly charred crust, about 1 minute per side. Transfer to a cutting board, and let rest 10 minutes. Cut between ribs into individual chops. Transfer to a platter, and sprinkle with sea salt. Serve with remaining mango honey. —GERARD CRAFT

WINE Smoky California Syrah: Andrew Murray Tous les Jours

LAMB SHOULDER CHOPS WITH HERB AND SUNFLOWER SEED SALAD

Lamb shoulder chops cook quickly; they're a very forgiving cut that's perfect for outdoor grilling. Here, F&W's Justin Chapple pairs the grilled lamb with a simple salad of parsley, cilantro, dill, mint, chives, and crunchy sunflower seeds—the tender herbs are a fresh foil for the lamb. Pick up one bunch of chives and two bunches each of parsley, cilantro, dill, and mint for the herb salad.

ACTIVE 30 MIN; TOTAL 45 MIN; SERVES 4 TO 6

- 5 Tbsp. extra virgin olive oil, divided
- 1 Tbsp. coriander seeds, coarsely ground
- 1 Tbsp. black peppercorns, coarsely ground
- 1 Tbsp. grated lemon zest plus 3 Tbsp. fresh lemon juice, divided
- 2½ tsp. kosher salt, divided
- 2½ lb. lamb shoulder blade chops (about 1 inch thick) or flanken-cut beef short ribs (about ½ inch thick)
- 1 tsp. honey
- 1½ cups loosely packed fresh flat-leaf parsley leaves
- 1½ cups loosely packed fresh cilantro leaves
- 1 cup loosely packed fresh dill sprigs
- 1 cup loosely packed fresh mint leaves
- ½ cup roughly chopped fresh chives
- ¼ cup salted roasted sunflower seed kernels (about 1 oz.)

1 Whisk together 2 tablespoons oil, ground coriander seeds, ground peppercorns, lemon zest, 1 tablespoon lemon juice, and 2 teaspoons salt in a small bowl. Prick lamb chops all over with a fork; rub evenly with coriander mixture. Arrange lamb chops in a single layer on a baking sheet lined with parchment paper. Let stand, uncovered, at room temperature 15 minutes.

2 Preheat grill to very high (500°F to 550°F). Place lamb on oiled grates; grill, uncovered, until charred and cooked to desired degree of doneness, 4 to 5 minutes per side for medium (about 130°F). (Reduce cook time to 2 to 3 minutes per side for medium doneness if using flanken-cut short ribs.) Remove from grill; let rest 5 minutes.

3 Meanwhile, whisk together honey, remaining 3 tablespoons oil, remaining 2 tablespoons lemon juice, and remaining ½ teaspoon salt in a large bowl. Add parsley, cilantro, dill, mint, chives, and sunflower seed kernels; toss to combine. Serve with lamb chops. —JUSTIN CHAPPLE

WINE Bright, peppery Grenache: Domaine Lafage Cuvée Nicolas

NOTE Flanken-cut short ribs are thinner than English-cut short ribs and can be purchased at Korean or Chinese grocery stores.

GRILLED LAMB SLIDERS WITH ROMAINE SALAD AND YOGURT-TAHINI SAUCE

A symphony of herbs—in the form of za'atar—and little bits of toasted pine nuts add bright flavor and texture to the ground lamb patties that accompany this fresh summer salad.

TOTAL 35 MIN; SERVES 4

SAUCE
- ½ cup plain whole-milk strained Greek-style yogurt
- 2 Tbsp. tahini
- 1 Tbsp. fresh lemon juice (from 1 lemon)
- 1 garlic clove, grated (about ½ tsp.)
- ¼ tsp. kosher salt

LAMB PATTIES
- 1½ lb. ground lamb
- ¾ cup finely chopped toasted pine nuts (from 1 cup pine nuts) (see Note)
- 2 Tbsp. za'atar
- 1 tsp. kosher salt
- 2 garlic cloves, grated (about 1 tsp.)
- ½ tsp. black pepper
- 2 Tbsp. pomegranate molasses

SALAD
- 4 cups torn romaine lettuce leaves (from 1 head lettuce)
- 1½ cups sliced Persian cucumbers (from 2 small [3-oz.] cucumbers)
- ⅓ cup thinly sliced red onion
- 1½ Tbsp. extra virgin olive oil
- 1 Tbsp. fresh lemon juice (from 1 lemon)
- ½ tsp. kosher salt
- ¼ tsp. black pepper

1 **Make the sauce:** Whisk together yogurt, tahini, lemon juice, garlic, and salt in a medium bowl until combined; set aside.

2 **Make the lamb patties:** Preheat grill to medium-high (400°F to 450°F). Place lamb in a large bowl. Add pine nuts, za'atar, salt, garlic, and pepper; mix with your hands until well combined. Divide mixture evenly into 8 (3½-ounce) portions; shape each portion into a ½-inch-thick patty. Arrange patties on oiled grates; grill, covered, until well marked and a thermometer inserted in thickest portion of meat registers 125°F, 3 to 4 minutes per side, brushing patties evenly with pomegranate molasses during final 1 to 2 minutes of grill time. Transfer cooked patties to a large platter.

3 **Make the salad:** Toss together lettuce, cucumbers, and onion in a medium bowl until combined. Drizzle with oil and lemon juice, and sprinkle with salt and pepper; toss gently to coat. Serve salad with lamb patties and sauce.
—ANN TAYLOR PITTMAN

MAKE AHEAD Sauce can be refrigerated in an airtight container up to 2 days.

WINE Spicy Mediterranean red: Cantele Salice Salentino Riserva

NOTE To toast pine nuts: Spread pine nuts on a parchment paper–lined baking sheet. Bake at 300°F for 13 to 15 minutes, stirring or shaking pan occasionally.

CHICKEN

This versatile bird can be prepared in so many different ways—whole, cut-up, just legs, or thighs, or breasts, or wings, roasted, grilled, poached, pan-fried, and more—and with a world of flavor profiles, you could eat it every night for a week and never elicit the question: "Chicken, again?"

CHICKEN WITH ROASTED GRAPES,
GARLIC, AND ROSEMARY (P. 82)

CRISPY CHICKEN THIGHS
WITH SPICE-ROASTED RADISHES

These chicken thighs, along with the simple Everyday Spice Blend, will be put to good use for dinner tonight.

ACTIVE 15 MIN; TOTAL 45 MIN; SERVES 6

6 bone-in, skin-on chicken thighs (about 3 lb.)

1½ lb. radishes (about 2 bunches), trimmed and halved lengthwise

3 Tbsp. extra virgin olive oil

2 Tbsp. Everyday Spice Blend (recipe follows)

6 cups baby arugula

Kosher salt

Preheat oven to 450°F. Toss together chicken thighs, radishes, olive oil, and Everyday Spice Blend on a large rimmed baking sheet until evenly coated. Spread in a single layer. Roast until an instant-read thermometer inserted in thickest portion of chicken registers 160°F, about 30 minutes. Divide arugula evenly among 6 plates, and top with chicken, radishes, and pan juices. Sprinkle with salt to taste. —KELSEY YOUNGMAN

WINE Lime-scented Australian dry Riesling: Leeuwin Estate Art Series

EVERYDAY SPICE BLEND

TOTAL 15 MIN; MAKES ¼ CUP

1 Tbsp. kosher salt

1 Tbsp. black peppercorns

1 tsp. cumin seeds

1 tsp. fennel seeds

½ tsp. crushed red pepper

1 Tbsp. chopped fresh rosemary

1 tsp. garlic powder

1 tsp. paprika

Combine salt, peppercorns, cumin seeds, fennel seeds, and crushed red pepper in a small skillet. Cook over medium, stirring often, until lightly toasted and fragrant, about 2 minutes. Transfer to a plate; let cool. With a mortar and pestle or spice grinder, grind to a coarse powder. Add rosemary, garlic powder, and paprika. Stir well to combine. — KELSEY YOUNGMAN

PEPPER JELLY–GLAZED CHICKEN THIGHS
WITH GRILLED PEPPERS

Sweet, spicy, and sticky pepper jelly–glazed chicken thighs pair perfectly with grilled shishito peppers, Anaheim chiles, and scallions in this dish from cookbook author and teacher Molly Stevens. Grilled limes squeezed over the cooked chicken add smoky acidity to the dish. Serve the chicken and vegetables with rice for a simple dinner.

TOTAL 35 MIN; SERVES 4

3 limes

8 boneless, skinless chicken thighs (about 2 lb. 5 oz.)

1 Tbsp. ground coriander

2½ tsp. kosher salt, divided

½ tsp. mellow red pepper flakes

¼ cup olive oil, divided

4 Anaheim chiles (10 to 12 oz.)

1 (8-oz.) pkg. shishito peppers (10 to 12 peppers)

1 bunch scallions, trimmed

½ cup hot pepper jelly

1 Preheat a grill to medium-high (400°F to 450°F). Cut limes in half. Squeeze 1 lime into a small bowl to equal 2 tablespoons juice; set juice aside, and discard juiced lime halves. Sprinkle chicken all over with coriander, 1½ teaspoons salt, and mellow red pepper flakes; rub evenly with 2 tablespoons oil. Set aside. Brush Anaheim chiles, shishito peppers, scallions, and cut sides of remaining 4 lime halves evenly with remaining 2 tablespoons oil. Sprinkle chiles, peppers, scallions, and lime halves evenly with remaining 1 teaspoon salt. Whisk together pepper jelly and reserved 2 tablespoons lime juice in a small bowl.

2 Arrange Anaheim chiles, shishito peppers, scallions, and limes, cut side down, on unoiled grill grates. Grill, uncovered, turning scallions often, chiles and peppers occasionally, and leaving limes undisturbed, until gently charred, 3 to 4 minutes for scallions and limes, 4 to 5 minutes for shishito peppers, and 6 to 8 minutes for Anaheim chiles. Transfer charred chiles, peppers, scallions, and limes to a baking sheet, and cover with aluminum foil to keep warm.

3 Arrange chicken thighs on unoiled grates; grill, covered, until nicely browned and a thermometer inserted in thickest portion of meat registers 165°F, 4 to 5 minutes per side. Brush tops of chicken thighs generously with some of the pepper jelly glaze, and grill, uncovered, until glaze is sizzling, about 1 minute. Flip chicken, and repeat with second side. Remove chicken from grill. Squeeze grilled lime halves over chicken; serve alongside chiles, peppers, and scallions.
—MOLLY STEVENS

WINE Peppery Rhône-style red: Bonny Doon Le Cigare Volant

NOTE Any mild to medium-heat fresh chile, such as poblano or Hatch, can be substituted for Anaheim chiles. Padrón peppers, the earthier and slightly spicier cousin to the shishito, would also make a nice substitute. Marash mellow red pepper flakes are available at zingermans.com.

SALT-AND-PEPPER CHICKEN THIGHS
WITH HERBY TOMATO SALAD

Accompanied by an heirloom tomato salad, these super-crispy thighs, inspired by Jess Hereth, Director of Restaurants at Olympia Provisions in Portland, Oregon, are gorgeous paired with orange wines. "Tomatoes are notoriously frustrating with wine, but the balance of acidity, tannin, and tropical flavors in orange wines seems to pair nicely," Hereth says. Depending on the sweetness of the tomatoes, adjust the lemon juice to taste; late-summer, super-ripe tomatoes may require a bit more acid. This recipe can also be prepared with four 4-ounce bone-in lamb chops; cook 4 minutes per side for medium-rare.

TOTAL 25 MIN; SERVES 2

- 4 bone-in, skin-on chicken thighs
- 2½ tsp. kosher salt, divided
- ½ tsp. black pepper
- ½ cup buttermilk, plain whole-milk yogurt, or kefir
- ¾ cup all-purpose flour (about 2½ oz.)
- ½ cup neutral oil (such as grapeseed or peanut oil)
- 2 cups cherry tomatoes, halved
- 1 small shallot, thinly sliced
- 2 Tbsp. extra virgin olive oil
- 1 Tbsp. chopped fresh oregano or thyme
- 1 lemon, cut into wedges

1 Sprinkle chicken all over with 1 teaspoon salt and the pepper. Place buttermilk in a shallow bowl; place flour on a separate plate. Working with 1 piece at a time, add chicken to bowl, and when lifting it out, let excess buttermilk drip back into bowl. Dip chicken in flour to coat on both sides. Transfer coated chicken to a separate plate.

2 Heat neutral oil in a large (10- to 12-inch) skillet over medium-high until oil is hot (about 350°F). Shake excess flour from chicken, and add chicken to oil (oil should come about two-thirds up the height of the chicken). Cook until exterior is golden brown and a meat thermometer inserted in chicken registers 165°F, about 6 minutes per side. Remove chicken from skillet using tongs, and transfer to a paper towel–lined plate or rack. Sprinkle evenly with 1 teaspoon salt; let rest 5 minutes.

3 Meanwhile, toss together tomatoes, shallot, olive oil, oregano, and remaining ½ teaspoon salt in a medium bowl. Divide chicken thighs and tomato salad evenly between 2 plates; serve with lemon wedges. —MARY-FRANCES HECK

WINE Rich, skin-contact Italian white: Paolo Bea Lapideus Umbria Bianco

CHICKEN WITH ROASTED GRAPES, GARLIC, AND ROSEMARY

PHOTO P. 75

Dinner doesn't get simpler or more elegant than this pan-roasted chicken. To make it, a whole chicken is cut into eight pieces, then roasted with grapes, garlic cloves, and sprigs of rosemary to yield crispy-skin chicken in a schmaltzy pan sauce that begs for a crusty piece of bread. "I'm on record as being a slavering fan of Angie Mar's glam-bomb fare," says Senior Editor Kat Kinsman, who is a super-fan of Mar (a 2017 Food & Wine Best New Chef) and first tried this dish to-go. "But the take-out foil pan filled with roasted grapes, garlic, and rosemary; fatty drippings; and the sloppiest, cook's-treat parts of a chicken (my favorite) may be the best thing she ever served me." Seek out a best-quality bird for this simple, focused dish, such as a pastured chicken from whiteoakpastures.com.

ACTIVE 15 MIN; TOTAL 45 MIN; SERVES 4

1 (4-lb.) whole chicken, cut into 8 pieces

4 tsp. kosher salt

⅓ cup extra virgin olive oil, divided

1 medium bunch red seedless grapes (about 2 cups), divided into small clusters

1 large garlic head, separated and cloves peeled (15 to 20 cloves)

1 (½-oz.) bunch fresh rosemary

¼ tsp. black pepper

1 Preheat oven to 400°F. Season chicken pieces with salt. Heat 1½ tablespoons oil in a large ovenproof skillet over high. Add chicken pieces, skin sides down, and cook, undisturbed, until skin is browned and crisp, about 10 minutes. Remove from heat, and transfer chicken to a plate. Add grapes, garlic cloves, and rosemary to skillet, stirring and scraping up any browned bits. Return chicken pieces to skillet, skin sides up, nestling between and atop grapes. Drizzle with remaining oil.

2 Roast in preheated oven until a meat thermometer inserted in chicken breast registers 155°F, 22 to 25 minutes. Let chicken rest 10 minutes; sprinkle with pepper. —ANGIE MAR

WINE Full-bodied, fruity white: Raeburn Russian River Valley Chardonnay

KOMBU ROAST CHICKEN
WITH KABOCHA SQUASH AND DAIKON

2019 Best New Chef Matthew Kammerer amps up butter with salty, mineral-rich seaweed at Harbor House Inn in Elk, California. We tried the butter under the skin of a roast chicken; it built major depth of flavor in this simple weeknight dinner.

ACTIVE 25 MIN; TOTAL 1 HR 40 MIN; SERVES 4

- 1 (2-lb.) kabocha or acorn squash, cut into 8 wedges, each wedge halved crosswise
- 1 (1-lb.) daikon, cut into 1-inch-thick rounds
- 2 Tbsp. olive oil
- 3¾ tsp. kosher salt, divided
- ½ tsp. black pepper
- ⅛ oz. dried kombu, broken into small pieces
- ¼ cup unsalted butter, at room temperature
- 1 Tbsp. grated garlic
- 2 tsp. lemon zest
- 1 (3- to 4-lb.) whole chicken, rinsed and patted dry

1 Preheat oven to 400°F. Toss together squash, daikon, oil, 1 teaspoon salt, and pepper in a large bowl. Arrange squash mixture in a roasting pan in a single layer.

2 Process kombu in a spice grinder until finely ground, about 25 seconds. Stir together 1 teaspoon ground kombu (reserve any remaining for another use), butter, garlic, lemon zest, and 1¾ teaspoons salt until thoroughly blended. Carefully run your fingers underneath skin of chicken breasts and thighs to loosen. Spread butter mixture under skin. Season outside of chicken with remaining 1 teaspoon salt. Place chicken on top of squash mixture.

3 Roast in preheated oven until a thermometer inserted into thickest portion of breast registers 155°F, about 1 hour, gently stirring squash mixture halfway through. Remove pan from oven; let chicken rest at least 15 minutes. Carve chicken, and serve with roasted vegetables. —LIZ MERVOSH

MAKE AHEAD Kombu butter can be made and refrigerated up to 1 week ahead.

WINE Earthy, exotic Loire natural white: La Grange Tiphaine Clef de Sol

ROAST CHICKEN WITH SAUCE CHASSEUR

Sauce chasseur is classically thickened with a rich demi-glace, but this version uses cream, which allows the flavors of the herbs, tomatoes, and acidic wine to come through.

ACTIVE 40 MIN; TOTAL 1 HR; SERVES 4

- 1 Tbsp. grapeseed or other neutral oil
- 4 (8-oz.) skin-on airline chicken breasts or boneless, skinless chicken breasts
- 1½ tsp. kosher salt, plus more to taste
- ½ tsp. black pepper
- 4 large shallots, halved lengthwise, root ends trimmed
- 8 fresh thyme sprigs
- ½ cup dry white wine (such as Aligoté or lightly oaked Chardonnay)
- 2 cups lower-sodium chicken broth
- 2 Tbsp. unsalted butter
- 8 oz. fresh wild mushrooms, cleaned and cut into bite-size pieces (about 3 cups)
- ½ cup heavy cream
- 1 large plum tomato, chopped
- 1 Tbsp. finely chopped fresh chives
- 1 Tbsp. finely chopped fresh tarragon

1 Preheat oven to 350°F. Heat oil in a 12-inch stainless-steel ovenproof skillet over medium-high. Season chicken with salt and pepper. Sear chicken in skillet, skin sides down, until skin is crisp and golden brown, about 4 minutes. Flip chicken; add shallots, cut sides down, and press into skillet. Cook chicken and shallots until shallots are browned, about 4 minutes. Add thyme and wine to skillet. Bring to a simmer over medium-high; add broth, and return to a simmer. Carefully transfer skillet (so skin of chicken stays dry) to preheated oven, and roast until thermometer inserted into thickest part of breasts registers 155°F, about 20 minutes.

2 Remove skillet from oven. Using tongs, place chicken breasts and shallots on a plate; tent with aluminum foil to keep warm while making sauce. Pour broth mixture through a fine wire-mesh strainer into a heatproof bowl or measuring cup, and set aside. Wipe skillet clean, and return to high heat.

3 Melt butter in skillet, and add mushrooms in a single layer. Cook, without stirring, until browned on one side, about 2 minutes. Shake skillet to loosen mushrooms; cook, without stirring, until mushrooms just begin to release their juices, about 2 minutes. Add strained broth mixture and cream to skillet, and bring to a boil over high. Reduce heat to medium-low, and simmer, stirring occasionally, until mushrooms are tender and sauce is thick enough to coat the back of a spoon, 10 to 15 minutes. Remove from heat, and stir in tomato, chives, and tarragon; season with salt to taste.

4 Slice chicken breasts crosswise into 1-inch-thick pieces. Divide chicken among plates, and serve with sauce chasseur. —MARY-FRANCES HECK

WINE Herb-scented village Burgundy: Louis Jadot Santenay Rouge

ROAST CHICKEN WITH HOT HONEY

Preseasoning these chicken legs with salt at least an hour before cooking ensures flavorful, juicy meat. Drizzle leftover hot honey on a cheese plate or pizza.

ACTIVE 30 MIN; TOTAL 2 HR 50 MIN; SERVES 4

2 Tbsp. kosher salt, divided

1½ tsp. black pepper

½ tsp. ground cardamom

4 chicken leg quarters

1 cup raw wildflower honey

⅓ cup unfiltered apple cider vinegar

1 Tbsp. cayenne pepper

1 tsp. smoked paprika

1 large garlic clove, roughly chopped

4 (3-inch) orange peel strips

1 fresh thyme sprig

¾ cup chopped toasted pecans

¼ cup thinly sliced radishes

¼ cup edible flowers (such as Micro Marigolds) (about ¼ oz.)

1 Stir together 4 teaspoons salt, black pepper, and cardamom. Sprinkle chicken all over with spice mixture. Arrange chicken, skin side up, on a wire rack set inside a rimmed baking sheet. Let stand at room temperature 1 hour, or chill, uncovered, 8 hours or overnight.

2 Heat 1 inch of water in a medium saucepan over low. Whisk together honey, vinegar, cayenne, paprika, garlic, and remaining 2 teaspoons salt in a medium-size heatproof glass bowl; add orange peel and thyme. Cover bowl tightly with 3 layers of plastic wrap. Place bowl in pan over warm water, ensuring bottom of bowl does not touch water. Let honey infuse 1 hour. Remove pan from heat; uncover and let mixture cool to room temperature, about 1 hour. Pour through a fine wire-mesh strainer into a bowl; discard solids.

3 Preheat oven to 450°F with rack in upper third of oven. Bake chicken in preheated oven until golden brown and a meat thermometer inserted in thickest portion registers 160°F, 30 to 35 minutes. Let rest 10 minutes. Drizzle each serving with about 3 tablespoons hot honey. Sprinkle each with 3 tablespoons pecans, 1 tablespoon radish slices, and 1 tablespoon edible flowers.
—KELSEY YOUNGMAN

MAKE AHEAD Hot honey can be made up to a week in advance. Store in an airtight container at room temperature.

WINE Fruit-forward Zinfandel: Cline Cellars Ancient Vines

FLORENTINE BUTTER CHICKEN

This recipe is inspired by Editor in Chief Hunter Lewis' trip to 150-year-old Trattoria Sostanza in Florence. Cultured butter has a higher butterfat content, with a slight tang from those cultures. The butterfat gives cultured butter a slightly higher smoke point and, when combined with olive oil, gives enough cooking time to finish the chicken and the sauce simultaneously. If the butter is darkening too quickly, remove it from the heat and continue to baste with the hot butter.

TOTAL 20 MIN; SERVES 2

1 large egg, beaten

¼ cup all-purpose flour

2 (7-oz.) boneless, skinless chicken breasts, lightly pounded to ¾-inch thickness

1 tsp. kosher salt

¼ tsp. coarsely ground black pepper

½ cup plus 2 Tbsp. (5 oz.) cold salted cultured butter (such as Vermont Creamery), cut into pieces, divided

3 Tbsp. olive oil

¼ cup fresh lemon juice (from 2 lemons)

1 Place beaten egg in a shallow bowl or pie plate. Spread flour in a separate shallow bowl or pie plate. Season chicken with salt and pepper. Working with 1 breast at a time, dip chicken in egg, letting any excess drip back into bowl, then dredge in flour, shaking off excess.

2 Melt ¼ cup butter with oil in a 10-inch stainless-steel skillet over medium-high, and cook, swirling occasionally, until milk solids begin to sink to bottom of skillet and start to brown, 4 to 5 minutes. Add chicken, rounded sides down, and cook, swirling skillet occasionally, until lightly golden, about 3 minutes. Carefully turn chicken over, and add remaining 6 tablespoons butter. Tilt skillet toward you so butter pools, and cook, basting chicken often, until chicken is just cooked through and golden brown, 4 to 5 minutes.

3 Remove from heat, and carefully pour in lemon juice (butter will start to bubble). Serve immediately. —FOOD & WINE

GRILLED CHICKEN WITH MARINATED TOMATOES AND ONIONS

In under an hour, heirloom tomatoes and slivers of red onion are transformed into a savory sauce that brings bright, summery flavor to this simple grilled chicken.

ACTIVE 45 MIN; TOTAL 50 MIN; SERVES 6

1 cup extra virgin olive oil, plus more for brushing

6 Tbsp. sherry vinegar

1½ tsp. dried oregano

1 small garlic clove, grated

2 tsp. kosher salt, divided

¾ tsp. black pepper, divided

12 oz. small heirloom tomatoes, cut into wedges (about 2 cups)

8 oz. cherry tomatoes and grape tomatoes, halved (about 1½ cups)

1 medium-size red onion, thinly sliced crosswise into rings (about 2 cups)

8 (4-oz.) chicken breast cutlets

Crusty bread, for serving

1 Whisk together oil, vinegar, oregano, garlic, ½ teaspoon salt, and ¼ teaspoon pepper in a large bowl or baking dish. Add tomatoes and onion; toss well. Let marinate at room temperature, tossing occasionally, 30 minutes to 1 hour.

2 Preheat a grill to medium-high (400°F to 450°F). Brush chicken with oil, and season with remaining 1½ teaspoons salt and ½ teaspoon pepper. Place chicken on oiled grates; grill, uncovered, until cooked through, 3 to 4 minutes per side.

3 Transfer chicken to a cutting board; let rest 5 minutes. Slice as desired, or leave whole. Transfer chicken to a serving platter; spoon tomato mixture and any remaining marinade in bowl over chicken. Serve with crusty bread. —JUSTIN CHAPPLE

WINE Supple Oregon white: Willamette Valley Vineyards Pinot Gris

GRILLED CHICKEN WITH
MARINATED TOMATOES
AND ONIONS

VERJUS-POACHED CHICKEN WITH HERBS

Made from unripe wine grapes, verjus (see Note) is high in acid but fresh-tasting. It's a killer poaching liquid for lean meats.

ACTIVE 30 MIN; TOTAL 9 HR 30 MIN; SERVES 6 TO 8

3 cups water

5 bone-in, skin-on chicken breasts
(4½ lb. total)

1 tsp. black peppercorns

2 cups plus 1½ Tbsp. verjus blanc,
divided

2 fresh flat-leaf parsley sprigs, plus
⅓ cup finely chopped fresh flat-leaf
parsley leaves, divided

2 fresh dill sprigs, plus ⅓ cup
chopped fresh dill, divided

1 fresh tarragon sprig, plus ⅓ cup
chopped fresh tarragon leaves,
divided

1½ Tbsp. kosher salt, divided

1 cup extra virgin olive oil

¾ Tbsp. flaky sea salt

1 Combine 3 cups water, chicken, peppercorns, 2 cups verjus blanc, herb sprigs, and 1 tablespoon salt in a large pot. Bring to a simmer over medium-high; reduce to low, and cook, uncovered, until an instant-read thermometer inserted in thickest portion of chicken registers 155°F, 25 to 30 minutes. Using tongs, transfer chicken to a plate; let cool 30 minutes. While chicken cools, pour about 1½ cups poaching liquid through a fine wire-mesh strainer into a medium bowl; discard solids. Set ¾ cup strained poaching liquid aside. Discard remaining poaching liquid.

2 Remove skin from chicken; carefully remove breast meat, whole, from bones. Discard skin and bones. Cut chicken breasts crosswise into ½-inch-thick slices; place in a 13- ×9-inch baking dish.

3 Whisk together olive oil, chopped herbs, remaining 1½ teaspoons salt, and reserved ¾ cup strained poaching liquid. Pour herb marinade over chicken in baking dish; cover with plastic wrap, and refrigerate 8 hours or up to overnight.

4 Let chicken come to room temperature, about 1 hour. Transfer to a serving platter, and spoon herb marinade over top. Drizzle with remaining 1½ tablespoons verjus blanc, and sprinkle with flaky sea salt. —KAY CHUN

NOTE If you can't find verjus, substitute 4 cups water and 1 cup of crisp white wine for the poaching liquid. For serving, drizzle with 1 tablespoon white wine vinegar.

WINE Lemony, lightly grassy Sancerre: Pascal Jolivet Sancerre

CHICKEN AND SHRIMP LAKSA

Top Chef *winner Buddha Lo shares this family recipe for the refreshing and brothy noodle dish popular throughout Southeast Asia. Lo's homemade laksa paste—made with fresh lemongrass, pungent shrimp paste, and nutty peanuts—forms the base of this fragrant noodle dish.*

TOTAL 45 MIN; SERVES 4

LAKSA PASTE

- 3 medium (1-oz.) shallots, chopped (about ¾ cup)
- 4 medium lemongrass stalks (about 4 oz.), sliced (about ½ cup)
- ¼ cup canola oil
- 1 (2-inch) piece fresh ginger, peeled and sliced (about ¼ cup)
- 1 (3-inch) piece fresh galangal, peeled and chopped (about ¼ cup)
- 4 small dried red chiles
- 3 large garlic cloves, smashed
- 1 cup chicken stock, divided
- ½ cup peanuts
- 2 tsp. dried shrimp paste (see Note)
- 2 tsp. ground turmeric
- 2 tsp. ground coriander
- 1 tsp. palm sugar or brown sugar

SOUP

- 2 Tbsp. canola oil
- 4 cups chicken stock
- 2 cups coconut cream (from 1 [15-oz.] can)
- 2 Tbsp. fish sauce, plus more to taste
- 8 oz. dried rice noodles
- 2 (8-oz.) cooked boneless, skinless chicken breasts, sliced
- 8 unpeeled raw jumbo shrimp, peeled, cleaned, and poached
- 1 cup fresh bean sprouts
- 4 scallions (about 1½ oz.), sliced (about ⅓ cup)
- ½ cup loosely packed fresh Vietnamese mint leaves
- ½ cup loosely packed fresh cilantro leaves
- ¼ cup fried shallots
- 1 lime, cut into 4 wedges

1 **Make the laksa paste:** Combine shallots, lemongrass, oil, ginger, galangal, red chiles, garlic, and ½ cup stock in a blender; process until mixture forms a thick, smooth paste, about 30 seconds. Add peanuts, shrimp paste, turmeric, coriander, sugar, and remaining ½ cup stock to blender; process until smooth, about 30 seconds.

2 **Make the soup:** Heat oil in a large Dutch oven over medium. Add laksa paste, and cook, stirring constantly, until fragrant, 4 to 6 minutes. Whisk in stock and coconut cream; bring to a boil. Reduce heat and simmer, covered, 10 minutes. Remove from heat. Whisk in fish sauce.

3 While stock mixture simmers, cook rice noodles according to package directions. Divide rice noodles evenly among 4 bowls. Arrange chicken and shrimp evenly on noodles. Ladle hot stock mixture evenly into bowls. Top evenly with bean sprouts, scallions, mint, cilantro, fried shallots, and lime wedges.

—BUDDHA LO

MAKE AHEAD Laksa paste can be made up to 3 days in advance and stored in an airtight container in refrigerator.

WINE Citrusy, off-dry Riesling: Fritz Haag Estate

NOTE Shrimp paste can be found at Asian grocery stores or online at foodsofnations.com.

KUNG PAO CHICKEN

At chef Ziqiang Lu's Birds of a Feather in Brooklyn, tingly heat from Szechuan peppercorns teams up with slightly sweet dark soy sauce and Shaoxing wine to build deep flavor into this quick stir-fry. Have all of the ingredients at the ready before heating the wok for best results. Lu recommends browning the dried chile peppers until well toasted. This helps tease out their aroma and leaves you with a warming mouthfeel that lingers.

TOTAL 20 MIN; SERVES 4 TO 6

- 3 Tbsp. vegetable oil, divided
- 2 lb. boneless, skinless chicken thighs, cut into 1-inch pieces
- 1 medium scallion, finely chopped
- 1 Tbsp. sliced peeled fresh ginger
- ½ tsp. Szechuan peppercorns, or more to taste
- 10 dried small red chiles (Tien Tsin or chile de árbol) (about ⅕ oz.)
- 2 garlic cloves, sliced
- 1 Tbsp. rice vinegar
- 2 tsp. soy sauce, or more to taste
- 2 tsp. granulated sugar
- 1 tsp. lao chou soy sauce (dark soy sauce)
- 1 tsp. Shaoxing wine or dry sherry
- 1 tsp. potato starch
- 2 Tbsp. crushed roasted peanuts
  Cooked short-grain rice, for serving

1 Heat 2 tablespoons oil in a large wok or skillet over high until shimmering and very hot. Add chicken; cook, stirring constantly, until chicken pieces have separated from each other and chicken is just cooked through, 3 to 5 minutes. Remove from heat. Transfer chicken to a plate lined with paper towels; set aside.

2 Return wok to heat over high; add remaining 1 tablespoon oil. Add scallion, ginger, peppercorns, chiles, and garlic; stir-fry until fragrant, 30 seconds to 1 minute.

3 Return chicken to wok; stir to combine. Stir in vinegar, soy sauce, sugar, dark soy sauce, wine, and potato starch; cook, stirring constantly, until fragrant and thick, about 1 minute. Add peanuts, and toss to combine. Remove from heat, and serve immediately with rice. —ZIQIANG LU

WINE Medium-bodied, red-fruited Beaujolais: Château du Moulin-à-Vent Couvent des Thorins

NOTE Find Szechuan peppercorns, Shaoxing wine, and dark soy sauce at Chinese grocery stores or online.

HULI HULI CHICKEN WINGS

Sheldon Simeon uses fresh ginger and pineapple juice to add bright heat and tang to the sweet, teriyaki-like homemade huli huli sauce that coats the chicken wings and pineapple slices in this recipe. The marinade helps the wings get smoky-sweet on the grill and retain a delicious juicy bite. Huli huli means "turn turn"—huli huli chicken is a local specialty on Oahu, where vendors thread chickens on a special rotating grill and broil it over charcoal. When grilling at home, be sure to turn the chicken wings often so they crisp evenly. The slices of fresh, glazed pineapple get smoky on the grill and play off the juicy, caramelized chicken.

ACTIVE 30 MIN; TOTAL 3 HR 30 MIN; SERVES 4

1 cup unsweetened pineapple juice

1 cup chicken stock

½ cup soy sauce

½ cup packed light brown sugar

⅓ cup ketchup

2 tsp. grated peeled fresh ginger (from 1 [2-inch] piece)

1½ tsp. finely chopped garlic

2 lb. whole chicken wings

½ tsp. kosher salt

1 (3-lb.) fresh pineapple, peeled and cut into ½-inch slices

Sliced scallions

1 Stir together pineapple juice, stock, soy sauce, brown sugar, ketchup, ginger, and garlic in a medium bowl. Reserve 1 cup marinade for basting and drizzling. Place chicken in a large resealable plastic freezer bag; add remaining marinade. Seal bag, and refrigerate at least 3 hours or up to overnight.

2 Remove chicken from marinade; discard marinade. Sprinkle chicken with salt. Preheat grill to medium (350°F to 400°F). Place chicken on oiled grates; grill, turning and basting often with ½ cup of the reserved marinade, until crispy and a meat thermometer registers 160°F, about 25 to 35 minutes. Transfer chicken to a platter. Baste pineapple slices with some of the remaining marinade; place on oiled grates, and grill, uncovered, until grill marks appear, about 4 minutes per side. Cut pineapple slices as desired. Add to platter, and garnish with scallions. Drizzle with remaining marinade. —SHELDON SIMEON

WINE Tropical-fruited California Chardonnay: La Crema Sonoma Coast

AUNTIE GEORGIA'S DAKGANGJEONG
(KOREAN FRIED CHICKEN WITH SOY SAUCE)

A sticky glaze of soy sauce and brown sugar gets subtle heat from fresh jalapeños to give these crispy fried wings the perfect level of spice, sweetness, and salt.

ACTIVE 25 MIN; TOTAL 40 MIN; SERVES 4 TO 6

- 2 lb. chicken wings, cut at joints, wing tips discarded
- 1 cup potato starch
- 4 cups vegetable oil, divided
- 2 small jalapeños, stemmed and thinly sliced (about ½ cup), plus more for garnish
- ¼ cup light brown sugar
- ¼ cup soy sauce
- 5 medium garlic cloves, sliced
- Chrysanthemum greens (optional)

1 Working in batches, toss together wings and starch in a large bowl to coat, shaking off excess. Repeat process, working in batches, to coat all wings a second time. Place in an even layer on a wire rack set inside a large rimmed baking sheet. Let stand at room temperature until starch begins to appear wet, about 15 minutes.

2 Heat 3½ cups oil in a large high-sided pan over medium-high until a deep-fry thermometer registers 350°F, adjusting heat as needed to maintain temperature. Working in batches, fry wings, turning often, until light golden brown, 3 to 4 minutes. Drain on a baking sheet lined with paper towels. Working in batches, return fried wings to hot oil; fry, turning often, until golden brown, about 2 minutes. Return to baking sheet.

3 Combine jalapeños, brown sugar, soy sauce, garlic, and remaining ½ cup oil in a medium skillet. Cook over medium-high, stirring occasionally, until oil begins to bubble, about 2 minutes. Place 5 wings in sauce in skillet; toss constantly using tongs until wings are deep golden brown and fully coated, about 30 seconds. Place wings on a serving platter. Quickly repeat process with remaining wings. Garnish with additional fresh jalapeño slices and, if using, chrysanthemum greens. —GEORGIA SONG

WINE Full-bodied, toasty Chardonnay: Newton Unfiltered

NOTE For a milder dish, remove seeds from jalapeños.

PERUVIAN CHICKEN SKEWERS

These Peruvian skewers are coated in a thick chile marinade that withstands the heat of the grill and clings to the chicken, yielding caramelized, charred bits.

ACTIVE 30 MIN; TOTAL 40 MIN; MAKES 8 SKEWERS

8 (12-inch) wooden skewers

½ cup ají panca paste (about 4 oz.)

5 Tbsp. extra virgin olive oil

3 Tbsp. red wine vinegar

2 Tbsp. gochujang

1 Tbsp. tamari or soy sauce

1½ tsp. toasted cumin seeds

¼ tsp. dried Mexican oregano

⅛ tsp. black pepper

1 large garlic clove

1½ lb. boneless, skinless chicken thighs, cut into 1-inch cubes

Huacatay Dipping Sauce (recipe follows)

1 Soak skewers in water 30 minutes.

2 Meanwhile, preheat grill to very high (500°F to 550°F). Place ají panca paste, olive oil, vinegar, gochujang, tamari, cumin, oregano, pepper, and garlic in a blender; process until smooth, about 1 minute. Transfer mixture to a medium bowl; add chicken, and stir to coat. Let stand 5 minutes at room temperature.

3 Remove skewers from water. Thread 4 or 5 chicken pieces onto each skewer, leaving a ½-inch space between pieces. Place kabobs on oiled grates; grill, covered, until charred and cooked through, about 4 minutes per side. Serve with Huacatay Dipping Sauce. —STEPHANIE IZARD

WINE Lively South American red: Veramonte Ritual Pinot Noir

HUACATAY DIPPING SAUCE

Huacatay, or Peruvian black mint, is related to the marigold. The jarred paste is smooth and creamy with notes of green tea; look for it online or in Latin markets.

ACTIVE 10 MIN; TOTAL 40 MIN; MAKES ABOUT 1⅔ CUPS

¼ cup neutral oil (such as grapeseed)

¼ cup roughly chopped red onion

1 jalapeño, seeded and sliced

4 garlic cloves, finely chopped

¾ cup huacatay paste

4 oz. cream cheese (about ½ cup), at room temperature

¼ cup fresh lime juice (from 2 limes)

¼ cup loosely packed fresh mint leaves, chopped

1 Heat oil in a medium skillet over medium. Add onion, jalapeño, and garlic; cook, stirring occasionally, until tender, about 4 minutes. Stir in huacatay paste. Remove from heat, and let cool to room temperature, about 30 minutes.

2 Transfer huacatay mixture to a blender; process until smooth, about 30 seconds. Add cream cheese, lime juice, and mint; process until fully incorporated, about 30 seconds. —STEPHANIE IZARD

MEATLESS

With many of us trying to eat less meat these days, these recipes sourced from chefs leaning into the exciting textures and flavors that plants offer will help you make nourishing, delicious, satisfying meals. Here, find crispy cheese-and-greens tacos, charred veggie steaks, Korean-inspired tofu stew— and much more.

KING OYSTER MUSHROOM
STEAKS WITH PESTO AND
ALMOND AILLADE (P. 106)

CRISPY RICOTTA-KALE TACOS

You'll see requesón in taco fillings in the central and northern states in Mexico. Whole-milk ricotta works well as a substitute; be sure to let it drain for 15 minutes before using. Leftover salsa is delicious slathered on grilled or roasted swordfish and lamb or with plantain chips for dipping.

ACTIVE 20 MIN; TOTAL 45 MIN; SERVES 4

SALSA

- 1 lb. fresh tomatillos, husks removed
- 1 unpeeled garlic clove
- 1¼ tsp. kosher salt
- ⅓ cup chopped salted roasted pistachios
- 2 Tbsp. fresh lime juice
- 1 small serrano chile, finely chopped (about 1 Tbsp.)
- 1 Tbsp. thinly sliced scallion

TACOS

- 1 Tbsp. olive oil
- 2 cups packed thinly sliced kale
- 1 tsp. plus a pinch of kosher salt, divided
- ½ tsp. plus a pinch of freshly ground black pepper, divided
- 8 (6- to 8-inch) corn tortillas
- 1 (15-oz.) container requesón or whole-milk ricotta cheese, drained in a colander 15 minutes
- ⅓ cup canola oil

1 **Make the salsa:** Preheat broiler to high with oven rack in upper third of oven. Place tomatillos and garlic in a 10-inch cast-iron skillet. Broil on upper rack, turning often, until evenly charred and tomatillos begin to release some of their liquid, about 10 minutes. Remove from skillet, and set aside. When garlic is cool enough to handle, remove and discard peel. Place tomatillos, garlic, and salt in a molcajete or mortar and pestle; mash until pulpy in texture. (To use a blender, pulse until roughly chopped, about 3 times, keeping some of the texture.) Transfer tomatillo mixture to a bowl, and stir in pistachios, lime juice, chile, and scallion.

2 **Make the tacos:** Heat olive oil in a clean 10-inch cast-iron skillet over medium. Add kale, a pinch of salt, and a pinch of pepper. Cook, stirring often, until kale is slightly wilted, about 4 minutes. Transfer to a medium bowl, and set aside to let cool slightly. Wipe out skillet.

3 Working with 1 tortilla at a time, place tortilla in skillet. Cook over medium until pliable, about 15 seconds per side. Wrap warmed tortillas in a clean kitchen towel, and set aside. Add drained requesón, remaining 1 teaspoon salt and remaining ½ teaspoon pepper to kale; stir until combined. Spoon about ¼ cup cheese filling down center of each tortilla; fold in half.

4 Add canola oil to skillet, and heat over medium-high until oil is shimmering but not smoking. Add a few tacos at a time, and fry until golden and lightly crisp, 20 to 30 seconds per side. (You're not deep frying until jaggedly crispy; you're only pan-frying for a little texture.) Drain tacos on a baking sheet lined with paper towels. Serve immediately with salsa. —PAOLA BRISEÑO GONZALÉZ AND JAVIER CABRAL

BEER Hoppy, piney IPA: Sierra Nevada Torpedo Extra IPA

DINKIES CHEEZESTEAK

This gloriously sloppy sub is the creation of Pinky Cole, founder of the popular Atlanta-based Slutty Vegan, and Derrick Hayes, Philly native and founder of Big Dave's Cheesesteaks. In Cole's Dinkies Cheezesteak, a plant-based version of Hayes' meat-packed hoagie, plant-based meat gets piled into toasted rolls with tender peppers, onions, and gooey pools of vegan cheese. Slutty Vegan's signature seasoning blend is available online, or substitute regular seasoned salt.

TOTAL 30 MIN; SERVES 4

1½ lb. plant-based ground meat (such as Impossible or Beyond Beef)

1 Tbsp. plus 1 tsp. all-purpose seasoning blend (such as Slutty Vegan Slut Dust)

1½ Tbsp. olive oil

1 medium-size green bell pepper, stemmed, seeded, and thinly sliced (about 2 cups)

1 small yellow onion, thinly sliced (about 2 cups)

6 (¾-oz.) vegan American cheese slices

6 (¾-oz.) vegan provolone cheese slices

1 Tbsp. water

6 Tbsp. vegan mayonnaise

4 (8-inch-long) vegan sub rolls, split horizontally and toasted

1 Using your hands, mix plant-based meat and seasoning blend in a medium bowl until well combined. Set aside.

2 Heat oil in a large skillet over medium-high. Add bell pepper, onion, and plant-based meat mixture; cook, stirring often to break mixture into small pieces, until bell pepper and onion are tender, plant-based meat is browned, and no liquid remains in skillet, 12 to 16 minutes. Reduce heat to medium-low. Spread mixture in an even layer in skillet, and top evenly with vegan cheese slices. Drizzle 1 tablespoon water around edge of skillet. Cover and cook until cheese is melted, 2 to 4 minutes. Remove from heat.

3 Spread 1½ tablespoons vegan mayonnaise over cut sides of each sub roll. Fill rolls evenly with plant-based meat mixture. Serve immediately. —PINKY COLE AND DERRICK HAYES

WINE Juicy, full-bodied Zinfandel: Marietta Cellars Román

NOTE Slut Dust seasoning blend is available online at sluttyvegan.shop.

KING OYSTER MUSHROOM STEAKS
WITH PESTO AND ALMOND AILLADE

PHOTO P. 101

Chef Julia Sullivan employs a duo of cast-iron skillets to prepare the tender, crispy-edged mushroom steaks at Henrietta Red in Nashville: one for cooking the mushrooms, the other for pressing them flat so they cook evenly. Buttery roasted almonds balance the sharper notes of garlic and lemon in this rustic French sauce.

ACTIVE 35 MIN; TOTAL 55 MIN; SERVES 6

½ cup raw almonds

¼ cup extra virgin olive oil, divided

1 garlic clove, coarsely chopped

1 tsp. grated lemon zest plus 1 Tbsp. fresh lemon juice, divided, plus more zest for garnish

1¾ tsp. kosher salt, divided, plus more to taste

6 king oyster mushrooms (about 2 lb.), trimmed and halved lengthwise

6 Tbsp. olive oil, divided

1 tsp. black pepper, divided

1¼ cups refrigerated pesto

Flaky sea salt, to taste

1 Preheat oven to 325°F. Spread almonds in an even layer on a rimmed baking sheet. Bake in preheated oven until toasted, 8 to 10 minutes, stirring once after 5 minutes. Let cool 5 minutes.

2 Coarsely chop almonds. Place almonds, 2 tablespoons extra virgin olive oil, garlic, lemon zest, and ¼ teaspoon kosher salt in a food processor. Pulse until mixture is finely chopped, about 12 pulses. Transfer mixture to a small bowl. Stir in remaining 2 tablespoons extra virgin olive oil; add kosher salt to taste. Let stand at room temperature at least 30 minutes.

3 Score the cut sides of each mushroom half with a ⅛-inch-deep diamond pattern. Heat 3 tablespoons olive oil in a large cast-iron skillet over medium-high. Place 6 mushroom halves, cut sides down, in hot oil. Sprinkle with ½ teaspoon kosher salt and ¼ teaspoon pepper. Wrap the bottom of a second large cast-iron skillet with aluminum foil, and place on top of mushrooms. (If using a lighter skillet, weight down with canned goods.) Reduce heat to medium; cook mushrooms, weighted down with skillet, until golden brown, 5 to 7 minutes. Remove top skillet; flip mushrooms, and sprinkle with ¼ teaspoon kosher salt and ¼ teaspoon pepper. Continue cooking mushrooms, weighted down with skillet, until tender and golden on both sides, 4 to 6 minutes. Remove mushrooms from skillet. Return skillet to medium-high, and repeat process with remaining olive oil, mushrooms, kosher salt, and pepper.

4 To serve, spoon about 3 tablespoons pesto on each of 6 plates. Top evenly with mushroom halves and almond aillade. Drizzle with lemon juice; sprinkle with flaky sea salt to taste, and garnish with additional lemon zest. —JULIA SULLIVAN

MAKE AHEAD Almond aillade can be made up to 3 hours in advance.

WINE Fresh, lightly almondy Orvieto: Antinori San Giovanni Della Sala

SMOKY MUSHROOM SKEWERS
WITH LABNEH AND SALSA VERDE

Thick-stemmed king trumpet mushrooms grill up meaty and tender, while feathery oyster mushrooms get nice and crispy—both are great options for these quick-cooking kabobs. Piled into warm pitas with a smear of tangy labneh and a drizzle of intensely herby salsa verde, this dish is a fun, fresh way to enjoy mushrooms.

TOTAL 30 MIN; SERVES 4

SALSA VERDE

- 1 cup loosely packed fresh flat-leaf parsley leaves (about ½ oz.)
- 1 cup loosely packed fresh cilantro leaves (about ½ oz.)
- 2 scallions, coarsely chopped (about ¾ cup)
- 3 Tbsp. fresh lemon juice
- 2 fresh serrano chiles, seeded (if desired) and coarsely chopped (about 3 Tbsp.)
- 2 (1½-inch) ice cubes
- ½ cup extra virgin olive oil
- ½ tsp. kosher salt
- ¼ tsp. black pepper

GRILLED MUSHROOMS

- ½ cup extra virgin olive oil
- 2 garlic cloves, minced
- 1¼ tsp. kosher salt, divided
- ¾ tsp. black pepper, divided
- 1 lb. fresh whole oyster mushroom heads (about 2 heads), trimmed and cut into 6 large pieces
- 1 lb. fresh medium-size king trumpet mushrooms (about 6 mushrooms), cut into 2- × ¾-inch pieces

ADDITIONAL INGREDIENTS

Labneh, warm pita rounds, and roasted sunflower seeds, for serving

1 **Make the salsa verde:** Pulse parsley, cilantro, scallions, lemon juice, chiles, and ice cubes in a food processor until roughly chopped, about 10 pulses. With processor running, pour oil through food chute, processing until mixture is smooth, about 15 seconds. Transfer mixture to a bowl; stir in salt and pepper. Set aside until ready to use, or refrigerate in an airtight container up to 2 days.

2 **Make the grilled mushrooms:** Preheat grill to medium-high (400°F to 450°F). Whisk together oil, garlic, ¼ teaspoon salt, and ¼ teaspoon pepper in a medium bowl until combined; set aside. Thread oyster mushrooms evenly onto 2 (9-inch) metal or wooden double-prong skewers; thread king trumpet mushrooms evenly onto similar skewers. Brush mushrooms with some of the garlic-oil mixture; sprinkle evenly with remaining 1 teaspoon salt and remaining ½ teaspoon pepper. Place mushroom skewers on oiled grill grates; grill, uncovered, until lightly charred, about 10 minutes, turning once or twice and basting with remaining garlic oil.

3 Serve mushrooms with salsa verde, labneh, warm pita, and sunflower seeds.
—JUSTIN CHAPPLE

WINE Peppery, cool-climate Syrah: Delas Les Launes Rouge

ROASTED BROCCOLI STEAKS
WITH TOMATO BUTTER AND TAPENADE

At his Philadelphia restaurant, Chef Greg Vernick treats broccoli like a steak, roasting it at a high temperature on a preheated pan to achieve a lightly charred crust. Cooked on the same pan, umami-packed tomatoes blend up into a super-quick sauce enriched with just the right amount of butter.

ACTIVE 20 MIN; TOTAL 50 MIN; SERVES 4

- 2 oz. bakery white or rye bread, torn into small pieces (about 1 cup)
- 6 Tbsp. olive oil, divided
- 3½ tsp. kosher salt, divided
- 1¾ tsp. black pepper, divided
- 2 medium broccoli heads, stems trimmed to 3 inches and heads cut lengthwise into 8 (¾-inch-thick) steaks
- 2 cups cherry tomatoes (about 10 oz.)
- 1 small red onion, cut into 1-inch wedges (root trimmed)
- 4 to 8 Tbsp. unsalted vegetable stock
- 2 Tbsp. unsalted butter, chilled and cut into ½-inch pieces
- ¼ cup jarred tapenade (such as Divina Olive Bruschetta)

1 Preheat oven to 475°F. Toss together bread, 2 tablespoons oil, ½ teaspoon salt, and ¼ teaspoon pepper on a rimmed baking sheet. Bake in preheated oven until bread is golden brown and crisp, 4 to 6 minutes, stirring once after 3 minutes. Remove from oven; set aside. Reduce oven temperature to 425°F.

2 Place a rimmed baking sheet in oven; let warm at 425°F 10 minutes. Toss together broccoli steaks, tomatoes, onion wedges, 2 teaspoons salt, 1 teaspoon pepper, and remaining ¼ cup oil in a large bowl. Arrange mixture in a single layer on preheated pan. Bake at 425°F until broccoli is tender and charred in spots, 20 to 25 minutes, flipping broccoli and onion after 10 minutes. Remove from oven.

3 Transfer tomatoes, onion, and ¼ cup stock to a blender. Secure lid on blender, and remove center piece to allow steam to escape. Place a clean towel over opening. Process until smooth, about 30 seconds, adding remaining ¼ cup stock, 1 tablespoon at a time, as needed to thin sauce to a pourable consistency. With blender running, gradually add butter, processing until sauce is glossy and thick, about 20 seconds. Stir in remaining 1 teaspoon salt and ½ teaspoon pepper.

4 Spoon about ¼ cup tomato sauce onto each of 4 plates. Top with broccoli steaks, tapenade, and toasted breadcrumbs. —GREG VERNICK

WINE Savory Rhône-style red: Joey Tensley Fundamental Red Blend

ROASTED BUTTERNUT SQUASH
WITH CHORIZO-SPICED KALE

With its earthy sweetness and dense texture, butternut squash makes a hearty vegetable steak. At Chaval in Portland, Maine, chef Damian Sansonetti highlights its complexity with his chorizo spice mix. He blooms the blend of cumin, pimentón, and coriander in oil to release their aroma, which provides a smoky foundation for this shoulder-season dish.

ACTIVE 15 MIN; TOTAL 35 MIN; SERVES 4

- 2 medium (3-lb.) butternut squash, necks peeled, each squash cut lengthwise into 4 (½-inch-thick) planks (squash bulbs reserved for another use)
- ¼ cup olive oil, divided
- 2¼ tsp. kosher salt, divided, plus more to taste
- 1¼ tsp. black pepper, divided
- 1 tsp. ground cumin
- ½ tsp. Pimentón de la Vera picante
- ¼ tsp. ground coriander
- ¼ cup thinly sliced red onion
- 2 garlic cloves, thinly sliced
- 1 medium bunch lacinato kale (about 8 oz.), stems removed and leaves cut into ½-inch-wide ribbons
- 1 tsp. apple cider vinegar
- 2 oz. Cotija cheese, crumbled (about ½ cup)
- ¼ cup salted roasted pepitas

1 Preheat oven to 475°F. Place a rimmed baking sheet in oven; let warm 10 minutes.

2 Meanwhile, drizzle squash planks evenly with 2 tablespoons oil; sprinkle with 2 teaspoons salt and 1 teaspoon pepper.

3 Arrange squash planks on hot baking sheet in a single layer. Roast in preheated oven until golden brown and tender, 22 to 30 minutes, flipping after 12 minutes.

4 While squash planks roast, heat remaining 2 tablespoons oil in a large skillet over medium. Add cumin, pimentón, and coriander; cook, stirring constantly, until fragrant, about 30 seconds. Add onion and garlic; cook, stirring constantly, until slightly softened, about 1 minute. Stir in kale, 2 tablespoons water, remaining ¼ teaspoon salt, and remaining ¼ teaspoon pepper. Cover and cook, stirring often, until kale is wilted and tender, 2 to 3 minutes. Remove from heat; stir in vinegar. Season with salt to taste.

5 Divide squash planks among 4 plates. Top squash with kale mixture, and sprinkle with cheese and pepitas. —DAMIAN SANSONETTI

MAKE AHEAD Roasted squash planks can be held at room temperature up to 2 hours and served at room temperature. Make the kale mixture just before serving.

WINE Full-bodied, spicy white: Tim Smith Eden Valley Viognier

NOTE Any hard winter squash, such as honeynut or buttercup, can be substituted for butternut in this recipe.

CREAMY POLENTA WITH BURST CHERRY TOMATO-AND-RED WINE RAGOUT

Laced with ribbons of hearty greens, Nashville chef Julia Sullivan's savory garden tomato ragout pops with bright flavor, the perfect accompaniment to a canvas of creamy polenta. The polenta is cooked with milk for a comforting vegetarian main. Garlic and basil punch up this modern classic; it's an easy addition to your weeknight rotation.

TOTAL 45 MIN; SERVES 4

POLENTA

- 3 cups whole milk
- 2 cups water
- 2 garlic cloves, smashed
- 4 (5-inch) fresh thyme sprigs
- 1 Tbsp. kosher salt
- ½ tsp. black pepper
- 1 cup uncooked coarse-ground polenta

RAGOUT

- ½ cup extra virgin olive oil
- 4 cups mixed cherry tomatoes (such as Black Cherry, Sun Gold, and Green Zebra)
- 1¼ tsp. kosher salt, divided
- ¼ tsp. black pepper
- 4 garlic cloves, minced
- ½ tsp. crushed red pepper, or more to taste
- 1 cup (8 oz.) dry red wine
- 2 cups thinly sliced leafy greens (such as Swiss chard, lacinato kale, tatsoi, or napa cabbage)
- ⅓ cup thinly sliced fresh basil, plus torn leaves, for garnish
- 2 Tbsp. unsalted butter, cut into pieces
- 1 tsp. fresh lemon juice

1 **Make the polenta:** Bring milk, 2 cups water, garlic, thyme, salt, and black pepper to a boil in a large saucepan over medium-high, stirring occasionally. Reduce heat to medium-low; remove and discard garlic and thyme, and bring to a gentle simmer. Gradually add polenta in a slow stream, whisking constantly until thickened. Return to a gentle simmer over medium-low. Reduce heat to low, and cook, stirring and scraping bottom of pot often, until tender and creamy, 30 to 35 minutes.

2 **While polenta cooks, make the ragout:** Heat oil in a large skillet over medium-high just until fragrant. Carefully add tomatoes, 1 teaspoon salt, and black pepper. Reduce heat to medium, and cook, stirring often, until most of the tomatoes have burst and juices start to release, 8 to 10 minutes. Cook, stirring occasionally, until tomatoes begin to stick to bottom of pan and sauce has thickened, 8 to 10 minutes. Add garlic and crushed red pepper; cook, stirring constantly, until fragrant, about 30 seconds. Add red wine, and cook, stirring occasionally, until a glossy sauce forms, about 10 minutes. Add greens, and cook, stirring constantly, until wilted, about 30 seconds. Stir in sliced basil and butter. Remove from heat, and stir in lemon juice. Season with remaining ¼ teaspoon salt.

3 Divide polenta evenly among 4 bowls; top with ragout. Garnish servings with torn basil. —JULIA SULLIVAN

MAKE AHEAD Ragout can be made up to 3 days ahead and stored in an airtight container in refrigerator.

WINE Medium-bodied, lightly herbal Italian red: Russiz Superiore Collio Cabernet Franc

TOFU BHURJI

Medium-firm tofu has just enough moisture to crumble into a scrambled egg–like texture in this breakfast dish inspired by Indian anda bhurji. Slightly pink in color, the kala namak (black salt) adds eggy, sulfurous flavors to this dish.

TOTAL 40 MIN; SERVES 2 TO 4

1 (19-oz.) pkg. medium-firm tofu, drained

2 Tbsp. neutral oil (such as canola)

1 tsp. cumin seeds

1 small red onion, finely chopped (about 1 cup)

1 small fresh Thai chile, unseeded and finely chopped (about ½ tsp.)

1 small tomato, finely chopped (about ½ cup)

1 garlic clove, finely chopped (about 1 tsp.)

1 (½-inch) piece fresh ginger, peeled and grated (about ¼ tsp.)

½ tsp. ground turmeric

¼ tsp. black pepper

¼ tsp. kala namak (black salt)

¾ tsp. kosher salt

¼ cup chopped fresh cilantro

Lime wedges and buttered toast, for serving

1 Place tofu in a medium bowl. Using a fork or your hands, crumble tofu into small pieces and curds, being careful not to overmash. Set aside.

2 Heat oil in a large skillet over medium-high. Add cumin seeds; cook, stirring constantly, until fragrant, about 30 seconds. Add onion and chile; cook, stirring often, until mixture is softened and onion is golden brown around edges, about 6 minutes. Add tomato, garlic, and ginger; cook, stirring often, until tomato breaks down into a chunky paste, about 2 minutes. Stir in turmeric, black pepper, and kala namak until combined. Add tofu and kosher salt; gently fold into tomato mixture until tofu turns light yellow. Cook, stirring occasionally and being careful not to overwork, until liquid has slightly evaporated, about 7 minutes. Stir in cilantro. Serve over toast with lime wedges. —ANTARA SINHA

NOTE Look for kala namak (black salt) at South Asian grocery stores or online.

KERALAN EGG CURRY

Coconut milk, tomatoes, and onions add vegetal sweetness that rounds out the fruity piquancy of Kashmiri chile powder and Thai chiles in this warmly-spiced egg curry. It's a South Indian dish that chef Margaret Pak of Thattu in Chicago, a 2020 Food & Wine Best New Restaurant, first learned to make from her husband, who is originally from Kerala. "The first time I had egg curry, my boyfriend (now husband) made it for me. I was mesmerized that a simple egg dish could be so comforting and delicious," she says. For the brightest flavor, toast and grind whole spices in small batches just before adding to this curry or any dish. Curry sprigs are tender and will continue to add flavor after cooking; feel free to leave them in for serving.

TOTAL 45 MIN; SERVES 4 TO 6

- 5 tsp. coriander seeds
- 4 tsp. fennel seeds
- 2 tsp. ground turmeric
- 2 tsp. Kashmiri chile powder or smoked paprika
- ¼ cup canola oil
- 2 Tbsp. finely chopped peeled fresh ginger
- 4 medium garlic cloves, finely chopped (about 2 tsp.)
- 4 to 6 fresh green Thai chiles, split lengthwise with stem ends left intact, seeds removed
- 2 (8-inch) curry sprigs
- 2 medium-size red onions (about 1½ lb.), chopped (about 4 cups)
- 4 medium-size plum tomatoes (about 14 oz.), cored and finely chopped (about 2 cups)
- ½ cup water, plus more as needed
- 2 tsp. kosher salt, plus more to taste
- 6 hard-cooked eggs, peeled and halved lengthwise
- 2 (13.5-oz.) cans unsweetened coconut milk, shaken and stirred
- Fresh cilantro, for garnish
- Cooked basmati rice, for serving

1 Toast coriander and fennel seeds in a small skillet over medium-low, stirring often, until fragrant, about 3 minutes. Remove from skillet, and let cool 5 minutes. Using a spice grinder or a mortar and pestle, grind coriander and fennel seeds until a fine powder forms. Transfer to a small bowl; add turmeric and chile powder, and set aside.

2 Heat oil in a large saucepan over medium. Add ginger, garlic, Thai chiles, and curry sprigs; cook, stirring constantly, until fragrant, about 20 seconds. Add onions; cook, stirring occasionally, until softened, 10 to 14 minutes. Stir in coriander mixture; cook, stirring constantly, until fragrant, about 1 minute. Add tomatoes, ½ cup water, and salt; cook, stirring often and scraping bottom of pan, until tomatoes begin to break down and mixture forms a coarse paste, about 5 minutes.

3 Add eggs, cut sides up, to mixture in pan. Pour in coconut milk, and gently stir to combine. Reduce heat to medium-low; cook, stirring occasionally, until flavors meld and eggs are heated through, about 10 minutes. Add additional water, 2 tablespoons at a time, if a thinner consistency is desired. Season with additional salt to taste. Garnish with cilantro. Serve with basmati rice. —MARGARET PAK

WINE Lemony, earthy, firmly acidic white: Domaine de l'Ecu Granite Muscadet

CITRUS AND BEET AGUACHILE

Chef Claudette Zepeda loves to experiment with different ingredients in her aguachiles, while still showcasing the dish's fundamental flavors of salt, acid, heat, and a little bit of sugar. For this gorgeous beet aguachile (which the chef nicknames "Vampiro" aguachile, for its deep purple-red color and for its inclusion of black garlic), Zepeda makes a bright, spicy broth out of beet juice. The unique, funky flavor from the black garlic and sweetness from the orange juice help balance the acidity of the lime juice. The beets and the broth can both be made a day ahead, making assembly a snap.

ACTIVE 30 MIN; TOTAL 2 HR 20 MIN; SERVES 4

- 8 small red and orange beets (about 1 lb.), scrubbed
- 2 cups kosher salt
- ¾ cup olive oil
- ½ cup store-bought beet juice
- ⅓ cup fresh lime juice (from 2 medium limes)
- 2 medium bunches fresh cilantro (about 2 oz. each), divided
- 1 medium (2-oz.) shallot, roughly chopped (about ⅓ cup)
- ¼ cup rice vinegar
- 1 Tbsp. grated orange zest, plus ⅓ cup fresh orange juice (from 1 orange)
- 1 small serrano chile (about ½ oz.), seeded (if desired) and roughly chopped (about 1 Tbsp.)
- 3 medium garlic cloves, roughly chopped (about 2 tsp.)
- 4 dried chiltepin or pequin chiles (unseeded), crushed
- 3 medium-size black garlic cloves, roughly chopped (optional)
- ½ tsp. fine sea salt
- 6 small radishes (about 3 oz.), thinly sliced (about 1/16 inch thick) on a mandoline
- 2 small Persian cucumbers (about 5 oz.), thinly diagonally sliced (about 1/16 to ⅛ inch thick)
- ½ cup thinly sliced red onion (from 1 small [5-oz.] onion)
- 8 (6-inch) tostada shells

1 Preheat oven to 400°F. Place beets in a rimmed baking dish; cover with kosher salt. Roast in preheated oven until beets are tender when poked with a skewer, 50 minutes to 1 hour. Remove from oven; let cool slightly, about 20 minutes. Uncover beets; using a paring knife or a paper towel, remove and discard skin. Cover beets; refrigerate until ready to use or up to 2 days.

2 While beets cook, combine oil, beet juice, lime juice, 1 cilantro bunch, shallot, vinegar, orange zest and juice, serrano chile, garlic, crushed chiltepin chiles, black garlic (if desired), and fine sea salt in a blender. Process until smooth, about 1 minute. Let stand, covered, in refrigerator 1 hour to allow flavors to meld. Pour through a fine wire-mesh strainer into a bowl, pressing on solids to extract all liquid; discard solids. Cover and refrigerate until completely chilled, at least 1 hour or up to 12 hours.

3 Remove beets from refrigerator. Cut lengthwise into quarters or sixths. Remove leaves from remaining cilantro bunch; discard stems. Ladle chilled beet broth onto a large plate, or ladle evenly into 4 shallow bowls. Arrange beet slices evenly among bowls. Top evenly with radishes, cucumbers, onion, and cilantro leaves. Serve with tostada shells. —CLAUDETTE ZEPEDA

MAKE AHEAD Beets can be prepared through Step 1 up to 2 days in advance and stored in an airtight container in refrigerator.

WINE Earthy, skin-contact orange wine: COS Ramí

NOTE Black garlic is fermented garlic that adds an earthy, sweet, umami punch to dishes and is available at nuts.com. Chiltepin or pequin chiles can be found at Latin groceries and mexgrocer.com.

WATERMELON CURRY

Sharp, pungent ajwain seeds permeate the curry with a thyme-like earthiness and complexity. Nigella seeds impart a slight bitterness and toasty onion flavor to play off the sweet melon.

ACTIVE 30 MIN; TOTAL 45 MIN; SERVES 4

- 1 small (4-lb.) seedless watermelon
- 2 Tbsp. canola oil
- 1 tsp. cumin seeds
- ½ tsp. ajwain seeds
- ½ tsp. nigella seeds
- 2 chiles de árbol
- 2 tsp. finely chopped peeled fresh ginger
- 1½ tsp. finely chopped garlic
- 1½ tsp. kosher salt, plus more to taste
- ½ tsp. ground turmeric
- 1 cup water
- 1½ Tbsp. chopped fresh cilantro

1 Using a sharp knife or a vegetable peeler, remove outer dark green skin from watermelon, and discard. Cut away pale green rind from red flesh, and chop rind into 1- to 2-inch pieces to measure about 4 cups (about 1 pound); place in a medium bowl, and set aside. Chop red flesh into 1- to 2-inch cubes to measure about 7 cups (about 1 pound, 6 ounces); set aside in a separate medium bowl.

2 Heat oil in a Dutch oven over medium-high until shimmering. Add cumin seeds, ajwain seeds, and nigella seeds; cook, stirring constantly, until fragrant, about 15 seconds. Add chiles, ginger, and garlic; cook, stirring constantly, until fragrant and garlic just picks up a little color, 20 to 30 seconds. Add pale green rind, salt, and turmeric. Reduce heat to medium; cook, stirring occasionally, until rind starts to deepen in color, about 5 minutes. Add 1 cup water; cover and reduce heat to medium-low. Cook, undisturbed, 15 minutes. If rind has not softened, cook up to 5 additional minutes, stirring and checking for softness occasionally. Uncover and gently stir in red flesh. Bring to a boil over high. Boil, stirring occasionally, until flesh has absorbed some liquid and rind has completely softened, about 5 minutes. Remove from heat. Let stand, stirring occasionally, 5 to 10 minutes to allow watermelon to marinate. Add additional salt to taste. Stir in cilantro, and serve. —VISHWESH BHATT

WINE Fragrant, floral rosé: Bonny Doon Vin Gris de Cigare

NOTE You can find ajwain and nigella seeds online at spicewallabrand.com or at your neighborhood Indian grocery store.

ORZO AND CHICKPEAS WITH TURMERIC-GINGER BROTH

Coconut milk and fresh lime juice are natural flavor partners to ginger and turmeric; here, they come together to form a restorative tea-based broth that's delicious studded with chickpeas and pasta.

ACTIVE 15 MIN; TOTAL 20 MIN; SERVES 2

- 4 single-serving turmeric-ginger tea bags (such as Rishi)
- ½ cup unsweetened coconut milk
- 3 Tbsp. fresh lime juice (from 2 limes), plus lime wedges, for serving
- ¾ tsp. kosher salt
- ½ tsp. fish sauce (such as Red Boat)
- 1 (15-oz.) can chickpeas, drained and rinsed
- 1 cup cooked orzo or other small pasta
  Thinly sliced shallot, fresh cilantro sprigs, and sambal oelek or Asian chile-garlic sauce, for serving

1 Bring 3 cups water to a boil in a teapot or small saucepan over high; remove from heat. Add tea bags, coconut milk, and lime juice; cover and steep 5 minutes. Remove and discard tea bags; stir in salt and fish sauce. Bring just to a simmer over medium. Remove from heat.

2 Divide chickpeas and orzo evenly between 2 bowls. Pour hot tea mixture evenly into bowls; serve immediately with lime wedges and desired toppings. —JUSTIN CHAPPLE

WINE Dry, lime-zesty California Riesling: Smith-Madrone Napa Valley

NOTE Look for Rishi turmeric-ginger tea at your local Asian market.

WATERMELON CURRY

SPICY TOFU AND ZUCCHINI STEW

Sommelier Annie Shi, co-owner of King in New York City, grew up going to Korean restaurants with her family. Memories of dishes like Soondubu Jjigae, a spicy Korean tofu stew, became inspiration for a quick and easy stew of tofu and vegetables that she makes for cozy weeknight dinners. Anna Theoktisto's rendition of Shi's recipe features an umami-rich broth powered by Korean fermented soybean paste and a smart shortcut dashi (made using a store-bought sachet filled with dried anchovies, shrimp, and kelp). Shi likes to pair this tofu stew with Beaujolais: "Beaujolais has an incredible ability to cut through spice, and the brambly red fruit complements stronger flavors. I like to serve my Beaujolais with a good chill to bring out the freshness—another wonderful point of contrast to the savory stew."

ACTIVE 30 MIN; TOTAL 40 MIN; SERVES 4

1 (16-oz.) pkg. firm tofu

5 cups water

1 (0.6-oz.) packet dried mixed seafood, anchovy, and dashi (such as GS Plus Seafood)

3 Tbsp. doenjang (fermented soybean paste)

3 Tbsp. gochujang

2 tsp. gochugaru, plus more for garnish

1 (1-inch) piece fresh ginger, peeled and minced (about 2 tsp.)

1 large garlic clove, minced

2 cups shredded napa cabbage

1 medium zucchini, cut into ⅛-inch-thick half-moons (about 1¾ cups)

1 small white onion, cut into ½-inch pieces (about 1 cup)

4 large scallions, cut into 1-inch pieces

1½ tsp. kosher salt

Toasted sesame oil, for garnish

Cooked white rice and kimchi, for serving

1 Cut tofu block in half crosswise. Drain half of tofu block; reserve remaining half for another use. Cut drained tofu into 1×½×½-inch rectangles; set aside.

2 Bring 5 cups water to a simmer in a medium Dutch oven over medium. Add dashi packet; simmer, covered, 10 minutes. Uncover. Discard dashi packet. Add doenjang, gochujang, gochugaru, ginger, and garlic; stir until doenjang and gochujang dissolve, about 1 minute. Increase heat to medium-high. Gently stir in tofu, cabbage, zucchini, and white onion; cook, uncovered, stirring occasionally, 4 minutes. Add scallions and salt; cook just until zucchini, onion, and scallions are cooked through but still crisp, about 2 minutes. Remove from heat. Divide stew among 4 bowls. Drizzle with sesame oil. Garnish with additional gochugaru. Serve with rice and kimchi. —ANNA THEOKTISTO

WINE Fresh, raspberry-scented Beaujolais: Domaine Jean-Claude Lapalu Beaujolais-Villages Vieilles Vignes

NOTE Find dashi packets, gochugaru, doenjang, and gochujang at Korean grocery stores or online.

FISH & SHELLFISH

The world's oceans, rivers, lakes, and streams yield a bounty of fresh fish and shellfish that can be prepared in myriad ways—just a few of which you'll find here, from the simplest hazelnut-crusted sole, to extra-crispy fish and chips, to a simple but elegant dish of seared scallops in lemon-butter-caper sauce.

PAN-SEARED BASS WITH GARLIC
SCAPE SALMORIGLIO (P. 128)

BROWN SUGAR-GLAZED SALMON
WITH BUTTERY ROASTED SQUASH

Chef Erick Williams of Virtue Restaurant & Bar in Chicago recommends thick cuts of salmon for this recipe; they cook quickly while remaining juicy and tender and are well balanced by the sweet, gingery glaze. If delicata or acorn squash aren't available, substitute 6 cups peeled and diced butternut squash.

ACTIVE 20 MIN; TOTAL 35 MIN; SERVES 4

- 2 acorn or delicata squash, halved lengthwise, seeded, and cut into ½-inch-thick slices (about 6 cups)
- 1 Tbsp. plus 2 tsp. canola oil, divided
- ¾ tsp. kosher salt, divided
- ½ tsp. black pepper, divided
- ⅜ tsp. ground ginger, divided
- 4 (6-oz., 2¼-inch-thick) wild salmon fillets (skin removed, if desired)
- ½ cup packed light brown sugar
- ¼ cup fresh orange juice
- 2 Tbsp. honey
- 2 Tbsp. chopped pecans, toasted
- 1½ Tbsp. unsalted butter, melted

1 Preheat oven to 425°F. Line a rimmed baking sheet with aluminum foil. Add squash to pan; toss with 2 teaspoons oil. Arrange squash in an even layer; sprinkle with ¼ teaspoon salt, ¼ teaspoon pepper, and ¼ teaspoon ginger. Roast in preheated oven until lightly browned, about 15 minutes, gently flipping halfway through cook time.

2 Meanwhile, remove salmon from refrigerator; let stand at room temperature 15 minutes. Combine brown sugar, orange juice, honey, and remaining ⅛ teaspoon ginger in a small saucepan. Bring to a simmer over low; simmer, stirring often, until thickened, 8 to 10 minutes. Remove from heat, and let cool at room temperature 10 minutes. Set glaze aside until ready to serve.

3 Transfer roasted squash to a large bowl. Add pecans and butter; gently toss to combine. Cover with aluminum foil to keep warm; set aside. Reduce oven temperature to 400°F.

4 Sprinkle salmon evenly with remaining ½ teaspoon salt and remaining ¼ teaspoon pepper. Heat remaining 1 tablespoon oil in a large ovenproof nonstick skillet over medium-high until shimmering. Add salmon, skin side up; cook, undisturbed, until edges begin to turn golden brown, about 2 minutes. Carefully flip fillets, and transfer skillet to oven. Roast at 400°F to desired level of doneness, 4 to 5 minutes for medium. Divide squash mixture among plates; top with salmon. Spoon glaze over salmon and squash. —ERICK WILLIAMS

WINE Full-bodied Sonoma Chardonnay: Rodney Strong Chalk Hill

GINGER-PONZU SALMON POKE

Salmon is tossed with ponzu and ginger to make this poke from Philadelphia-based food writer Kiki Aranita perfect for serving over cooked rice. Ask your fishmonger about sushi-grade salmon suitable for poke.

TOTAL 20 MIN; SERVES 4

2 Tbsp. ponzu (such as Poi Dog Maui Lavender Ponzu), plus more to taste

2 Tbsp. finely chopped scallions (from 2 medium scallions), plus more to taste

1 Tbsp. finely sliced fresh shiso (Japanese or Vietnamese) (about 6 leaves), plus more to taste

1 Tbsp. crushed unsalted roasted macadamia nuts, plus more to taste

2 tsp. perilla oil, plus more to taste

1½ tsp. grated peeled fresh ginger (from 1 [2-inch] piece), plus more to taste

1 lb. skinless sushi-grade salmon fillet

Alaea sea salt or Maldon sea salt, to taste

Toasted shiso seeds (perilla seeds) or white sesame seeds

Cooked short-grain white rice, fried wonton skin chips, or gim (dried seaweed), for serving (optional)

1 Stir together ponzu, scallions, shiso, macadamia nuts, perilla oil, and ginger in a medium bowl. (Mixture will be slightly creamy.)

2 Cut salmon into bite-size (about ¾-inch) cubes using a sharp knife. Add salmon to ponzu mixture in bowl; gently stir together until well coated.

3 Season with salt to taste. Adjust flavors with additional ponzu (umami tang), scallions (pungency), shiso (brightness), macadamia nuts (creaminess), perilla oil (velvety richness), ginger (heat), and/or salt (texture) to taste. Garnish with shiso seeds; serve immediately with desired accompaniments. —KIKI ARANITA

MAKE AHEAD Poke can be made up to 1 day in advance and stored in an airtight container in refrigerator. Reseason before serving.

WINE Substantial, spicy rosé: Domaine de la Begude Bandol Rosé

NOTE Perilla oil is available at Korean markets and online at gothamgrove.com. Poi Dog Maui Lavender Ponzu is available online at poidogphilly.com. Alaea sea salt is available online at thespicehouse.com.

PAN-SEARED BASS WITH GARLIC SCAPE SALMORIGLIO

PHOTO P. 123

Salmoriglio is a traditional Southern Italian sauce, and its pungent, acidic, herbal bite complements sweet summer tomatoes and light striped bass. Substitute the bass with another sweet, mildly fatty fish; too rich of a fish will overpower the sauce and potatoes.

TOTAL 45 MIN; SERVES 4

- 2 to 3 garlic scapes (or 1 garlic clove and 3 scallions)
- ¾ cup extra virgin olive oil
- 1 tsp. lemon zest plus ¼ cup fresh lemon juice (from 2 lemons), divided
- 1 Tbsp. water
- 1 tsp. dried Greek oregano
- ½ tsp. crushed red pepper
- 1 fresh bay leaf
- ½ tsp. kosher salt, plus more to taste
- ¼ tsp. black pepper
- 4 (5-oz., 1-inch-thick) skin-on striped bass, black sea bass, or bluefish fillets, patted dry with paper towels
- 1 cup chopped tomato
- 1 Tbsp. fresh oregano leaves
- 2 Tbsp. vegetable oil
- 1 cup loosely packed arugula
- ½ cup chopped fresh flat-leaf parsley

1 Rinse garlic scapes, and pat dry with paper towels. Trim and discard woody ends and curly tops. Cut scapes into ⅛-inch-thick slices to equal ⅓ cup. (If using scallions and garlic, slice scallions to equal ⅓ cup, and thinly slice garlic to equal 1 teaspoon.) Combine garlic scapes, olive oil, lemon juice, 1 tablespoon water, dried oregano, red pepper, and bay leaf in a small saucepan. Season with salt and black pepper. Bring to a simmer over medium. Reduce heat to low; cook, stirring often, until mixture is softened and darkened, about 5 minutes. Remove from heat; let cool 20 minutes. Discard bay leaf; stir in lemon zest.

2 Cut 2 shallow diagonal slashes across skin of each fillet; arrange in a single layer on a rimmed baking sheet lined with parchment paper. Brush both sides of fillets with 3 tablespoons garlic scape oil, and season with salt to taste. Stir tomato and fresh oregano into remaining oil; set salmoriglio aside.

3 Preheat oven to 450°F. Heat a large ovenproof skillet over medium-high until very hot, about 4 minutes. Add vegetable oil; heat until very hot, about 1 minute. Add fillets, skin sides down. Press fillets gently with a spatula. Reduce heat to medium, and cook until skin begins to brown around edges, about 4 minutes. Transfer skillet to preheated oven, and roast until fish is opaque and just cooked through, about 4 minutes. Flip fillets, and divide among 4 plates, skin sides up. Spoon salmoriglio evenly over each fillet. Sprinkle servings with arugula and parsley. —JODY ADAMS

WINE Crisp Sicilian white: Regaleali Bianco

MONKFISH PICCATA

Monkfish, with its tender, springy bite reminiscent of lobster, is firm and sweet enough to stand up to this lemony butter sauce enriched with white miso. Plenty of briny capers and caperberries help cut through the richness.

TOTAL 30 MIN; SERVES 4

½ cup plus 1 tablespoon unsalted butter, divided

12 thinly sliced garlic cloves plus 2 smashed garlic cloves, divided

1 cup unsalted chicken stock

¼ cup white miso

2 Tbsp. fresh lemon juice plus 1 lemon, thinly sliced

½ cup instant flour (such as Wondra)

¾ tsp. granulated garlic

4 (7-oz.) monkfish fillets, trimmed

1 tsp. kosher salt

3 Tbsp. canola oil, divided

2 fresh thyme sprigs, divided

14 caperberries, whole or halved

1 Tbsp. drained capers

Fresh flat-leaf parsley sprigs, for garnish

1 Cook ½ cup butter in a medium saucepan over medium-high, stirring often, until browned, about 5 minutes. Stir in sliced garlic; cook 1 minute. Whisk in stock and miso until combined. Bring to a boil; cook until reduced to about 1 cup, 10 to 12 minutes. Transfer to a blender; secure lid, and remove center piece to allow steam to escape. Place a towel over opening. Process until smooth, about 1 minute. Stir in lemon juice and reserve.

2 Stir together flour and granulated garlic on a plate. Sprinkle fish with salt; dredge fish in seasoned flour. Heat 1 tablespoon oil in a large skillet over high until it begins to smoke. Add lemon slices; cook until just browned, about 1 minute per side. Wipe skillet clean.

3 Heat 1 tablespoon oil in same skillet over medium-high. Add 2 fillets; cook until golden brown, 4 to 5 minutes per side. During the last minute of cooking, add 1½ teaspoons butter, 1 smashed garlic clove, and 1 thyme sprig to skillet; spoon mixture over fish. Discard garlic and thyme; transfer fish to a platter and keep warm. Repeat with remaining oil, fish, butter, smashed garlic, and thyme. Add caperberries, capers, and lemon slices to skillet; toss until warmed, about 1 minute. To serve, spoon reserved sauce onto 4 plates; top with fish. Spoon caperberries, capers, and lemon over each fillet. Garnish with parsley. —TIFFANI FAISON

WINE Vibrant, citrusy Sonoma Coast Chardonnay: Chalk Hill

HAZELNUT-CRUSTED SOLE WITH ROSEMARY

Crusting fish with nuts creates a crisp and very flavorful exterior and a steamy, flaky interior. Mild sole and woodsy rosemary complete this 15-minute main course, the perfect accompaniment to crisp Loire Chenin Blanc.

TOTAL 15 MIN; SERVES 4

1 cup coarsely ground hazelnuts

4 tsp. finely chopped fresh rosemary

4 (5½- to 6-oz.) skinless sole fillets

1¼ tsp. fine sea salt, plus more for serving

2 large eggs, beaten

½ cup unsalted butter (4 oz.), divided

Lemon wedges, for serving

1 Stir together hazelnuts and rosemary on a plate. Sprinkle fillets evenly on both sides with salt. Brush 1 side of each fillet with some of the egg. Place fillets, egg sides down, in hazelnut mixture, pressing lightly to adhere.

2 Melt ¼ cup butter in a large skillet over medium-high. Add 2 fillets, hazelnut sides down, to skillet; cook, undisturbed, until browned, about 3 minutes. Carefully flip fillets; cook, spooning butter in skillet over tops of fillets, until fish is flaky and opaque, about 1 minute. Transfer fillets to a plate. Wipe skillet clean. Repeat process with remaining ¼ cup butter and 2 fillets.

3 Season fillets with additional salt; serve with lemon wedges. —JACQUES THOREL

WINE Loire Chenin Blanc: Domaine de la Taille aux Loups Clos de Mosny

GRILLED MAHI-MAHI WITH LEMONGRASS-LIME AÏOLI

Sweet, mild grilled mahi-mahi harmonizes with an aïoli featuring lemongrass and lime. The creamy aïoli comes together in seconds using an immersion blender, resulting in a silky texture that's less likely to break and adding richness and zest to a classic summer meal.

TOTAL 25 MIN; SERVES 4

1 large egg yolk

1 Tbsp. grated lemongrass (grated using a Microplane, see Note)

1 tsp. grated lime zest plus 2 Tbsp. fresh lime juice (from 1 lime)

1 large garlic clove, grated (about ½ tsp.)

¾ tsp. fine sea salt, divided

3 Tbsp. avocado oil or other neutral cooking oil

5 Tbsp. extra virgin olive oil, divided

4 (6-oz.) skinless mahi-mahi fillets

¼ tsp. black pepper

1 Preheat a grill to medium-high (400°F to 450°F). Combine egg yolk, lemongrass, lime zest and juice, garlic, and ¼ teaspoon salt in a 1-pint Mason jar. Place an immersion blender inside jar, and process until mixture is well incorporated, about 3 seconds. Stir together avocado oil and 3 tablespoons olive oil in a small bowl; with immersion blender running, drizzle oil mixture into egg yolk mixture, processing until smooth and combined, 10 to 15 seconds. Set aside.

2 Brush fish fillets evenly with remaining 2 tablespoons olive oil; sprinkle evenly with pepper and remaining ½ teaspoon salt. Arrange fillets on oiled grill grates; grill, covered, until fish flakes easily and is just cooked through, 4 to 5 minutes per side. Transfer fillets to plates or a large serving platter; serve alongside aïoli.

—ANN TAYLOR PITTMAN

MAKE AHEAD Aïoli can be made up to 1 day in advance and stored in an airtight container in refrigerator.

WINE Bright, citrusy white: Adelaida Vineyards Picpoul Blanc

NOTE To grate lemongrass on a Microplane and easily break down the fibrous herb, peel away the tough outer leaves, and trim off the root end with a serrated knife. Grate the pale, softer bottom of the stalk, and reserve the woodier tops (about two-thirds of the way up the stalk) for infusing in broths, soups, and stews.

EXTRA-CRISPY FRIED FISH

Adam Evans features this fried fish recipe at his restaurant, Automatic Seafood and Oysters in Birmingham, Alabama. The gluten-free batter gets extra flavor from the spice blend, which includes garlic powder, onion powder, turmeric, and gochugaru. Evans uses skinless mahi-mahi or flounder fillets, or skin-on brown trout fillets at the restaurant; Pacific cod and haddock also work nicely here. Delicious on its own, this fish also makes great sandwiches and tacos.

ACTIVE 20 MIN; TOTAL 25 MIN; SERVES 2 TO 4

DREDGE

- ¼ cup plus 1 Tbsp. white rice flour (about 1⅜ oz.)
- ¼ cup tapioca flour (about 1⅛ oz.)
- 1 tsp. kosher salt
- ½ tsp. black pepper

BATTER

- ½ cup plus 2 Tbsp. white rice flour (about 2⅝ oz.)
- ½ cup tapioca flour (about 2⅛ oz.)
- 1¼ tsp. onion powder
- 1¼ tsp. garlic powder
- ¾ tsp. gochugaru or ½ tsp. crushed red pepper
- ¾ tsp. baking powder
- ¾ tsp. ground turmeric
- ¾ tsp. black pepper
- ½ tsp. kosher salt
- ½ tsp. granulated sugar
- 1 cup cold club soda

ADDITIONAL INGREDIENTS

- 8 cups peanut oil
- 1 lb. (1- to 1½-inch-thick) skinless mahi-mahi or flounder fillets, or skin-on brown trout fillets (4 fillets)
- 1½ tsp. kosher salt, divided
- ¾ tsp. black pepper, divided
- French fries and tartar sauce, for serving

1 **Make the dredge:** Whisk together rice flour, tapioca flour, salt, and black pepper in a large bowl until well combined.

2 **Make the batter:** Whisk together rice flour, tapioca flour, onion powder, garlic powder, gochugaru, baking powder, turmeric, black pepper, salt, and sugar in a large shallow bowl until well combined. Just before frying fish, whisk in club soda until well combined.

3 Heat oil in a 10-inch straight-sided skillet or Dutch oven to 375°F. Season fillets evenly with 1 teaspoon salt and ½ teaspoon black pepper.

4 Place 2 fillets in dredge mixture, pressing mixture onto fillets; gently shake off excess. Dip fillets in batter, allowing any excess batter to drip off. Place battered fillets in hot oil, and cook, turning occasionally, until golden brown and cooked through, 3 to 4 minutes. Transfer fillets to a wire rack set inside a rimmed baking sheet; season with ¼ teaspoon salt and ⅛ teaspoon black pepper. Repeat frying process with remaining fillets, salt, and pepper. Serve with fries and tartar sauce. —ADAM EVANS

WINE Lime-scented dry Riesling: Penfolds Bin 51

NOTE Look for gochugaru at Korean grocery stores, or find it online at spicejungle.com.

HERB-ROASTED TROUT WITH BUTTERY ALMONDS

Lemon slices and a bounty of hardy herbs flavor these tender whole trout from the inside out, while toasted almonds provide a crunchy finish. Tucked inside and underneath the fish, sprigs of rosemary, thyme, oregano, and sage release their essential oils during roasting without getting too crisp in the oven. Serve these roasted trout over a simple spring salad of arugula and thinly sliced fennel and radishes.

ACTIVE 20 MIN; TOTAL 40 MIN; SERVES 4

3 lemons, thinly sliced, divided

1 (½-oz.) bunch fresh rosemary, divided (about 10 [5-inch] sprigs)

1 (½-oz.) bunch fresh thyme, divided (about 12 [5-inch] sprigs)

1 (½-oz.) bunch fresh oregano, divided (about 35 sprigs)

1 (½-oz.) bunch fresh sage, divided (about 8 [6-inch] sprigs)

4 (12-oz.) whole trout, cleaned

3 Tbsp. extra virgin olive oil, divided

2¾ tsp. kosher salt, divided

1½ tsp. black pepper

¼ cup unsalted butter

½ cup sliced almonds (about 3¾ oz.)

1 Preheat oven to 450°F. Spread half of lemon slices and half of fresh herb sprigs on a large rimmed baking sheet lined with parchment paper. Rub trout all over with 2 tablespoons oil; sprinkle inside and outside of trout with 2½ teaspoons salt and the pepper. Stuff trout cavities evenly with remaining lemon slices and herb sprigs. Arrange trout on prepared baking sheet. Roast in preheated oven until a thermometer inserted into thickest portion of fish near the head registers 140°F, 16 to 20 minutes. Transfer trout to a large serving platter.

2 Heat butter and remaining 1 tablespoon oil in a medium skillet over medium. Add sliced almonds, and cook, stirring often, until light golden, 2 to 4 minutes. Remove from heat (almonds will continue to brown), and stir in remaining ¼ teaspoon salt. Spoon almond mixture evenly over trout. —JUSTIN CHAPPLE

WINE Fragrant, lightly off-dry Riesling: Zilliken Butterfly

SALVADORAN-STYLE PESCADO FRITO (FRIED FISH)

This recipe by chef and food writer Karla Vasquez, inspired by her mother's cooking, celebrates this popular style of cooking fish in El Salvador. Many families use mojarra, a fish found in agua dulce (fresh water), but trout makes a great substitute. Salsa inglesa, or Worcestershire sauce, is a frequent find in Salvadoran condiment drawers and teams up with the mustard to create a punchy, umami-packed crust. Delicate, meltingly tender whole trout gets crispy skin from a quick sear in a cast-iron skillet.

TOTAL 20 MIN; SERVES 4

2 Tbsp. coarse sea salt

4 (10- to 12-oz.) whole trout, cleaned and skin scored

¼ cup yellow mustard

2 Tbsp. Worcestershire sauce

1 Tbsp. garlic powder

½ medium-size red onion, thinly sliced (about 1 cup)

1 cup vegetable oil

Lime wedges, rice, and salad, for serving

1 Rub 1½ teaspoons salt evenly over outside and inside of each fish. Stir together mustard, Worcestershire sauce, and garlic powder in a small bowl. Spread evenly over outside and inside of each fish, covering completely.

2 Stuff cavities of fish evenly with onion slices. Heat oil in a large, deep skillet over medium-high to 350°F. Carefully place 2 fish in hot oil, and cook until skin is browned and crispy, about 4 minutes. Flip fish, and cook just until flesh is white throughout, 2 to 3 minutes. Transfer to a wire rack. Repeat with remaining 2 fish.

3 Serve fish with lime wedges, rice, and salad. —KARLA T. VASQUEZ

BEER Pleasingly bitter, lightly malty beer: New Glarus Brewing Two Women Lager

**HERB-ROASTED TROUT
WITH BUTTERY ALMONDS**

SHAOXING-STEAMED STEELHEAD TROUT AND MUSHROOMS

Oyster, beech, and shiitake mushrooms cook alongside fatty, succulent steelhead trout fillets in a bath of steam from the Shaoxing wine simmering in the wok beneath the steamer. Serve the fish alongside cooked rice to soak up the aromatic sauce.

ACTIVE 20 MIN; TOTAL 30 MIN; SERVES 4

1 small fresh red Fresno chile or serrano chile (unseeded), stemmed and finely chopped (about 1 Tbsp.)

1 Tbsp. granulated sugar

2 tsp. very finely chopped peeled fresh ginger (from 1 [½-inch] piece)

2 small garlic cloves, very finely chopped (about 1½ tsp.)

2 tsp. kosher salt, divided

4 (5- to 6-oz.) skin-on steelhead trout fillets

8 oz. mixed fresh mushrooms (such as oyster mushrooms, beech mushrooms, and shiitake mushroom caps) (about 4 cups)

1 cup Shaoxing wine

1 cup water

1 Tbsp. fresh lime juice

2 medium scallions (about ¾ oz.), cut crosswise into 2-inch pieces and thinly sliced lengthwise (julienned)

1 Combine chile, sugar, ginger, garlic, and 1 teaspoon salt in a medium-size heatproof bowl; set aside. Line each of 2 trays of a 14-inch bamboo steamer with a 6-inch square of parchment paper, leaving space around sides of parchment square for steam to rise. Sprinkle trout evenly with remaining 1 teaspoon salt. Place 2 fillets, skin side down, in each steamer tray on parchment paper. Tear mushrooms into large bite-size pieces, if needed; scatter mushrooms between and around fillets. Stack steamer trays; cover basket with lid.

2 Pour wine and 1 cup water into a nonreactive 14-inch flat-bottomed wok. Bring to a boil over medium-high. Place prepared steamer over wok. Steam until fish is just cooked through and mushrooms are tender, 5 to 6 minutes.

3 Remove bamboo steamer from wok. Immediately ladle ¼ cup of the boiling wine mixture from wok over chile mixture in bowl, and stir in lime juice. The sauce should be sharply flavored, tart, salty, and a little sweet. Discard remaining wine mixture in wok.

4 Arrange trout fillets, skin side down, on a platter. Scatter mushrooms on top of and around fish. Pour chile-ginger sauce over fish and mushrooms, and sprinkle with scallions. —ANDREA SLONECKER

WINE Minerally, lightly off-dry Riesling: Peter Lauer Senior Fass 6

SNAPPER WITH PRESERVED CITRUS GREMOLATA AND FREGOLA

Inspired by the Middle Eastern flavors that chefs Ori Menashe and Genevieve Gergis wield so deftly at Bavel in L.A., we created this quick-preserved citrus gremolata using thin-skinned clementines and tangerines. It adds a fragrant, briny flavor to this snapper, and is the perfect way to wake up your winter palate.

ACTIVE 35 MIN; TOTAL 45 MIN; SERVES 4

2 tangerines or clementines, cut crosswise into ¼-inch-thick rounds and seeded

½ cup plus 2 Tbsp. fresh tangerine or clementine juice (from about 6 tangerines or clementines), divided

4 tsp. kosher salt, divided

1 cup chopped fresh flat-leaf parsley

5½ Tbsp. olive oil, divided

2 Tbsp. finely chopped shallot

¼ tsp. crushed red pepper

4 (6-oz.) skin-on snapper fillets, skin scored and fillets patted dry

Cooked fregola sarda pasta, for serving

1 Stir together tangerine rounds, ½ cup tangerine juice, and 1 tablespoon salt in a small saucepan. Bring to a boil over high. Cook, stirring occasionally, until salt is dissolved. Reduce heat to low; cover and simmer until citrus peels are tender, about 10 minutes. Remove from heat, and let cool 10 minutes. Remove 5 tangerine rounds from juice, allowing excess juice to drip off; cut rounds into quarters. Set quarters aside.

2 Gently stir together parsley, ¼ cup oil, shallot, crushed red pepper, tangerine quarters, 1½ teaspoons cooked tangerine juice, and remaining 2 tablespoons fresh tangerine juice in a small bowl; set aside.

3 Heat remaining 1½ tablespoons oil in a large skillet over medium-high. Season snapper fillets evenly with remaining 1 teaspoon salt. When oil is very hot, add snapper fillets, skin sides down. Immediately press fillets gently with a spatula until skin stays flat in skillet. Sear until skin is browned and crisp, 5 to 7 minutes. Flip fillets; cook until bottom half of flesh is opaque, about 30 seconds. Transfer fillets to 4 plates; spoon gremolata over fillets, and serve with fregola sarda.
—KELSEY YOUNGMAN

MAKE AHEAD Preserved tangerines may be stored in an airtight container in refrigerator up to 6 months.

WINE Unoaked coastal Chardonnay: Scribe Winery Carneros

NOTE Use organic citrus whenever possible, and scrub any waxy residue off peels before preserving.

BRANZINO WITH MESCLUN AND TOMATO–HERBES DE PROVENCE VINAIGRETTE

Branzino, known as loup de mer, or "wolf of the sea" in French, is mild and sweet. Its delicate flavor pairs nicely with a summery tomato–and–mixed-herb vinaigrette. Scoring the fish skin before cooking prevents the fillets from curling in the pan.

TOTAL 30 MIN; SERVES 4

- 1 **small beefsteak tomato (about 6 oz.), halved crosswise**
- ½ **cup extra virgin olive oil, divided**
- 3 **Tbsp. Champagne vinegar**
- 2 **tsp. herbes de Provence**
- 2 **tsp. kosher salt, divided**
- ¾ **tsp. black pepper, divided**
- 1 **small garlic clove, finely grated (about ¼ tsp.)**
- 4 **(5-oz.) skin-on branzino fillets**
- 5 **oz. mesclun greens (about 10 cups)**
- 1 **cup loosely packed fresh flat-leaf parsley leaves**
- ½ **cup sliced (¼- to ½-inch pieces) fresh chives**
- ⅓ **cup loosely packed fresh tarragon leaves**
- 1 **tsp. fresh chervil leaves (optional)**

1 Grate cut sides of tomato halves on small holes of a box grater into a medium bowl until only tomato skin remains in your hand; discard tomato skins. Add 6 tablespoons oil, vinegar, herbes de Provence, ½ teaspoon salt, ¼ teaspoon pepper, and garlic to grated tomato in bowl; whisk until well combined. Set vinaigrette aside.

2 Place 1 branzino fillet, skin side up, over rim of a plate. Gently fold fillet over the rim to pull the skin taut. Using a sharp paring knife, score only the skin by making 3 or 4 shallow slashes, being careful not to cut too deep into the fillet. Repeat scoring process with remaining 3 fillets. Sprinkle both sides of fillets evenly with 1 teaspoon salt.

3 Heat remaining 2 tablespoons oil in a large nonstick skillet over medium-high. Add fillets, skin side down, to skillet; using a fish spatula (see Note), gently press each fillet to flatten. Cook, undisturbed, until skin is browned and crisp, about 4 minutes. Flip fillets; cook until just cooked through, 30 seconds to 1 minute. Transfer fillets, skin side up, to plates or a platter.

4 While fillets cook, toss together mesclun, parsley, chives, tarragon, and, if using, chervil in a large bowl to combine. Add ⅓ cup tomato vinaigrette, remaining ½ teaspoon salt, and remaining ½ teaspoon pepper; toss well to coat.

5 Serve salad alongside branzino fillets, passing remaining vinaigrette (about ½ cup) at the table. —JUSTIN CHAPPLE

WINE Medium-bodied Oregon Pinot Gris: Ponzi Willamette Valley

NOTE The large surface area and flexible paddle of a fish spatula make it perfect for pressing fish fillets flat as they cook.

SEARED TUNA TIRADITO

At Cabra in Chicago, 2011 F&W Best New Chef Stephanie Izard channels her love of Peruvian cuisine to deliver inspired takes on traditional ceviche and tiradito. At the restaurant, Izard dresses raw sushi-grade tuna steak with a creamy Kewpie mayonnaise-laced sauce, thinned with lime and orange juices and studded with spicy serrano chiles. For a twist, try giving the tuna a quick sear in a screaming-hot skillet to add another layer of complexity to the dish.

ACTIVE 15 MIN; TOTAL 45 MIN; SERVES 4

- 2 cups packed fresh cilantro leaves and tender stems, roughly chopped
- ½ cup fresh lime juice
- ⅓ cup Kewpie mayonnaise
- ¼ cup roughly chopped seeded fresh serrano chile
- ¼ cup roughly chopped seeded fresh poblano chile
- 2 Tbsp. fresh orange juice
- 2 tsp. kosher salt
- ⅓ cup plus 4 tsp. extra virgin olive oil, divided
- 1 (6-oz.) sushi-grade tuna steak, chilled
- 2 Tbsp. finely chopped peeled jicama
- 2 Tbsp. passion fruit pulp
- 2 Tbsp. diced peeled mango
- Flaky sea salt, to taste

1 Combine cilantro, lime juice, mayonnaise, serrano, poblano, orange juice, kosher salt, and ⅓ cup oil in a food processor. Process until mostly smooth with flecks of cilantro still visible, about 20 seconds. Transfer to a medium bowl; cover and chill until cold, at least 30 minutes or up to 3 days.

2 Heat 2 teaspoons olive oil in a medium skillet over high. When oil is shimmering, add tuna to skillet. Cook until browned but rare in the center, about 1 minute per side. Immediately remove from skillet, and transfer to a cutting board. Cut tuna into 24 (⅛-inch-thick) slices.

3 Spoon 2 tablespoons of cilantro-chile sauce onto each of 4 serving plates. Reserve remaining sauce for another use. Top each serving with 6 tuna slices, 1½ teaspoons jicama, 1½ teaspoons passion fruit pulp, and 1½ teaspoons mango. Drizzle each plate with ½ teaspoon oil, and sprinkle with flaky sea salt to taste. Serve immediately. —STEPHANIE IZARD

MAKE AHEAD The cilantro-chile sauce can be made up to 3 days in advance, covered, and stored in refrigerator.

WINE Tart, lemony Assyrtiko: Estate Argyros

GRILLED SHRIMP AND LETTUCES
WITH CHARRED GREEN GODDESS DRESSING

Green goddess dressing—a retro favorite—gets a smoky upgrade from charred parsley and scallions. Barely grilled baby lettuces double down on the flavor while retaining their sweet crunch.

ACTIVE 30 MIN; TOTAL 45 MIN; SERVES 4 TO 6

6 medium scallions, roots trimmed

1 bunch fresh flat-leaf parsley, stems tied

1 cup packed fresh basil leaves

1 cup mayonnaise

⅓ cup fresh lemon juice

½ oz. drained canned anchovy fillets (about 5 fillets)

1 garlic clove, finely grated

2¾ tsp. kosher salt, divided, plus more to taste

1¼ tsp. black pepper, divided, plus more to taste

2 medium ears fresh corn, husks removed

5 Tbsp. olive oil, divided, plus more for grill grates

1 lb. peeled and deveined tail-on raw large shrimp

4 medium heads Little Gem lettuce, halved lengthwise

1 medium romaine lettuce heart, halved lengthwise

½ cup smoked almonds, chopped

1 avocado, sliced

1 Preheat grill to very high (about 550°F). Place scallions and parsley on oiled grates; grill, uncovered, turning often, until just wilted and lightly charred, 30 seconds to 2 minutes. Remove from grill. Remove and discard parsley stems. Place scallions, parsley leaves, basil, mayonnaise, lemon juice, anchovies, garlic, 1½ teaspoons salt, and ½ teaspoon pepper in a food processor; process until smooth, about 15 seconds. Refrigerate until chilled, about 30 minutes.

2 Meanwhile, brush corn evenly with 1 tablespoon oil; sprinkle with ¼ teaspoon salt and ¼ teaspoon pepper. Toss together shrimp, 2 tablespoons oil, and remaining 1 teaspoon salt and ½ teaspoon pepper in a large bowl. Place corn and shrimp on oiled grates; grill, uncovered, turning occasionally, until corn is lightly charred and shrimp is just cooked through, 2 to 3 minutes for shrimp and 6 to 8 minutes for corn. Remove from grill; let cool slightly, about 5 minutes. Cut corn kernels off cobs; discard cobs. Set corn kernels and shrimp aside.

3 Brush cut sides of lettuces with remaining 2 tablespoons oil. Place lettuces, cut sides down, on oiled grates; grill, uncovered, until grill marks appear but lettuce is still mostly crisp and not yet wilted, 2 to 3 minutes. Remove from grill; let cool slightly. Chop into 1½-inch pieces.

4 Place corn kernels, shrimp, lettuces, almonds, and 1 cup dressing in a large bowl; toss until evenly coated. Add avocado; season with additional salt and pepper to taste, and gently toss to combine. Serve with remaining dressing. —JUSTIN CHAPPLE

MAKE AHEAD Dressing can be made 1 day ahead and stored in an airtight container in refrigerator.

WINE Flinty, citrusy Pouilly-Fumé: Ladoucette

CHILE SHRIMP

Aromatic lemongrass and ginger are paired with wok-cooked head-on shrimp in this chile-studded dish from California-based chef, master sommelier, and winemaker Rajat Parr.

TOTAL 40 MIN; SERVES 4

- 2 lb. raw large shrimp, tail-on, preferably head-on (see Note)
- 2 Tbsp. ketchup
- 2 Tbsp. dry sherry
- 2 Tbsp. sweet chile sauce (such as Mae Ploy)
- 2 Tbsp. fresh lemon juice (from 1 lemon)
- 2 Tbsp. soy sauce
- 1 Tbsp. granulated sugar
- 3 Tbsp. vegetable oil, divided
- 2 medium (1-oz.) jalapeños, seeded and finely chopped (about ⅓ cup)
- 1 small (1-oz.) lemongrass stalk, tender inner white bulb only, finely chopped (about 1 Tbsp.)
- 1 Tbsp. minced peeled fresh ginger (from 1 [1-inch] piece)
- 2 medium garlic cloves, finely chopped (about 2 tsp.)
- 4 scallions (about 2 oz.), thinly sliced (about ⅔ cup)
- ¼ cup chopped fresh cilantro
- Steamed long-grain white rice, for serving

1 Using scissors, cut down the back of each shrimp shell, and remove vein, leaving shell intact. Stir together ketchup, sherry, chile sauce, lemon juice, soy sauce, and sugar in a small bowl. Set aside.

2 Heat 2 tablespoons oil in a large wok over high until smoking. Add shrimp in an even layer on bottom and sides of wok. Cook, flipping once or twice, until shrimp start to curl and turn pale pink, about 4 minutes.

3 Add jalapeños, lemongrass, ginger, garlic, and remaining 1 tablespoon oil to shrimp; cook over high, stirring constantly, until fragrant, about 1 minute. Add scallions and ketchup mixture; cook, stirring constantly, until shrimp are coated in sauce, about 30 seconds. Stir in cilantro. Spoon shrimp mixture evenly onto 4 plates, and serve with rice. —RAJAT PARR, CAMBRIA, CALIFORNIA

WINE Lightly off-dry German Riesling: Forstmeister Geltz Zilliken Saarburger Kabinett

NOTE For a creamier and more shrimp-forward sauce, use head-on shrimp.

BUTTERY SHRIMP WITH PEAS AND POTATOES

Unlike their larger, late-season siblings, baby veggies are supremely quick to cook. Creamy new potatoes add substance to this quick one-pan skillet dinner of tender shrimp, fresh shelling peas, and dill, which come together in a sweet and buttery broth laced with cream.

TOTAL 30 MIN; SERVES 4

5 cups water

2 Tbsp. plus 1 tsp. kosher salt, divided, plus more to taste

8 oz. baby gold potatoes, cut into ¼-inch-thick slices (about 1¾ cups)

8 oz. shelled fresh or frozen English peas (about 1½ cups)

¼ cup unsalted butter

¼ cup extra virgin olive oil

1 medium shallot, finely chopped (about ⅓ cup)

1 medium-size fresh Fresno chile, stemmed, seeded (if desired), and finely chopped (about 2 Tbsp.)

4 medium garlic cloves, finely chopped (about 4 tsp.)

⅓ cup dry white wine

12 oz. peeled and deveined tail-on raw large shrimp

¼ tsp. black pepper, plus more to taste

1 cup lower-sodium chicken broth

¼ cup heavy cream

⅓ cup chopped fresh dill

Crusty bread, for serving

1 Bring 5 cups water to a boil in a 12-inch skillet over medium-high. Stir in 2 tablespoons salt. Add potatoes; cook, stirring occasionally, until barely tender, 5 to 7 minutes. Using a slotted spoon, transfer to a plate. Add peas to boiling water; cook, stirring occasionally, until crisp-tender, 2 to 3 minutes. Remove skillet from heat. Drain peas in a colander; rinse under cold water until cool to the touch, about 15 seconds. Set aside.

2 Wipe skillet dry using paper towels. Add butter and oil to skillet; cook over medium-high until butter is melted. Add shallot, chile, garlic, and ½ teaspoon salt; cook, stirring often, until mixture is fragrant and softened, 2 to 3 minutes. Add wine; cook, stirring occasionally, until wine is almost completely reduced, about 2 minutes.

3 Add shrimp to skillet in a single layer; sprinkle with black pepper and remaining ½ teaspoon salt. Cook, undisturbed, until shrimp are partially opaque, about 2 minutes. Flip shrimp, and immediately add broth and potatoes to skillet. Bring to a simmer over medium-high; simmer, stirring occasionally, until shrimp are almost cooked through, about 1 minute. Add peas and cream; cook, stirring occasionally, until heated through, about 30 seconds. Remove from heat. Season with additional salt and black pepper to taste. Sprinkle with dill, and serve with crusty bread. —JUSTIN CHAPPLE

WINE Crisp, steely California Chardonnay: Balletto Vineyards Teresa's Unoaked

SUMMER SQUASH AND SHRIMP FRICASSEE

"Once the summer starts, there are inevitably big baskets of zucchini and yellow squash that we just don't know what to do with," says Oxford, Mississippi–based chef Vishwesh Bhatt. "This fricassee is a terrific place to use them. It's really light, it's really quick, and it's really easy to cook a big batch of it, making it an ideal centerpiece for summer gatherings." Fricassee is a cross between a quick sauté and a stew. This recipe calls for a habanero chile, which can be very hot but has beautiful floral notes that you can't replicate with other peppers. If you take care to remove the seeds, the heat will be more manageable. "This recipe is inspired by a dish my friend Nina Compton served us for dinner one night at her restaurant, Compere Lapin," Bhatt says. It's a great one to reach for in summer, but because good-quality frozen shrimp and yellow squashes can be found year-round in grocery stores, this dish can be thrown together almost any time of the year.

TOTAL 20 MIN; SERVES 2 TO 4

- 2 (5-oz.) bunches scallions
- 2 Tbsp. olive oil
- 6 medium garlic cloves, thinly sliced (about 2½ Tbsp.)
- 2 fresh or dried bay leaves
- 1½ cups fresh corn kernels (from 2 ears corn)
- 1 lb. peeled and deveined raw large shrimp, tail-on
- ½ cup shrimp stock or fish stock
- 1 small fresh habanero chile (about ½ oz.), seeded and minced (about 1 tsp.) (see Note)
- 1 lb. summer squash, chopped into ¼-inch pieces (about 3⅔ cups)
- 1 medium tomato (about 8 oz.), finely chopped (about 1 cup)
- ½ cup dry white wine
- 3 Tbsp. chopped fresh flat-leaf parsley
- 2 Tbsp. fresh thyme leaves
- 2 Tbsp. fresh lemon juice (from 1 lemon)
- 2 tsp. kosher salt
- 1 tsp. black pepper
- 2 Tbsp. unsalted butter

1 Thinly slice scallions, dividing the white and light green parts from the dark green parts. Set dark green parts aside.

2 Heat oil in a Dutch oven over medium-high. Add white and light green scallion parts, garlic, and bay leaves; cook, stirring occasionally, until scallions just soften, about 2 minutes. Add corn; cook, stirring constantly, 1 minute. Add shrimp, shrimp stock, and habanero; cook, stirring constantly, until shrimp just start to turn opaque but are not cooked through, about 45 seconds. Add squash, tomato, wine, parsley, thyme, lemon juice, salt, and black pepper. Cook, stirring constantly, until shrimp are just cooked through, about 1 minute. Add butter; cook, stirring vigorously, until butter melts and makes a creamy sauce, about 1 minute.

3 Remove from heat. Stir in dark green scallion parts. Serve immediately.
—VISHWESH BHATT

WINE Lemony, medium-bodied Chardonnay: Roserock Eola-Amity Hills Chardonnay

NOTE Wear gloves when seeding and mincing the habanero chile.

CILANTRO-LIME SHRIMP SCAMPI

Although "scampi" are technically langoustines, in the United States the term has come to describe the famous dish of shrimp cooked with butter, garlic, and white wine. Here, the use of tequila, cilantro, and fresh lime juice offer a bold twist on the classic. Tender cilantro stems mellow slightly after a quick sauté, accenting the fresh cilantro leaves used to finish this dish. Serve it with a torn baguette to sop up the juices.

TOTAL 20 MIN; SERVES 4

- ¼ cup unsalted butter
- ¼ cup extra virgin olive oil
- ¼ cup finely chopped fresh cilantro stems plus ½ cup chopped fresh cilantro leaves, divided
- 4 large garlic cloves, finely chopped
- 1 crushed chile de árbol or ½ tsp. crushed red pepper
- 3 Tbsp. (1½ oz.) tequila blanco
- 1½ lb. peeled and deveined raw large shrimp, tail-on
- 1 tsp. kosher salt, plus more to taste
- ¾ tsp. black pepper
- 3 Tbsp. fresh lime juice
- Torn baguette, for serving

1 Heat butter and oil in a large skillet over medium-high, stirring often, until butter is melted. Add cilantro stems, garlic, and chile. Cook, stirring constantly, until very fragrant, 1 to 2 minutes. Remove skillet from heat, and turn off heat.

2 Carefully add tequila to skillet. Return to heat over medium-high; cook, stirring occasionally, until liquid has evaporated, about 1 minute. Add shrimp, salt, and black pepper; cook, stirring occasionally, until shrimp are opaque and cooked through, 4 to 5 minutes. Remove from heat. Stir in lime juice and cilantro leaves. Season with additional salt to taste. Serve immediately with torn baguette.

—JUSTIN CHAPPLE

WINE Lime-scented, dry Australian Riesling: Jim Barry Watervale

HERBED LEMONGRASS BROTH WITH SHRIMP

The citrusy flavor of lemongrass is an ideal companion for shrimp, while the earthiness of spinach and mushrooms makes for a hearty and wholesome dish.

ACTIVE 15 MIN; TOTAL 20 MIN; SERVES 2

- 4 single-serving lemongrass tea bags
- ¼ cup finely chopped fresh chives
- ¼ cup finely chopped fresh curly parsley
- ¼ cup finely chopped fresh tarragon
- 1 Tbsp. rice vinegar
- ¾ tsp. kosher salt
- 6 oz. cooked peeled and deveined medium shrimp, halved lengthwise
- 2½ oz. fresh baby spinach, chopped into 1-inch pieces (about 2 cups)
- 4 button mushrooms, very thinly sliced
- ½ cup thawed frozen sweet peas
- Extra virgin olive oil

1 Bring 3 cups water to a boil in a teapot or small saucepan over high; remove from heat. Add tea bags; cover and steep 5 minutes. Remove and discard tea bags; stir in chives, parsley, tarragon, vinegar, and salt. Bring tea just to a simmer over medium. Remove from heat.

2 Divide shrimp, spinach, mushrooms, and peas evenly between 2 shallow bowls. Pour hot tea mixture evenly into bowls; drizzle with olive oil, and serve.

—JUSTIN CHAPPLE

WINE Bright, lemony Semillon: L'Ecole No. 41 Columbia Valley

NOTE If you can't find pure lemongrass tea, substitute one mixed with lemon.

SCALLOP GRENOBLOISE

PHOTO P. 1

Grenobloise means in the style of the southeastern French city of Grenoble, and refers to a classic French sauce of lemon and capers. Here, beautifully seared scallops with a golden crust are served in a sauce popping with acidity from lemon, brininess from capers, and slight warmth from mildly piquant jalapeños. Toss them with a favorite pasta for a quick, simple meal. For the best results, seek out Massachusetts dayboat scallops. They are harvested daily and are dry-packed, which yields the best flavor and sear.

TOTAL 20 MIN; SERVES 4

- 1 large lemon
- 16 jumbo sea scallops
- 1 tsp. kosher salt, divided
- ½ tsp. black pepper, divided
- 2 Tbsp. extra virgin olive oil
- ¼ cup unsalted butter, cut into cubes
- 2 Tbsp. capers, drained
- 1 medium jalapeño, stemmed, seeded, and minced (about 1½ Tbsp.)
- 2 Tbsp. finely chopped fresh flat-leaf parsley

1 Using a paring knife, remove outer peel and bitter white pith from lemon; discard. Cut in between membranes to remove lemon segments, and discard membranes. Cut segments into ¼-inch pieces; remove and discard seeds. Set lemon segments aside.

2 Sprinkle scallops evenly with ½ teaspoon salt and ¼ teaspoon black pepper. Heat oil in a large nonstick skillet over medium-high. Add scallops; cook until well seared and golden brown on bottoms, about 3 minutes. Flip scallops; cook until just opaque throughout, 2 to 3 minutes. Transfer scallops to a platter, and cover with foil to keep warm. Wipe skillet clean.

3 Add butter to skillet, and melt over medium-high. Add capers and jalapeño; cook, stirring often, until sizzling and fragrant, about 1 minute. Stir in lemon segments, parsley, and remaining ½ teaspoon salt and ¼ teaspoon black pepper. Spoon mixture over scallops. Serve immediately. —JUSTIN CHAPPLE

WINE Bright, grapefruity Sauvignon Blanc: Dry Creek Vineyard

GRILLED SCALLOPS WITH MISO-CORN SALAD

Scallops take well to an infinite array of preparations and cooking techniques, adapt to almost any cuisine, and can be cooked incredibly quickly, making them the ultimate canvas for everything from black truffles to black bean sauce, citrus to sambal. This take from cookbook author and Top Chef *judge Gail Simmons is a favorite for quick and easy backyard dinners. It incorporates miso, ginger, and toasted sesame, adding a savory dimension to the salad and a rich contrast to the corn and scallops' inherent sweetness. To achieve the best sear on your scallops, set them uncovered on a paper towel in the refrigerator for a few hours before grilling.*

TOTAL 30 MIN; SERVES 4

MISO VINAIGRETTE

- **2 Tbsp. white miso**
- **1 Tbsp. soy sauce**
- **1 Tbsp. unseasoned rice wine vinegar**
- **1 tsp. toasted sesame oil**
- **1 tsp. lime zest plus 2 Tbsp. fresh lime juice (from 1 lime)**
- **1 tsp. light brown sugar**
- **½ tsp. grated peeled fresh ginger (from 1 [1-inch] piece)**
- **1 small jalapeño or serrano chile, seeded and finely chopped (optional)**
- **3 Tbsp. canola oil**

SALAD

- **3 medium ears fresh yellow corn, shucked**
- **4 medium scallions**
- **2 Tbsp. canola oil, divided**
- **12 dry-packed U12 sea scallops (about 1 lb.)**
- **¼ tsp. kosher salt**
- **1 cup cooked and shelled fresh or frozen edamame**
- **1 cup halved cherry or grape tomatoes**
- **2 Tbsp. fresh small basil leaves or mint leaves, or a combination of both, torn, plus more for serving**
- **2 tsp. toasted sesame seeds, divided**

1 **Make the miso vinaigrette:** Whisk together miso, soy sauce, vinegar, sesame oil, lime zest and juice, brown sugar, ginger, and jalapeño, if using, in a small bowl until miso is dissolved. Whisk in canola oil in a slow, steady stream until well combined. Set aside, or cover and refrigerate up to 1 week.

2 **Make the salad:** Preheat a grill to high (450°F to 500°F), or heat a grill pan over high. Brush corn and scallions with 1 tablespoon canola oil, and place on grates (or grill pan). Grill, uncovered, turning occasionally, until just tender and slightly charred, about 4 minutes for scallions and 10 minutes for corn. Remove from heat. When cool enough to handle, cut kernels off cobs, and roughly chop scallions into ½-inch pieces; set corn and scallions aside.

3 Remove and discard the small side muscle from each scallop; rinse under cold running water, and pat dry. Thread 3 scallops on 2 parallel skewers, and repeat with remaining 9 scallops on 6 skewers. Brush scallops with remaining 1 tablespoon canola oil, and season both sides with salt. Grill scallops, uncovered, until grill marks appear, about 1 minute and 30 seconds. Turn scallops, and grill until desired degree of doneness, about 30 seconds for medium (warm translucent center). Remove from grill, and set aside.

4 Toss together corn, scallions, edamame, and tomatoes in a large bowl. Add herbs, miso vinaigrette, and 1 teaspoon sesame seeds; toss to combine. Divide salad among 4 shallow bowls. Top each with a skewer of scallops. Sprinkle with remaining 1 teaspoon sesame seeds and additional herbs. —GAIL SIMMONS

WINE Lime-zesty Australian dry Riesling: Pikes Hills & Valleys

LITTLENECK CLAMS IN THE
STYLE OF ESCARGOT

LITTLENECK CLAMS IN THE STYLE OF ESCARGOT

Easy-to-find little neck clams stand in for snails in this riff on the French classic. The quick wine-brightened garlic butter melts into the clam liquor to create an irresistible broth; have plenty of bread on hand for nonstop sopping.

ACTIVE 25 MIN; TOTAL 55 MIN; SERVES 4

2 lb. littleneck clams (about 24 clams), scrubbed

4 cups ice cubes

¼ cup plus ¼ tsp. fine sea salt, divided

¼ cup unsalted butter, softened

2 garlic cloves, finely chopped

1 Tbsp. minced shallot

1 Tbsp. finely chopped fresh flat-leaf parsley

1 Tbsp. dry white wine

¼ tsp. black pepper

Crusty bread, for serving

1 Place clams in a large bowl; add ice cubes and ¼ cup salt. Add just enough cold water to cover clams by 1 inch. Let clams purge 30 minutes.

2 Meanwhile, preheat oven to 550°F with oven rack about 6 inches from heat. Mash butter, garlic, shallot, parsley, wine, pepper, and remaining ¼ teaspoon salt in a bowl with a fork until mixture is smooth.

3 Lift clams from bowl, shake dry, and place, hinge sides down, in the wells of four 6-well escargot trays (or place clams on their sides on a foil-lined rimmed baking sheet). Roast until clams just begin to open, 4 to 5 minutes. Remove clams from oven. Increase oven temperature to broil on high. Spoon about ½ teaspoon garlic butter into each clam shell, and return to oven. Broil until clams completely pop open and butter is bubbling, about 6 minutes. (Discard any clams that do not open.) Serve with crusty bread. —MARY-FRANCES HECK

WINE Crisp white Burgundy: Joseph Drouhin Saint-Véran

MANILA CLAMS WITH SHIRO DASHI AND BASIL

Clams are often covered and gently steamed until they open. Here, F&W Best New Chef 2020 Trigg Brown cooks them uncovered over high heat to coax steam from the cooking liquid and concentrate its flavor at the same time. The result: tender, juicy clams with a rich, reduced broth in only 15 minutes.

TOTAL 15 MIN; SERVES 2 TO 4

2 Tbsp. grapeseed oil

4 garlic cloves, finely chopped

2 lb. small clams (about 16 per lb.), such as cockle, baby Manila, or littleneck, scrubbed and purged

½ cup Asian-style lager beer (such as Taiwan Beer)

½ cup Shaoxing cooking wine or dry sherry

¼ cup shiro dashi

1½ cups halved Sun Gold cherry tomatoes

1 cup fresh basil leaves, plus more for garnish

2 Tbsp. unsalted butter

1 tsp. toasted sesame seeds

½ tsp. gochugaru

1 Heat oil in a wok or large high-sided skillet over high. Add garlic, and cook, stirring constantly, until fragrant, about 15 seconds. Add clams, beer, Shaoxing cooking wine, and shiro dashi; cook, uncovered, stirring often, until clams open, 10 to 15 minutes. Discard any clams that do not open.

2 Add tomatoes, basil, and butter; cook, stirring constantly, until butter is melted. Transfer mixture to a serving bowl. Sprinkle with sesame seeds and gochugaru. Garnish with basil leaves. —TRIGG BROWN

WINE Vivid, lightly herbal Sémillon: Mother Rock Force Celeste

NOTE Shiro dashi is a concentrated soup base available at Asian markets.

PASTA, GRAINS & EGGS

These three simple ingredients are among the most versatile in your kitchen—and all make a flexible foundation for a satisfying dinner. Their universal appeal is seen—and enthusiastically tasted— in these around-the-world recipes.

KIMCHI FRIED RICE WITH
SPICY SHRIMP-AND-
SESAME SAUCE (P. 168)

PULLING-FROM-THE-PANTRY PUTTANESCA

West Coast–based F&W Best New Chef 2015 Zoi Antonitsas is passionate about preserved fish. The salty, briny fillets are her favorite powerhouse pantry ingredient. They can make almost anything into a meal—and a delicious one at that. Use high-quality tins, like Matiz España brand, for the best results.

TOTAL 30 MIN; SERVES 2 TO 3

- 3 Tbsp. extra virgin olive oil
- 1 garlic clove, thinly sliced
- 2 anchovy fillets, chopped
- ¼ tsp. crushed red pepper, or to taste
- 1 cup dry white wine
- 1 (28-oz.) can plum tomatoes, drained
- 1 (4.2-oz.) can Spanish sardines (such as Matiz España)
- ¼ cup chopped Castelvetrano olives
- 2 Tbsp. drained nonpareil capers
- 1 tsp. chopped fresh marjoram
- 8 oz. uncooked spaghetti
- 2 Tbsp. chopped fresh flat-leaf parsley

1 Heat oil in a skillet over low; add garlic, and cook, stirring often, until brown, about 3 minutes. Add anchovies, and, cook, stirring constantly, until anchovies melt into oil, about 1 minute and 30 seconds. Stir in red pepper. Increase heat to medium, and stir in wine. Cook until reduced by half, about 6 minutes.

2 Add tomatoes; break up using a wooden spoon. Bring sauce to a low simmer. Add sardines, olives, capers, and marjoram. Simmer, uncovered, stirring occasionally, 20 minutes. Taste for seasoning, and adjust if needed.

3 Meanwhile, bring a large pot of salted water to a boil over high. Cook spaghetti according to package directions. Drain pasta, reserving 1 cup cooking liquid. Toss spaghetti with tomato sauce, adding reserved cooking liquid as needed to reach desired consistency. Sprinkle with parsley, and serve immediately.
—ZOI ANTONITSAS

WINE Fruity southern Italian Masseria Li Veli Orion Primitivo

SPAGHETTI ALL'ASSASSINA

This spicy "assassin's spaghetti" is made by gradually adding a mixture of tomato paste and boiling water to pasta in a skillet, where it simmers, allowing the spaghetti to soften to a perfect al dente and then develop a crispy, caramelized texture as it absorbs flavor. Sliced peperoncini peppers infuse the quick-cooking dish with a warming piquancy, and a drizzle of high-quality olive oil adds a rich finish.

ACTIVE 25 MIN; TOTAL 35 MIN; SERVES 4

- 10 cups water
- 3 Tbsp. no-salt-added tomato paste
- 2 tsp. fine sea salt, plus more to taste
- ¼ cup extra virgin olive oil
- 2 medium garlic cloves, chopped (about 2 tsp.)
- 2 fresh peperoncini peppers, sliced, or 2 tsp. crushed red pepper
- ¾ cup tomato puree (passata di pomodoro) (such as Mutti), divided
- 12 oz. uncooked spaghetti
- High-quality extra virgin olive oil, for drizzling
- Chopped fresh flat-leaf parsley

1 Pour 10 cups water into a large pot; bring to a boil over medium-high. Whisk tomato paste and salt into boiling water; reduce heat to medium-low to maintain a simmer.

2 Heat a large enameled cast-iron skillet or Dutch oven (at least 12 inches or wider) over medium. Add oil, and heat until oil shimmers, about 30 seconds. Add garlic and peperoncini; cook, stirring constantly, until fragrant, about 15 seconds. Stir in half of the tomato puree, and increase heat to medium-high. Spread spaghetti over mixture in skillet, trying to get as much spaghetti in contact with skillet as possible. Pour remaining tomato puree over spaghetti. Cook noodles in tomato puree mixture, undisturbed, until starting to soften and become pliable, about 2 minutes. Using a spatula or tongs, lift noodles to check that they are in contact with skillet to make sure they're getting crispy; if needed, spread and separate noodles more on bottom of skillet to keep in direct contact with skillet. Continue cooking 2 minutes. Move noodles around using tongs to allow other noodles to make contact with skillet.

3 Add 2 ladlefuls (about 1 cup) of simmering tomato water to spaghetti mixture in skillet. Cook until noodles are al dente, 8 to 10 minutes, adding more tomato water, 1 ladleful at a time, when previous addition of tomato water has been absorbed by noodles (adding 2 to 2½ cups tomato water total). As mixture cooks, attentively watch the noodles and the liquid content in skillet. To ensure the noodles keep those crispy bits, do not inundate them with the broth—only add more broth as needed once noodles have soaked up what was previously ladled. The red hues of the tomato sauce will brown.

4 Taste spaghetti and sauce; add more salt to taste, if desired. Using kitchen tweezers or tongs, swirl spaghetti noodles inside the cup of your ladle, creating a compact and rather perfect swirl of noodles. Place ladles of spaghetti all'assassina on individual plates or a large platter. Finish with a drizzle of high-quality extra virgin olive oil, and sprinkle with chopped parsley. —KATIE QUINN

WINE Spicy, lively Southern Italian red: Colosi Nero d'Avola

NOTE Tomato passata is strained pureed uncooked tomatoes. It can be found at most grocery stores or at eataly.com.

SOBA AND ZUCCHINI SALAD
WITH GOCHUJANG DRESSING

This soba salad offers bracing heat that's most welcome on a hot day when the coldest beers are at hand. Tender buckwheat noodles and crispy strands of zucchini soak up a pleasantly piquant dressing laced with both gochugaru and gochujang for a double hit of spicy Korean peppers, mellowed by a touch of brown sugar. Perfect served chilled or at room temperature, it's an easy make-ahead dish for summer entertaining.

TOTAL 25 MIN; SERVES 4

8 oz. uncooked soba noodles

3 Tbsp. gochujang (see Note)

3 Tbsp. rice vinegar

2 Tbsp. gochugaru

2 Tbsp. light brown sugar

2 Tbsp. toasted sesame oil

½ tsp. kosher salt

1 large garlic clove, grated (about ½ tsp.)

3 cups zucchini spirals (about 10 oz.) (from 2 small [6-oz.] zucchini)

2 cups thinly sliced red cabbage (from 1 small [2-lb.] head cabbage)

½ cup matchstick-cut carrots

1 small yellow bell pepper (about 7 oz.), cut into thin strips

1 Bring a large pot of water to a boil over high. Add noodles, and cook according to package directions, being careful not to overcook. Drain and rinse with cold water until noodles are cool. Drain well.

2 Whisk together gochujang, vinegar, gochugaru, brown sugar, sesame oil, salt, and garlic in a large bowl. Add noodles, zucchini, cabbage, carrots, and bell pepper; toss well to coat. Serve chilled or at room temperature.
—ANN TAYLOR PITTMAN

MAKE AHEAD Salad can be prepared up to 1 day in advance and stored in an airtight container in refrigerator.

NOTE Be sure to use real gochujang paste—the miso-thick, glossy-shiny paste sold in tubs in Asian markets. Gochujang sauce, sold in many grocery stores, is thinner and milder and doesn't have as deep a flavor.

SPRING HERBS SOUP WITH FREGOLA AND PANCETTA

Inspired by s'erbuzzu, a classic Sardinian soup packed with more than a dozen varieties of herbs and spring greens, this recipe delivers big flavor with fresh parsley, tarragon, and chives. White beans, crispy bits of pancetta, and fregola sarda—tiny balls of dried semolina pasta—add heft; orzo or Israeli couscous are delicious substitutes. Stirring in a handful of tarragon, parsley, and chives just before serving this soup preserves the color and flavor of the delicate herbs.

TOTAL 45 MIN; SERVES 6

3 Tbsp. extra virgin olive oil

4 oz. pancetta, finely diced

1 medium-size yellow onion, finely chopped (about 2 cups)

½ tsp. kosher salt, plus more to taste

½ tsp. black pepper, plus more to taste

½ cup (4 oz.) dry white wine

1¼ cups uncooked fregola sarda, orzo, or Israeli couscous

3 Tbsp. finely chopped fresh flat-leaf parsley stems plus 1½ cups finely chopped parsley leaves, divided

2 large garlic cloves, thinly sliced

1 tsp. fennel seeds

½ tsp. crushed red pepper

8 cups lower-sodium chicken broth

1 (15-oz.) can cannellini beans, drained and rinsed

½ cup finely chopped fresh chives

¼ cup finely chopped fresh tarragon

Finely grated Pecorino Romano cheese, for garnish

Lemon wedges, for serving

1 Heat oil in a medium Dutch oven over medium. Add pancetta; cook, stirring occasionally, until fat is rendered, 4 to 6 minutes. Add onion, salt, and black pepper; cook, stirring occasionally, until softened, 8 to 12 minutes. Add wine; cook, stirring occasionally, until liquid has almost completely reduced, 4 to 5 minutes. Add fregola, parsley stems, garlic, fennel seeds, and crushed red pepper; cook, stirring constantly, until fragrant, 2 to 4 minutes. Add broth; bring to a boil over medium-high. Reduce heat to medium-low; cook, stirring occasionally, until fregola is al dente, 14 to 16 minutes (8 to 10 minutes for orzo or couscous).

2 Reduce heat to low. Stir in cannellini beans; cook until heated through, about 2 minutes. Remove from heat. Stir in chives, tarragon, and parsley leaves. Season with additional salt and black pepper to taste. Garnish with Pecorino Romano, and serve with lemon wedges. —JUSTIN CHAPPLE

WINE Crisp Sardinian white: Argiolas Costamolino Vermentino

ITALIAN WEDDING RISOTTO

Inspired by the classic Italian wedding soup, this heartier risotto is filled with just-wilted spinach and topped with crispy, garlicky meatballs. Remove the risotto from the heat while it's still a little soupy—it will thicken slightly as it rests.

TOTAL 45 MIN; SERVES 4 TO 6

- 1 lb. ground pork
- ½ cup panko
- 1½ oz. Parmigiano-Reggiano cheese, finely grated with a Microplane (about ⅔ cup), divided, plus more for garnish
- ¼ cup finely chopped fresh flat-leaf parsley, plus more for garnish
- 1 large egg, lightly beaten
- 4 garlic cloves, finely chopped, divided
- 2 tsp. kosher salt, plus more to taste
- 1 tsp. black pepper, plus more to taste and for garnish
- 4 cups lower-sodium chicken stock or broth
- 2 cups water
- 2 Tbsp. extra virgin olive oil, plus more for drizzling
- ¼ cup unsalted butter (2 oz.), divided
- 1 medium-size yellow onion, finely chopped (about 2 cups)
- 1 medium celery stalk, finely chopped (about ⅓ cup)
- 1½ cups uncooked Arborio rice (about 10½ oz.)
- ¾ cup dry white wine
- 3 cups packed fresh baby spinach, torn (about 3 oz.)

1 Preheat oven to broil with rack 9 inches from heat. Combine pork, panko, ⅓ cup of the cheese, parsley, egg, 2 teaspoons chopped garlic, salt, and pepper in a medium bowl. Mix gently until just combined. Roll mixture into 20 meatballs (about 2 tablespoons each). Place 1 inch apart on a broiler-safe baking sheet lined with foil. Broil until browned and cooked through, 6 to 9 minutes.

2 Combine stock and 2 cups water in a medium saucepan; bring to a simmer over medium. Reduce heat to medium-low.

3 Heat oil and 2 tablespoons butter in a large saucepan over medium. Add onion, celery, and remaining chopped garlic; cook, stirring often, until softened, about 5 minutes. Add rice, and cook, stirring constantly, until translucent, 1 to 2 minutes. Add wine, and cook, stirring often, until almost completely reduced, 1 to 2 minutes. Add 1 cup warm stock mixture, and cook, stirring constantly, until most of the liquid has been absorbed. Add remaining stock mixture, 1 cup at a time, stirring until liquid has been absorbed after each addition, until rice is al dente, about 20 minutes.

4 Remove from heat. Stir in remaining ⅓ cup cheese and remaining 2 tablespoons butter. Add spinach. Stir until just wilted, about 30 seconds. Divide risotto and meatballs among bowls. Drizzle with additional oil; garnish with additional cheese, parsley, and pepper. —JUSTIN CHAPPLE

MAKE AHEAD Uncooked meatballs can be frozen up to 2 months. Place on a rimmed baking sheet; freeze 2 hours. Transfer to a freezer bag. Let thaw before broiling.

WINE Herbal, red-fruited Chianti Classico: Ruffino Riserva Ducale

LOBSTER RISOTTO

A small pinch of saffron goes a long way in imparting a vibrant golden hue and floral fragrance to this creamy, indulgent lobster risotto. Precooked lobster and bottled clam juice deliver robust layers of flavor with a minimum amount of effort, making this a perfect weeknight supper. Pair it with a bottle of white Bordeaux, recommends sommelier Tonya Pitts, of Les Dames D'Escoffier International, San Francisco. "I love white Bordeaux with this easy dish. It highlights the lobster and creaminess of the risotto, ultimately becoming intertwined with the flavor and textures."

TOTAL 30 MIN; SERVES 4

3 cups bottled clam juice (such as Bar Harbor)

3 cups water

2 Tbsp. olive oil

1 cup finely chopped yellow onion

½ cup cubed (⅛-inch pieces) carrot

½ cup cubed (⅛-inch pieces) celery

1½ cups uncooked Arborio rice

Pinch of best-quality saffron threads (such as Diaspora Co.)

½ cup (4 oz.) dry white wine

1 lb. cooked lobster meat (such as Luke's Lobster) (about 3 cups)

1 tsp. kosher salt

¼ tsp. black pepper

3 oz. Parmesan cheese, grated (about ¾ cup)

Sliced fresh chives, for garnish

1 Cook clam juice and 3 cups water in a medium saucepan over medium, undisturbed, until steaming, about 10 minutes. Reduce heat to medium-low, and keep warm.

2 Meanwhile, heat oil in a large saucepan over medium-high. Add onion, carrot, and celery; cook, stirring often, until slightly softened, about 5 minutes. Add rice and saffron; cook, stirring constantly, until rice is toasted, about 1 minute. Add wine; cook, stirring often, until almost absorbed, 30 seconds to 1 minute. Reduce heat to medium.

3 Add 1 cup hot clam juice mixture to rice mixture; cook, stirring often, until almost absorbed, 2 to 3 minutes. Continue adding clam juice mixture, ½ cup at a time, stirring until clam juice mixture is almost absorbed after each addition, until rice is al dente and mixture is creamy, 15 to 20 minutes.

4 Remove rice mixture from heat; gently stir in lobster, salt, and pepper. Gradually stir in Parmesan. Stir in additional clam juice mixture, a splash at a time, to loosen risotto, if needed. Discard remaining clam juice mixture. Divide risotto evenly among 4 bowls; garnish with chives. —ANNA THEOKTISTO

WINE Citrusy, supple white Bordeaux: Château de Fieuzal

SALMON OCHAZUKE

Japanese ochazuke—rice served in green tea, water, or broth—is the epitome of simple. The soothing toasty-sweet flavor of Japanese green tea provides a brothy, effective base for leftover rice and other accompaniments like hot-smoked salmon and scallion. Don't have all the listed garnishes on hand? Don't fret, any combination will work just fine.

ACTIVE 15 MIN; TOTAL 20 MIN; SERVES 2

3 single-serving genmaicha (Japanese green tea with roasted brown rice) tea bags

½ tsp. kosher salt, divided

1½ cups hot cooked white sushi rice

2 (4-oz.) hot-smoked salmon fillets, skin discarded and flesh flaked

Sliced scallion, shredded roasted nori, pickled ginger, furikake seasoning, and wasabi paste, for serving

1 Bring 2 cups water to a boil in a teapot or small saucepan over high; remove from heat. Add tea bags and ¼ teaspoon salt. Cover and steep 2 to 3 minutes.

2 Divide rice and salmon evenly between 2 bowls. Remove and discard tea bags; pour tea around salmon and rice. Sprinkle evenly with remaining ¼ teaspoon salt. Serve with desired toppings. —JUSTIN CHAPPLE

WINE Lightly herbal Grüner Veltliner: Domäne Wachau Terrassen Federspiel

NOTE Genmaicha is available on Amazon; we like the Yamamotoyama brand.

KIMCHI FRIED RICE WITH SPICY SHRIMP-AND-SESAME SAUCE

PHOTO P. 155

Chef Roy Choi's Kimchi Fried Rice is the best way to reinvigorate day-old rice with spicy, potent kimchi. The kimchi actually sweetens when heated and adds not only its signature funk, tang, and spice but also a delicious crunch. The briny, spicy dipping sauce is the perfect punchy accompaniment.

TOTAL 15 MIN; SERVES 2

SPICY SHRIMP-AND-SESAME SAUCE

1 cup salted dried baby shrimp, rinsed (about 1 oz.)

½ cup thinly sliced scallions

½ cup soy sauce

¼ cup water

1 large jalapeño, stemmed and finely chopped

2 Tbsp. finely chopped garlic

4 tsp. gochugaru

1 Tbsp. toasted sesame oil

FRIED RICE

3 Tbsp. canola oil

3½ cups cooled cooked short-grain rice (day-old rice is best)

1 cup chopped kimchi (about 6 oz.)

¼ cup low-sodium chicken broth

2 Tbsp. unsalted butter

1 Make the spicy shrimp-and-sesame sauce: Stir together all sauce ingredients in a medium bowl. Set aside.

2 Make the fried rice: Heat oil in a large skillet over high until shimmering. Add rice to hot oil, and spread in an even layer. Cook, without stirring, until rice is crispy and a light golden brown, about 4 minutes. Stir in kimchi, broth, and 3 tablespoons sauce. Cook, stirring often, until crispy, about 3 minutes. Add butter, and stir until melted. Remove from heat. Divide rice mixture between 2 bowls, and serve with remaining sauce. —ROY CHOI

SALMON OCHAZUKE

NASI GORENG JAWA (JAVANESE FRIED RICE)

Nasi goreng is a classic Indonesian fried rice. Whether you make it at home or you pick it up from a street cart, it makes for a fantastic breakfast (or late-night snack) that uses up leftovers. "Nasi goreng is a comfort food," says Indonesian chef and TV personality William Wongso, who is very particular about that comfort. He makes his version in small batches, in a hot wok, with cold rice, and with distinct colors—yellow from scrambled egg, red from sambal bajak (a sweet and spicy condiment), and green from a scattering of scallions. This, Wongso's favorite style, is one he grew up eating in Surabaya, a city in East Java. Bumbu, the spice paste that flavors this rice, is richly savory, aromatic, and only mildly spicy. Toasting shrimp paste mellows out its pungent flavors and adds silky richness to the fried rice.

TOTAL 25 MIN; SERVES 2

BUMBU (SPICE PASTE)

- ⅔ cup seeded and coarsely chopped fresh red Kashmiri or other mild red chiles (from about 3½ oz. chiles)
- ½ cup coarsely chopped shallots
- ¼ cup coarsely chopped garlic
- ¼ tsp. kosher salt
- ¼ cup neutral oil (such as grapeseed oil), divided
- 1 tsp. terasi (fermented shrimp paste, such as Shrimp & 6A brand)

NASI GORENG JAWA (FRIED RICE)

- 2 Tbsp. neutral oil (such as grapeseed oil)
- 2 large eggs, beaten
- 2 cups cooked and chilled long-grain white rice (such as jasmine), preferably day-old
- Kosher salt or lower-sodium soy sauce, to taste
- 1 large scallion, thinly diagonally sliced (about ⅓ cup)

1 **Make the bumbu:** Process chiles, shallots, garlic, and salt in a food processor or blender until very finely chopped, about 20 seconds, stopping to scrape down sides as needed. Heat 1 tablespoon oil in a medium skillet over medium. Add terasi to skillet, and cook, mashing terasi into oil, until toasted and pungent, about 40 seconds. Transfer mixture to a small bowl. Add remaining 3 tablespoons oil to skillet over medium. Add chile mixture; cook, stirring constantly, until slightly softened but still vibrant in color, 1 minute and 30 seconds to 2 minutes. Stir in toasted terasi mixture. Remove from heat; transfer bumbu to a small bowl.

2 **Make the nasi goreng Jawa:** Heat oil in a wok or a large nonstick skillet over medium-high until shimmering. Pour in eggs, tilting wok to spread eggs evenly; cook, stirring gently and constantly, until eggs are set but still creamy looking, about 25 seconds. Add cooked rice, stirring to break up any clumps. Add 3 tablespoons bumbu; cook, stirring constantly, until rice is heated through and tinted the color of bumbu, about 2 minutes. Season with salt or soy sauce to taste. Remove from heat; stir in sliced scallion. —WILLIAM WONGSO

MAKE AHEAD Bumbu can be stored in an airtight container in refrigerator up to 2 weeks.

BEER Malty dark lager beer: Shiner Bock

NOTE Find fermented shrimp paste (sold as terasi or belacan) in South Asian grocery stores or online at indofoodstore.com.

NORI-AND-SHRIMP FRIED RICE

"One of the best things I ate recently was Rachel Yang's nori fried rice at her restaurant, Joule, in Seattle. I was so bowled over by its richness and piscine umami-ness, I went home to Santa Cruz, California, and worked up a version of my own," says James Beard Award–winning cookbook author Andrea Nguyen. "You don't need anything fancy for the nori dust. Just whirl up sheets of sushi nori with a small amount of coarse salt in a blender. Then deploy the nori dust to add vegetal savoriness and visual flair; it's a nimble seasoning and handsome garnish. To ensure the rice grains take on flavors and fry up to a delicate deliciousness, use dry-ish rice. Long-grain and medium-grain are my go-tos, but feel free to try this with basmati or even leftover takeout rice. Fry it in two batches to ensure the grains cook fast and evenly."

ACTIVE 25 MIN; TOTAL 55 MIN; SERVES 2

¾ tsp. kosher salt, divided

5 nori sheets (about ½ oz.)

3 cups cooked long-grain white rice (such as basmati) or medium-grain white rice (such as Calrose)

3 Tbsp. canola oil or European-style unsalted butter (such as Plugrá), divided

2 garlic cloves, finely chopped

5 oz. peeled and deveined raw extra-large shrimp, patted dry with paper towels and cut into ½-inch pieces

2 tsp. fish sauce

1 small scallion, sliced

1 Place ½ teaspoon salt in a blender. Tear or cut nori sheets into 1- to 2-inch pieces; add to blender. Process on medium-high speed until mixture resembles graphite-color glitter, about 1 minute. Transfer to an airtight container.

2 If using hot freshly cooked rice, spread in an even layer on a baking sheet lined with paper towels; let cool until rice is room temperature and grains are dry, about 30 minutes. If using chilled day-old rice, spread in an even layer on a baking sheet lined with paper towels; let come to room temperature. Gently rub rice back and forth between your hands to separate the grains. Place rice and remaining ingredients near stove so you can cook quickly.

3 Heat 2 tablespoons oil in a 12-inch carbon-steel or nonstick skillet over medium. When oil is nearly shimmering, add garlic, and cook, stirring constantly, until garlic is toasted and fragrant, 10 to 15 seconds. Add shrimp, and stir to combine. Season with remaining ¼ teaspoon salt. Cook, stirring constantly, until shrimp are nearly cooked through, 45 seconds to 1 minute.

4 Add 1½ cups rice to skillet, and stir to combine. Increase heat to high. Cook, undisturbed, 20 seconds; stir. Repeat cooking-and-stirring process until a dry skin forms around some of the rice grains, 2 to 3 minutes. Transfer mixture to a medium bowl. Repeat procedure with remaining 1 tablespoon oil and 1½ cups rice. Return rice-shrimp mixture to skillet, and stir to combine. Drizzle with fish sauce, and cook, stirring constantly, 20 seconds. (This will ensure rice grains are well-seasoned.)

5 Remove from heat. Stir in sliced scallion, and let stand until scallion is just softened, 10 to 15 seconds. Stir in 1 tablespoon nori dust. —ANDREA NGUYEN

MAKE AHEAD Nori dust may be stored in an airtight container at room temperature up to 3 months.

WINE Dry, lychee-scented Gewürztraminer: Tiefenbrunner Turmhof

KHICHDI

Khichdi is a fortifying, easily digestible dish made from mung beans, rice, and a wide variety of spices. It is a staple of meals at Thikse Monastery in Ladakh, India, and reflects the Thikse monks' belief that food should be consumed not only to quell hunger but also to contribute to optimal health. Chef and cookbook author Cortney Burns, who spent time at the monastery learning from the monks, uses a warming spice mixture including fenugreek, turmeric, cumin, and ginger to perfume this soothing, comforting porridge.

ACTIVE 30 MIN; TOTAL 40 MIN; SERVES 6 TO 8

- 1¼ cups dried split yellow mung beans (such as Pride of India)
- ¾ cup uncooked white basmati rice
- ½ cinnamon stick (about 1½ inches)
- 6 whole cloves
- 1½ tsp. ground cumin
- 1 tsp. ground coriander
- 1 tsp. brown mustard seeds
- 1 tsp. ground turmeric
- ½ tsp. fennel seeds
- ½ tsp. ground fenugreek seeds
- Generous pinch of cayenne pepper
- 2 garlic cloves, finely chopped
- 2 tsp. finely chopped peeled fresh ginger
- 6½ cups water
- 2 fresh bay leaves
- Pinch of kosher salt, plus more to taste
- Whole-milk yogurt and fresh cilantro leaves, for serving

1 Place mung beans and rice in a fine wire-mesh strainer; rinse under cold water, stirring with your hands, until water runs clear, about 3 minutes.

2 Place cinnamon stick, whole cloves, cumin, coriander, mustard seeds, turmeric, fennel seeds, fenugreek, and cayenne in a large heavy-bottomed pot or a medium Dutch oven. Heat over medium, stirring constantly with a wooden spoon, until very fragrant, about 3 minutes. Add garlic and ginger; cook, stirring constantly, 1 minute. Add mung bean mixture; stir to coat in spices. Add 6½ cups water, bay leaves, and salt.

3 Bring mixture to a vigorous simmer over medium-high, stirring occasionally. Cover and reduce heat to low; simmer, stirring and running spoon along bottom of pot occasionally, until mung bean mixture is tender but rice still holds its shape, 12 to 15 minutes. (Mixture will be slightly runny, but it will thicken as it sits.) Remove from heat. Remove and discard cinnamon, whole cloves, and bay leaves. Gently stir in salt to taste. Divide evenly among bowls; dollop with yogurt, and sprinkle with cilantro. —CORTNEY BURNS

MAKE AHEAD Khichdi can be made up to 1 day ahead.

NOTE Find split yellow mung beans at Indian grocery stores or online.

QUINOA WITH SPICE-RUBBED SHRIMP AND PISTOU

Oxford, Mississippi–based chef John Currence coats shrimp with a potent mix of fennel seeds, dried oregano, and garlic and onion powders. He flavors the quinoa with a vibrant, pesto-like pistou, made with a judicious amount of oil.

ACTIVE: 30 MIN; TOTAL: 1 HR; SERVES 4

- ½ lb. peeled and deveined raw medium shrimp
- ½ tsp. garlic powder
- ½ tsp. onion powder
- ½ tsp. smoked paprika
- ½ tsp. dried oregano, crumbled
- ½ tsp. fennel seeds, chopped
- ¼ tsp. dried thyme
- ¼ cup canola oil
- ½ tsp. salt, plus more to taste
- ½ tsp. freshly ground black pepper, plus more to taste
- ¼ cup (packed) fresh basil leaves
- 2 Tbsp. fresh flat-leaf parsley leaves
- 1 Tbsp. fresh rosemary leaves
- 1½ tsp. fresh thyme leaves
- 1 garlic clove, smashed
- 2 Tbsp. freshly grated Parmigiano-Reggiano cheese
- 1½ cups quinoa, rinsed
- 2¼ cups water

1 In a resealable plastic bag, toss the shrimp with the garlic and onion powders, paprika, oregano, fennel seeds, dried thyme, 1 tablespoon oil, and ½ teaspoon each of salt and pepper until coated. Let stand at room temperature 30 minutes.

2 Meanwhile, preheat oven to 425°F. To make the pistou, pulse basil, parsley, rosemary, thyme leaves, garlic, and cheese in a food processor. Add 2 tablespoons oil, and puree until smooth. Season to taste with salt and pepper.

3 In a saucepan, combine the quinoa, water and the remaining 1 tablespoon of oil. Season lightly with salt and bring to a boil. Cover and simmer over low heat until the quinoa is tender, about 15 minutes. Let stand for 5 minutes. Transfer to a bowl; keep warm.

4 Arrange shrimp on a baking sheet, and roast in the preheated oven about 8 minutes, until curled and pink. Cut the shrimp into thirds, and add to quinoa with the pistou. Toss well, season with salt and pepper, and serve. —JOHN CURRENCE

SANTA FE QUINOA SALAD

At L.A. Bento in Los Angeles, chef Chad Aaland makes quinoa salad with three types of beans and house-pickled onions. This streamlined version with black beans and jarred cocktail onions is tasty, too.

ACTIVE: 20 MIN; TOTAL: 45 MIN; SERVES 4

¾ cup quinoa (about 5 oz.)

1½ cups water

Kosher salt

1 tsp. cumin seeds

2 Tbsp. fresh lime juice

6 Tbsp. vegetable oil

Freshly ground pepper

1 (15-oz.) can black beans, rinsed

1 small red bell pepper, finely diced

½ cup finely chopped fresh cilantro

1 (3-oz.) jar cocktail onions, drained and finely chopped

1 Combine quinoa, 1½ cups water, and a pinch of salt in a medium saucepan; bring to a boil. Cover and simmer over low until the water is absorbed, about 15 minutes. Spread the quinoa on a baking sheet; refrigerate about 20 minutes.

2 Meanwhile, toast cumin seeds in a small skillet over high, shaking the pan, until fragrant, about 2 minutes; transfer to a blender. Add lime juice and oil, and blend. Season with salt and pepper.

3 Pour the dressing into a bowl and add the black beans, bell pepper, cilantro and cocktail onions. Scrape the quinoa into the bowl, season with salt and pepper and serve. —CHAD AALAND

ROASTED DELICATA SQUASH WITH QUINOA SALAD

Quinoa is definitely a superfood: a grain-like seed, it's a "complete" protein containing all eight essential amino acids. (Another plus: It cooks much more quickly than most grains.) To create a terrific vegetarian main course, Michael Symon of Cleveland's Lola tosses quinoa with arugula, apple, raisin, and fresh herbs, then spoons the salad into a halved baked squash (a great source of iron and vitamins A and C).

ACTIVE: 30 MIN; TOTAL: 1 HR; SERVES 4

2 delicata squash (about 1 lb. each), halved lengthwise and seeded

2 Tbsp. extra virgin olive oil, divided

Salt and freshly ground black pepper

1 cup quinoa

2 Tbsp. golden raisins

1 Tbsp. sherry vinegar

1 tsp. honey

1 Granny Smith apple, finely diced

1 large shallot, minced

1 garlic clove, minced

2 Tbsp. chopped fresh mint

2 Tbsp. chopped fresh parsley

2 oz. arugula (2 cups)

1 Preheat oven to 350°F. Brush the cut sides of the squash with 1 teaspoon olive oil, and season the cavities with salt and pepper. Place the squash, cut sides down, on a baking sheet, and roast in the preheated oven about 45 minutes, until tender.

2 Meanwhile, in a saucepan, bring 2 cups of lightly salted water to a boil. Add quinoa, cover, and simmer 10 minutes. Stir in raisins, and simmer, covered, until the water is absorbed, about 5 minutes. Transfer quinoa to a large bowl, and let cool.

3 Whisk the vinegar, honey, and remaining 1 tablespoon plus 2 teaspoons olive oil in a small bowl; season with salt and pepper. Add the dressing to the quinoa along with apple, shallot, garlic, mint, and parsley, and toss well. Add arugula, and toss gently.

4 Set the squash halves on plates. Fill with the salad, and serve. —MICHAEL SYMON

MAKE AHEAD The quinoa can be refrigerated overnight. Bring to room temperature and add the arugula just before serving.

EGGS BENNY TOAST

The secret to this super-simple eggs Benedict? Cornstarch. It stabilizes the emulsion in the hollandaise, helping to prevent the sauce from breaking while it cooks over direct heat. Easier than poaching, gently steaming eggs results in delicately tender whites and smooth, creamy yolks.

TOTAL 30 MIN; SERVES 4

3 large egg yolks

1 Tbsp. cold water

1 tsp. cornstarch

1 tsp. Dijon mustard

1½ Tbsp. fresh lemon juice, divided

1 tsp. kosher salt, divided

12 Tbsp. unsalted butter (6 oz.), melted, plus 2 Tbsp. cold unsalted butter, divided

⅛ tsp. cayenne pepper

Warm water, as needed

4 cold large eggs

4 (½-inch-thick) sourdough bread slices, toasted

8 thin prosciutto or speck slices (about 4 oz.)

2 Tbsp. roughly chopped fresh soft herbs (such as tarragon and chives)

Freshly ground black pepper (optional)

1 Whisk egg yolks in a small saucepan until smooth, about 1 minute. Add 1 tablespoon cold water, cornstarch, Dijon, 1 tablespoon lemon juice, and ½ teaspoon salt; whisk until thoroughly combined. Prepare a bowl of ice water large enough to dip bottom of saucepan into; set aside.

2 Add 1 tablespoon cold butter to egg yolk mixture; place over very low heat. Cook, whisking constantly, until thickened and bubbles have disappeared, 1 to 2 minutes, being careful not to curdle egg mixture. (If egg mixture looks anything but perfectly smooth, remove from heat, and briefly plunge saucepan into ice water, whisking constantly.) When butter is completely incorporated and mixture has thickened, immediately add remaining 1 tablespoon cold butter; remove from heat, and whisk until smooth.

3 While whisking egg yolk mixture constantly, slowly add 2 tablespoons melted butter, ¼ teaspoon at a time, until mixture begins to thicken, about 1 minute. Whisking constantly, add remaining 10 tablespoons melted butter, 1 tablespoon at a time, until sauce is smooth, about 2 minutes. Whisk in cayenne, remaining ½ tablespoon lemon juice, and remaining ½ teaspoon salt. Add warm water, 1 teaspoon at a time, as needed until sauce is thin enough to spread out but still thick and billowy. Cover pan, and keep warm over very low heat. Add more warm water to thin if needed after resting.

4 Set a steamer basket in a medium saucepan, and fill pan with 1 inch of water. Bring to a simmer over medium; add cold eggs. Cover and cook eggs 7 minutes for runny yolks, increasing time by 30-second increments up to 8 minutes and 30 seconds for less runny yolks. Transfer eggs to ice bath; let stand 1 to 2 minutes. Carefully peel eggs.

5 To assemble, drape each piece of sourdough toast with 2 prosciutto slices. Cut peeled eggs carefully in half lengthwise, and top each toast with 2 egg halves. Spoon ¼ cup hollandaise over each toast; sprinkle with herbs and, if desired, black pepper. —SUSAN SPUNGEN

WINE Toasty brut Champagne: NV Laurent-Perrier La Cuvée Brut

BOURSIN OMELET

This beautifully basic omelet is the sleeper hit of chef Michael Tusk's French-inflected bar à vin menu at Verjus in San Francisco. An homage to his love of dairy, spreadable garlic-herb cheese melts richly into the creamy center of the tender eggs. While it makes for a delicious and satisfying breakfast, this omelet is best with some crusty baguette, a crisp salad, and a glass of chilled sparkling wine.

TOTAL 20 MIN; SERVES 1

- 2 Tbsp. plus 1 tsp. unsalted butter, divided
- 1 cup finely chopped yellow onion
- ¼ tsp. kosher salt, divided, plus more to taste
- 2 large eggs
- 1 tsp. heavy cream
- 1 Tbsp. garlic-and-herb spreadable cheese (such as Boursin), at room temperature
- ½ tsp. thinly sliced fresh chives

1 Heat 1 tablespoon butter in an 8½-inch nonstick skillet over medium-high. Add onion, and spread in an even layer. Cook, undisturbed, until onion begins to brown, about 4 minutes. Add 2 tablespoons water and ⅛ teaspoon salt; cook, stirring constantly, until onion is golden brown and softened, 8 to 10 minutes. Transfer onion to a bowl. Wipe skillet clean.

2 Using a fork, stir together eggs, cream, and remaining ⅛ teaspoon salt in a medium bowl until well combined, being careful not to incorporate too much air.

3 Heat same skillet over medium-high. Add 1 tablespoon butter (it should melt almost immediately); swirl to evenly coat bottom of skillet. Just as butter stops foaming but before it begins to brown, add egg mixture all at once. Cook, stirring constantly with a heatproof rubber spatula, until mixture thickens slightly into very soft scrambled eggs with thin ribbons of set curd running throughout, 10 to 20 seconds. Gently shake skillet to form an even sheet of eggs on bottom of skillet.

4 Reduce heat to low. Crumble cheese over eggs. Sprinkle 1 tablespoon caramelized onion in a straight line separating the upper third from the bottom two-thirds of omelet. (Reserve remaining onion for another use.) Cook omelet, undisturbed, until filling heats and cheese melts, about 1 minute. Using spatula and starting with upper third side, gently fold omelet over, just covering filling. Starting at top of folded side, roll up entire omelet. Turn off heat, and let stand 10 seconds. Transfer to a warm plate, and rub hot omelet with remaining 1 teaspoon butter. Sprinkle with chives, and add salt to taste. Serve immediately.
—MICHAEL TUSK

MAKE AHEAD Caramelized onion may be covered and refrigerated up to 5 days.

WINE Zesty California sparkling wine: Domaine Carneros Estate Brut

CHILAQUILES ROJOS WITH FRIED EGGS AND COTIJA

Charring the tomato and onion before adding them to the red chile sauce is a quick way to create rich, slow-cooked flavor in this hearty dish from San Diego–based chef and culinary entrepreneur Claudette Zepeda. Thick-cut fresh tortilla chips soak up the sauce and runny egg yolks without getting soggy.

ACTIVE 35 MIN; TOTAL 50 MIN; SERVES 4

1½ lb. plum tomatoes (about 8 medium), halved lengthwise

1 medium-size white onion, cut into 1-inch wedges

2 dried chiles de árbol, stemmed and seeded

5 dried guajillo chiles, stemmed and seeded

1 dried chipotle chile, stemmed and seeded

3 medium garlic cloves, unpeeled

2½ Tbsp. fresh oregano leaves

1 Tbsp. kosher salt

1 bunch fresh cilantro, leaves and stems separated, divided

1 Tbsp. olive oil

4 large eggs

12 cups thick corn tortilla chips (such as Montes)

2 avocados, sliced

8 oz. queso fresco, crumbled (about 2 cups)

½ cup Mexican crema, for serving

1 Preheat broiler with oven rack in middle of oven. Place tomatoes, cut sides up, and onion on a rimmed baking sheet, and broil in preheated oven on middle rack until charred, 16 to 22 minutes. Let cool 15 minutes, and set aside.

2 Meanwhile, heat a large cast-iron skillet over medium. Add chiles and garlic cloves, and cook, turning often, until chiles are fragrant, about 4 minutes. Remove chiles from skillet. Continue cooking garlic cloves, turning occasionally, until blackened in spots and softened, about 10 minutes total. Let garlic cloves cool 10 minutes; peel and set aside.

3 Bring 1 quart water to a boil in a small saucepan over medium-high. Add toasted chiles, and boil, stirring occasionally, until chiles are softened, about 10 minutes. Drain, reserving 1½ cups cooking liquid.

4 Combine tomatoes, onion, garlic, chiles, oregano, salt, reserved cooking liquid, and 1 cup cilantro stems in a blender. (Reserve any remaining cilantro stems for another use.) Process until smooth, about 20 seconds. Pour mixture through a fine wire-mesh strainer into a bowl; discard solids. Set red chile sauce aside.

5 Heat oil in a large (12-inch) nonstick skillet over medium. Crack eggs into skillet, leaving 1 inch between them. Cook until edges are set and starting to brown, about 2 minutes. Cover skillet, and cook until whites are set and yolks reach desired degree of doneness, 2 to 3 minutes for runny yolks. Transfer eggs to a plate; tent with aluminum foil to keep warm. Add red chile sauce to skillet over medium. Bring to a simmer. Pour red chile sauce over chips in a large bowl; toss to coat. Divide chip mixture evenly among 4 plates. Top evenly with eggs, avocado slices, queso fresco, crema, and desired amount of cilantro leaves. Serve immediately. —CLAUDETTE ZEPEDA

MAKE AHEAD Red chile sauce can be chilled in an airtight container up to 3 days.

WINE Brambly, rich Zinfandel: Ridge Vineyards East Bench

BASTED EGG TARTINES WITH CREAMED MUSTARD

This open-face sandwich is an ideal breakfast but also makes for a light, simple lunch. The creamed mustard pairs with lightly bitter greens and rich, runny egg yolk; try leftover sauce on baked salmon.

TOTAL 15 MIN; SERVES 2

2 Tbsp. sour cream

1½ Tbsp. whole-grain mustard

1 tsp. Dijon mustard

2 tsp. fresh lemon juice, divided

2 (⅓-inch-thick) rustic bread slices, toasted

1 cup fresh baby mustard greens

Kosher salt, to taste

Black pepper, to taste

1 Tbsp. extra virgin olive oil

2 large eggs

⅓ cup hot water

1 Whisk together sour cream, whole-grain mustard, Dijon mustard, and 1 teaspoon lemon juice in a small bowl. Spread mixture evenly on one side of toast slices. Toss together mustard greens and remaining 1 teaspoon lemon juice in a separate bowl; season to taste with salt and pepper. Mound greens evenly on toasts.

2 Heat oil in a large nonstick skillet over medium. Crack eggs into skillet, spacing at least 1 inch apart; cook until whites just start to change color, about 30 seconds. Add ⅓ cup hot water to skillet; cook, basting eggs with water, until whites are just set and yolks are still runny, about 2 minutes. Place 1 egg on each prepared toast. Season with salt and pepper to taste. Serve immediately. —JUSTIN CHAPPLE

MAKE AHEAD Creamed mustard can be made and stored in an airtight container in refrigerator up to 5 days ahead.

CHAWANMUSHI WITH SHRIMP AND CELERY

Celery leaves, scallion, and sweet, tender shrimp add texture to these smooth steamed custards.

ACTIVE 15 MIN; TOTAL 40 MIN; SERVES 2

3 large eggs

1½ cups lower-sodium chicken broth

1½ tsp. fish sauce (such as Red Boat)

½ tsp. kosher salt

⅓ cup torn celery leaves, plus more for garnish

1 scallion, thinly sliced, plus more for garnish

6 peeled and deveined raw medium shrimp, cut in half lengthwise

1 Whisk together eggs, broth, fish sauce, and salt in a bowl. Divide celery leaves and scallion evenly between 2 (12-ounce) bowls. Pour egg mixture through a fine wire-mesh strainer evenly into bowls. Wrap each bowl in plastic wrap (use rubber bands to secure plastic if it doesn't adhere to sides).

2 Place bowls in a large steamer basket set over a large saucepan of simmering water. Cover and cook until custards are just set, 15 to 18 minutes.

3 Carefully remove bowls from steamer basket; remove and discard plastic wrap. Let custards stand 5 minutes.

4 Meanwhile, place shrimp in a single layer in steamer basket. Cover and cook until opaque and cooked through, about 1 minute. —JUSTIN CHAPPLE

5 Top custards evenly with shrimp; garnish with celery leaves and scallion.

WINE Dry Australian Riesling: Pikes Traditionale

**BASTED EGG TARTINES WITH
CREAMED MUSTARD**

MAIN-DISH SALADS, SANDWICHES & PIZZAS

The ultimate in casual cooking and eating is tossing together a few beautiful ingredients from the farmers market plus a protein for a big, crisp, cool seasonal salad—or tucking into something yummy you can eat with your hands.

CACIO E PEPE BROCCOLINI
WITH CRISPY WHITE BEANS
AND BURRATA (P. 188)

CHARRED FOCACCIA AND STEAK SALAD

PHOTO P. 5

Sturdy focaccia croutons stand up to bold ingredients like the steak and chile in this recipe.

ACTIVE 30 MIN; TOTAL 35 MIN; SERVES 4

- 1 (8-oz.) strip steak (about 1½ inches thick), trimmed
- 6½ Tbsp. extra virgin olive oil, divided, plus more for grill grates
- 2¼ tsp. kosher salt, divided, plus more to taste
- 1 tsp. black pepper, divided, plus more to taste
- 8 oz. focaccia (preferably day-old), split horizontally
- 3½ Tbsp. white wine vinegar
- 1 to 2 Tbsp. finely chopped jarred Calabrian chiles
- 2 cups watercress, roughly torn
- 2 cups baby arugula
- 1 medium heirloom tomato, cut into 1½-inch pieces (about 2 cups)
- 3 medium Persian cucumbers, cut into ¾-inch pieces (about 1½ cups)
- 1 cup thinly sliced red onion

1 Preheat grill to very high (about 550°F). Rub steak with ½ tablespoon oil; sprinkle with ½ teaspoon salt and ¼ teaspoon black pepper. Place on oiled grates; grill, uncovered, to desired degree of doneness, 4 to 5 minutes per side for medium-rare. Transfer steak to a cutting board; let rest 10 minutes. Slice against the grain.

2 While steak rests, brush focaccia pieces evenly with 1 tablespoon oil; sprinkle with ½ teaspoon salt and ¼ teaspoon black pepper. Grill, uncovered, turning often, until crisp and lightly charred all over, 4 to 6 minutes. Remove from grill; let cool slightly, about 5 minutes. Tear or cut into 1-inch pieces.

3 Whisk together vinegar, Calabrian chiles, remaining 5 tablespoons oil, remaining 1¼ teaspoons salt, and remaining ½ teaspoon black pepper in a small bowl. Place steak, watercress, arugula, tomato, cucumbers, and onion in a large bowl; add ½ cup dressing, and toss to coat. Add focaccia pieces; toss to combine. Let salad stand 5 minutes. Season with salt and black pepper to taste. Transfer salad to a large serving bowl; drizzle with remaining dressing. —JUSTIN CHAPPLE

MAKE AHEAD Focaccia croutons can be made 1 day ahead and stored in an airtight container at room temperature.

WINE Savory, medium-bodied Tuscan red: Banfi Centine Rosso

SHRIMP WEDGE SALAD WITH OLD BAY BREADCRUMBS AND HOT SAUCE DRESSING

Taking a cue from chef Nina Compton at Bywater American Bistro, we're adding a Crystal hot sauce–spiked dressing to this mash-up of a wedge salad and a po'boy sandwich.

TOTAL 20 MIN; SERVES 4

- 1 Tbsp. vegetable oil
- 20 peeled and deveined raw large shrimp (about 1 lb.)
- ½ tsp. kosher salt
- ⅛ tsp. black pepper
- 1¼ cups fresh breadcrumbs (about 3⅜ oz.)
- ½ tsp. Old Bay seasoning
- ½ cup mayonnaise
- 2 Tbsp. whole milk
- 4 tsp. hot sauce (such as Crystal)
- 1 (20-oz.) head iceberg lettuce, cut into 4 wedges
- Capers, for garnish

1 Heat oil in a 12-inch nonstick skillet over medium-high. Add shrimp; cook until pink and cooked through, 1 to 2 minutes per side. Sprinkle with salt and pepper. Remove from skillet; set aside.

2 Add breadcrumbs and Old Bay seasoning to skillet; cook over medium, stirring occasionally, until golden brown, about 4 minutes. Remove from heat; set aside.

3 Whisk together mayonnaise, milk, and hot sauce in a small bowl until smooth.

4 Arrange lettuce wedges on a platter. Top with shrimp, dressing, and breadcrumbs. Garnish with capers. —KELSEY YOUNGMAN

WINE Zesty California Sauvignon Blanc: Duckhorn Vineyards Napa Valley

SHRIMP WEDGE SALAD WITH
OLD BAY BREADCRUMBS AND
HOT SAUCE DRESSING

CACIO E PEPE BROCCOLINI WITH CRISPY WHITE BEANS AND BURRATA

PHOTO P. 185

Hetty McKinnon used to pedal around Sydney on her bike, delivering salads. As the sole owner of a meal-delivery business, McKinnon dreamed up salads in her home kitchen and built a community around sharing meals. Now based in Brooklyn, McKinnon, the author of three previous cookbooks, has filled her latest book, Family, *with comforting, uncomplicated recipes meant to be shared. This Cacio e Pepe Broccolini with Crispy White Beans and Burrata captures the rich, elegant, simple flavors of the classic Italian pasta and rounds them out with bitter charred Broccolini and crispy, creamy, flash-fried white beans. It's a hearty and healthy late-summer meal.*

TOTAL 40 MIN; SERVES 4

- 2 bunches fresh Broccolini (about 1 lb.), trimmed, stems halved lengthwise
- 7 Tbsp. extra virgin olive oil, divided, plus more for drizzling
- 1 tsp. fine sea salt, divided
- 2 (15.5-oz.) cans cannellini or navy beans, drained, rinsed, and patted dry
- 1 red Fresno chile, thinly sliced
- 1 garlic clove, finely chopped
- ¼ cup chopped fresh flat-leaf parsley
- 8 oz. Burrata cheese
- 1½ oz. Pecorino Romano cheese, grated (about ⅓ cup)
- ½ to 1 tsp. black pepper
- ½ lemon, cut into 4 wedges

1 Heat a large skillet over medium-high until very hot, 4 to 5 minutes. Toss together Broccolini and 3 tablespoons oil in a large bowl until coated. Add half of Broccolini to skillet, and spread in an even layer. Cook until slightly charred and crisp-tender, 2 to 3 minutes per side. Transfer to a large bowl, and repeat with remaining Broccolini. Toss Broccolini with ¾ teaspoon salt.

2 Carefully wipe skillet clean, and return to heat over medium-high. Add 2 tablespoons oil; swirl to coat. Add half of the beans; spread in an even layer. Cook, undisturbed, until outer skins of beans begin to peel back, crisp, and brown slightly, about 1 minute and 30 seconds. Add chile and garlic; stir, and cook, undisturbed, until fragrant, 15 to 30 seconds. Transfer to bowl with Broccolini. Repeat with remaining 2 tablespoons oil and beans.

3 Gently toss Broccolini and beans with parsley and remaining ¼ teaspoon salt. Arrange Burrata in center of serving bowl, and surround with Broccolini and beans mixture. Sprinkle with Pecorino Romano and black pepper. Drizzle with oil, and serve with lemon wedges. —HETTY MCKINNON

WINE Lemony, zesty Italian white: Principe Pallavicini Frascati Superiore

WAX BEAN SALAD WITH POTATOES, CAPERS, AND EGGS

One of cookbook author Sarah Copeland's favorite ways to start the weekend is to visit her local farmers market; she changes up this easy riff on Niçoise salad based on her finds. Yellow wax beans make a beautiful addition when they're in season, but haricots verts are the perfect stand-in.

ACTIVE 30 MIN; TOTAL 45 MIN; SERVES 4

8 oz. fingerling potatoes or new potatoes

6 Tbsp. extra virgin olive oil

2 Tbsp. sherry vinegar

1 tsp. fine sea salt

Black pepper, to taste

4 oz. green, yellow, or purple wax beans, trimmed

¼ cup thinly sliced red onion

¼ cup pitted Castelvetrano olives

1 Tbsp. undrained capers

¼ cup fresh flat-leaf parsley leaves or fresh tarragon leaves

8 anchovy fillets, drained (optional)

4 hard-cooked eggs, peeled and cut into halves or quarters

Flaky sea salt (such as Maldon)

1 Place potatoes in a medium saucepan; cover with salted water, and bring to a boil over high. Reduce heat to medium-high, and simmer until tender when pierced with a knife, 12 to 15 minutes; drain.

2 Whisk together oil, vinegar, fine sea salt, and pepper; set aside. Cut potatoes into quarters or halves; arrange on a platter in an even layer. Spoon ⅓ cup dressing over potatoes; set aside.

3 Bring another pot of water to a boil over high. Prepare a bowl of ice water for an ice bath. Cook beans until their color is deeply saturated, about 3 minutes. Remove with a slotted spoon, and plunge into ice water. Drain, and pat dry.

4 Toss together beans, onion, olives, capers and brine, parsley, and anchovies, if using, with remaining dressing in a large bowl; spread over potatoes. Top with eggs, and sprinkle with flaky sea salt. —SARAH COPELAND

CHARRED SHALLOT AND ARUGULA SALAD
WITH SUNNY-SIDE-UP EGGS

Peppery arugula, nutty Parmesan, savory prosciutto, and sunny-side-up eggs pair with a garlicky dressing in this hearty salad. Charring shallots makes them tender and coaxes out their sweetness.

TOTAL 25 MIN; SERVES 4

DRESSING

- ¼ tsp. grated lemon zest plus 2 Tbsp. fresh lemon juice (from 1 lemon)
- 4 garlic cloves, grated on a Microplane (about 2 tsp.)
- 1 tsp. Dijon mustard
- ¼ tsp. dry mustard
- ¼ tsp. dried oregano leaves
- ¼ tsp. dried basil
- 2 Tbsp. olive oil

SALAD

- 4 large shallots (about 6 oz.), thinly sliced (about 1 cup)
- 2 tsp. avocado oil, divided
- 4 large eggs, at room temperature
  Kosher salt, to taste
- 6 cups loosely packed arugula (about 3 oz.)
- 2 oz. Parmesan cheese, shaved (about 1 cup)
- ½ tsp. coarsely ground black pepper, plus more to taste
- 2 oz. prosciutto, torn into bite-size pieces (about 1 cup)

1 **Make the dressing:** Whisk together lemon zest and juice, garlic, Dijon, dry mustard, oregano, and basil in a medium bowl until combined. Gradually drizzle in olive oil, whisking constantly, until oil is incorporated and dressing is smooth.

2 **Make the salad:** Preheat broiler to high with oven rack 6 inches from heat. Toss together shallots and 1 teaspoon avocado oil in a small bowl; spread in an even layer on a small baking sheet. Broil shallots in preheated oven until slightly charred, about 3 minutes. Remove from oven. Let cool 5 minutes.

3 Meanwhile, heat remaining 1 teaspoon avocado oil in a large nonstick skillet over medium. Crack eggs into skillet, and sprinkle with salt to taste. Cook until whites are set and yolks are runny, about 3 minutes. Remove from heat. Transfer eggs to a plate, and set aside.

4 Drizzle 1 tablespoon dressing in a large bowl. Add arugula, and drizzle with 1 tablespoon dressing. Top with shallots, Parmesan, and pepper. Toss to combine, or cover bowl with a baking sheet or lid, and shake to combine. Transfer salad to a large platter. Top with eggs and prosciutto. Season with additional salt and pepper to taste. Drizzle with additional dressing, if desired.

—MARVE MCCLAIN

MAKE AHEAD Dressing can be stored in an airtight container in refrigerator up to 3 days.

WINE Full-flavored Italian rosé: Benanti Etna Rosato

GRILLED PEPPER AND ONION PANZANELLA
WITH PEPERONCINI VINAIGRETTE

Molly Stevens' panzanella uses grilled sweet peppers and onions in place of tomatoes as the centerpiece of this dinner salad. The charred vegetables are tossed with cubes of grilled bread, drizzled with a peperoncini vinaigrette, and topped with creamy feta and crisp slices of peperoncini, which add pops of flavor and contrasting texture. This is a highly adaptable salad; try incorporating your favorite sweet or hot peppers and grilling other vegetables, such as squash and eggplant planks, alongside the peppers, if you like.

ACTIVE 35 MIN; TOTAL 40 MIN; SERVES 4

- **10 to 12 oz.** rustic bread (such as ciabatta or Pugliese) (from 1 [20-oz.] loaf), sliced 1 inch thick
- **3** small red and/or yellow bell peppers (about 5 oz. each), each cut lengthwise into 4 planks
- **1** large red onion (about 16 oz.), sliced into ½-inch-thick rounds
- **¼ cup plus 1 Tbsp.** extra virgin olive oil, divided, plus more to taste
- **1½ tsp.** kosher salt, divided, plus more to taste
- **¼ tsp.** black pepper, divided, plus more to taste
- **8** peperoncini, sliced into thin rounds, plus ¼ cup peperoncini brine (from 1 [15-oz.] jar), divided
- **3 oz.** feta cheese, crumbled into large pieces (about ½ cup)
- **¼ cup** torn fresh basil

1 Preheat grill to medium-high (400°F to 450°F). Brush bread slices, bell peppers, and onion rounds evenly with 2 tablespoons oil, and sprinkle evenly with 1 teaspoon salt and ⅛ teaspoon black pepper. Whisk together peperoncini brine, remaining 3 tablespoons oil, remaining ½ teaspoon salt, and remaining ⅛ teaspoon black pepper in a small bowl; set vinaigrette aside.

2 Arrange bread on unoiled grates; grill, uncovered, until nicely marked and toasted, 2 to 3 minutes per side. Transfer to a cutting board. Grill bell peppers and onion, covered, turning occasionally, until charred and tender, 8 to 10 minutes. Transfer to cutting board.

3 Cut bread into 1-inch cubes, and transfer to a large bowl. Slice bell peppers into thin strips, and separate onion rounds into rings; add to bread in bowl. Toss to combine. Drizzle with peperoncini vinaigrette, and toss again. Add additional salt and black pepper to taste, and add a drizzle of oil if salad seems dry. Top with peperoncini rounds, feta, and basil. Serve panzanella warm or at room temperature. —MOLLY STEVENS

MAKE AHEAD Salad can be prepared through Step 2 up to 2 hours in advance and held at room temperature. Proceed with Step 3 just before serving.

WINE Substantial Italian rosé: Leone de Castris Five Roses Rosato

NOTE Grilling the bread adds a smoky flavor and dries it out, allowing it to absorb the flavorful vinaigrette.

CRUNCHY EGGPLANT AND CORN SALAD
WITH MINT AND FETA

Slicing the eggplant into thin, even slabs is the key to knocking this salad from Michigan-based chef and cookbook author Abra Berens out of the park; at that thickness, the crunchy coating gets nice and brown while the eggplant flesh roasts to the perfect tenderness. The corn can get a little rowdy in the skillet; keep it partially covered during cooking to catch popping kernels.

ACTIVE 35 MIN; TOTAL 1 HR 50 MIN; SERVES 4

2½ cups fresh breadcrumbs

½ cup canola oil, divided

2½ tsp. kosher salt, divided

1¼ tsp. black pepper, divided

4 medium ears fresh sweet corn (about 1¾ lb.), shucked

1 (1-lb.) eggplant, striped with a Y-shape peeler and cut crosswise into 16 (⅓-inch-thick) rounds

¼ cup mayonnaise

4 oz. feta cheese, crumbled (about 1 cup)

¼ cup fresh mint leaves

Chile Oil (recipe follows), for serving

1 Preheat oven to 400°F. Combine breadcrumbs, 2 tablespoons oil, ½ teaspoon salt, and ¼ teaspoon pepper in a medium bowl; toss to coat. Set aside. Cut kernels from corn cobs (you will have about 2½ cups kernels). Set aside.

2 Toss together eggplant rounds, ¼ cup oil, 1 teaspoon salt, and ½ teaspoon pepper in a medium bowl until well coated. Arrange eggplant in a single layer on a lightly greased, foil–lined baking sheet. Brush top of each eggplant round with about ¾ teaspoon mayonnaise and sprinkle with about 2½ tablespoons breadcrumb mixture. Bake until eggplant is tender and breadcrumbs are golden brown, 20 to 22 minutes.

3 Meanwhile, heat remaining 2 tablespoons oil in a large skillet over high. Add corn kernels, remaining 1 teaspoon salt and remaining ½ teaspoon pepper. Partially cover skillet, leaving about a 2-inch gap (for steam to escape and to prevent corn from popping out of skillet). Cook, shaking skillet occasionally, until corn is well charred, about 8 minutes. Remove from heat, and let cool in skillet, partially covered, 1 minute. Transfer charred corn to a bowl.

4 Arrange 4 eggplant rounds on each of 4 serving plates. Top servings with about ⅓ cup corn, ¼ cup crumbled feta, and 1 tablespoon mint. Drizzle with Chile Oil.
—ABRA BERENS

WINE Berry-scented Greek rosé: Gai'a 14-18h Agiorgitiko

CHILE OIL

Double this simple recipe and drizzle the spicy oil over pizza or grilled vegetables.

TOTAL 1 HR 10 MIN; MAKES ½ CUP

½ cup canola oil, divided

1 Tbsp. crushed red pepper

¼ tsp. kosher salt

Heat ¼ cup oil in a small saucepan over medium until shimmering, about 3 minutes. Remove from heat, and stir in red pepper and salt. Let stand until fragrant, 1 to 2 minutes. Stir in remaining ¼ cup oil. Let cool completely, about 1 hour. —ABRA BERENS

MAKE AHEAD Store Chile Oil in an airtight container at room temperature up to 5 days.

PATTY MELTS WITH CHARRED SCALLION-CHIPOTLE MAYO

Classic versions of the patty melt often include caramelized onions, but those take time, so here cookbook author Molly Stevens leans on quick-charred scallions instead. Chipotle-spiked mayonnaise adds an extra dose of lushness and a punch of smoky heat. For the cheese, semisoft cheeses like Oaxaca or Monterey Jack add a satisfying tang, but any good melting cheese works—cheddar or Swiss are perfectly delicious stand-ins. You'll need a heavy skillet (cast-iron works great) that can hold four sandwiches; otherwise work in batches or in two skillets. Form the ground beef patties to match the size of the bread, ensuring every bite of the finished sandwich achieves a proper bread-to-cheese balance.

TOTAL 30 MIN; SERVES 4

- 1 lb. 80% lean ground beef
- 1 bunch scallions (6 to 8 scallions), root ends trimmed
- 1 tsp. olive oil
- 1 tsp. plus a pinch of kosher salt, divided
- 1 tsp. plus a pinch of black pepper, divided
- ½ cup mayonnaise, divided
- 2 tsp. minced canned chipotle chiles plus 3 tsp. adobo sauce from can
- 2 Tbsp. unsalted butter
- 1 (12-oz.) bakery white or rye sandwich bread loaf, cut into 8 (½-inch) slices
- 8 oz. Oaxaca cheese (quesillo) or Monterey Jack cheese, cut into 8 slices

1 Shape ground beef into 4 thin patties to match the size and shape of bread slices. Set aside.

2 Toss together scallions, oil, a pinch of salt, and a pinch of black pepper in a bowl. Heat a large skillet over medium-high. Add scallions; cook, turning occasionally, until charred in spots and tender, about 4 minutes. Transfer scallions to a cutting board, and coarsely chop. Stir together chopped scallions, ¼ cup mayonnaise, chipotle chiles, and adobo sauce in a small bowl; set aside. Wipe skillet clean.

3 Add butter to skillet; melt over medium-high. Add beef patties, and sprinkle evenly with ½ teaspoon salt and ½ teaspoon black pepper. Cook patties, pressing tops occasionally using a spatula to keep patties thin and flat, until bottoms are well browned, about 2 minutes. Flip patties; sprinkle evenly with remaining ½ teaspoon salt and remaining ½ teaspoon black pepper. Cook patties, pressing tops occasionally, until a crust forms on bottoms and beef is cooked to desired degree of doneness, 2 to 3 minutes for medium-rare (about 145°F). Transfer patties to a plate lined with paper towels. Wipe skillet clean.

4 Spread about 1 tablespoon scallion-chipotle mayonnaise on 4 bread slices. Top each with 1 cheese slice, 1 patty, and 1 additional cheese slice. Cover with remaining bread slices.

5 Return skillet to heat over medium. Spread 1 outer side of each sandwich with ½ tablespoon mayonnaise; place sandwiches, mayonnaise side down, in skillet. Cook sandwiches, pressing tops with a spatula, until bottoms are golden, 1 minute and 30 seconds to 3 minutes. Spread top of each sandwich with ½ tablespoon mayonnaise; flip sandwiches. Cook sandwiches, pressing tops occasionally with spatula, until bottoms of sandwiches are toasty and cheese is melted, 2 to 3 minutes. Cut sandwiches in half, and serve. —MOLLY STEVENS

WINE Juicy, smoky Washington Syrah: Dusted Valley Boomtown

THE ORIOLE "HAM SANDOVAL"

Nutty raclette cheese melted on toasted baguette gets piled high with rich country ham and silky mortadella studded with cinnamon and black pepper in this exquisite ham sandwich from 2017 F&W Best New Chef Noah Sandoval of Oriole in Chicago. Tangy walnut mustard aïoli, peppery arugula, and poppy-citrus dressing cut through the richness and add fresh flavor to every bite.

TOTAL 15 MIN; SERVES 1

- 1 (6-oz.) demi baguette
- 2 oz. thinly sliced Roelli Cheese Haus raclette cheese
- 3 Tbsp. Sur Les Quais Moutarde aux Noix (mustard with walnut)
- 1 Tbsp. Hellmann's mayonnaise
- 3 oz. Smoking Goose mortadella, thinly shaved
- 4 oz. Edwards Virginia Smokehouse country ham, thinly shaved
- 1 Tbsp. fresh lemon juice (from 1 lemon)
- 1 Tbsp. Agrumato Lemon Extra Virgin Olive Oil & Lemon
- 1 tsp. poppy seeds
- ⅛ tsp. kosher salt
- 1½ cups arugula (about ¾ oz.)

1 Preheat broiler to high with oven rack in middle position. Split baguette in half, and shingle bottom half with raclette cheese. Place baguette halves on a baking sheet, and broil until cheese is melted, 2 to 4 minutes.

2 Stir together mustard and mayonnaise; smear evenly over top half of toasted baguette. Line bottom half of baguette with shaved mortadella. Top with ham.

3 Whisk together lemon juice and oil in a medium bowl. Whisk in poppy seeds and salt. Add arugula, and toss to coat well. Top country ham with dressed arugula, and crown with top half of baguette. Slice in half diagonally, and serve immediately. —NOAH SANDOVAL

WINE Juicy, berry-rich Rhône-style blend: Bonny Doon Le Cigare Volant

NOTE Edwards country ham is available online at edwardsvaham.com. Mortadella is available online at smokinggoose.com. Walnut mustard is available from rareteacellar.com.

CHORIZO-AND-KIMCHI DOGS

At Claudette Zepeda's regional Mexican restaurant in San Diego, this dish is served as an homage to the Sonoran hot dog. Easy hacks like crumbled chorizo make this restaurant favorite easy to pull off for backyard entertaining.

TOTAL 20 MIN; SERVES 4

CILANTRO CREMA

- ½ cup Mexican crema
- ½ bunch fresh cilantro, roughly chopped
- 1 serrano chile, stemmed and roughly chopped
- 1 scallion, roughly chopped
- 2 Tbsp. fresh lime juice

KIMCHI SLAW

- 3 oz. drained kimchi (preferably Mother-in-Law's), thinly sliced
- 2 Tbsp. kimchi liquid from jar
- 3 oz. thinly sliced bok choy
- 2 scallions, thinly sliced
- 2 Tbsp. chopped fresh cilantro

HOT DOGS

- 4 oz. fresh Mexican chorizo
- 4 (3½-oz.) Wagyu beef hot dogs
- ½ cup mayonnaise
- 4 hot dog buns, split
- 1½ oz. chicharróns, crushed
- Thinly sliced scallions, for garnish

1 **Make the cilantro crema:** Process all cilantro crema ingredients in a blender until smooth. Set aside.

2 **Make the kimchi slaw:** Toss together all kimchi slaw ingredients in a large bowl until combined. Set aside.

3 **Make the hot dogs:** Cook chorizo in a skillet over medium-high, stirring to crumble, until lightly browned, 5 to 6 minutes. Remove from skillet. Add hot dogs to skillet, and cook until seared on all sides, 6 to 7 minutes. Remove from skillet.

4 Spread mayonnaise inside buns, and sear cut sides of buns in skillet over medium-high until lightly browned. Place hot dogs in buns. Add chorizo and kimchi slaw; drizzle with cilantro crema. Sprinkle with chicharróns; garnish with sliced scallions, and serve immediately. —CLAUDETTE ZEPEDA

MAKE AHEAD Cilantro crema and kimchi slaw may be made up to 2 days ahead; cover and chill until ready to serve.

BEER Crisp Mexican-style lager: 21st Amendment Brewery El Sully

HERBY CHICKEN BURGERS

Cookbook author Leah Koenig's secret for the juiciest chicken burgers is grinding chicken breasts in the food processor, which guarantees the freshest blend and the best texture for these moist, tender burgers. Cutting whole chicken breasts into chunks and pulsing them in the food processor yields the smooth consistency needed for the burgers to hold together, and stirring a bit of mayonnaise into the mixture yields burgers that are juicy, tender, and light. Flavored with scallions, parsley, basil, and lemon zest, these chicken burgers are delicious enough to stand alone, but for a fuller meal, serve them with coconut rice and a green salad, or on brioche with harissa-honey mayo.

TOTAL 35 MIN; SERVES 6

BURGERS

- 1 bunch scallions, roughly chopped
- ½ cup roughly chopped fresh flat-leaf parsley
- ¼ cup roughly chopped fresh basil
- 1 tsp. packed finely grated lemon zest
- ¼ tsp. crushed red pepper
- 1 lb. boneless, skinless chicken breasts, cut into 1-inch chunks
- 2 large eggs
- 1½ tsp. kosher salt, plus more to taste
- ¼ cup all-purpose flour (or gluten-free all-purpose flour)
- 2 Tbsp. mayonnaise
- Vegetable oil, for frying

ADDITIONAL INGREDIENTS

- ½ cup mayonnaise
- ¼ cup finely chopped fresh basil
- 2 tsp. honey
- 2 tsp. sriracha
- 6 brioche buns, toasted
- Bibb lettuce leaves, thinly sliced English cucumber, and thinly sliced red onion, for topping

1 **Make the burgers:** Combine scallions, parsley, basil, lemon zest, and red pepper in a food processor; pulse until finely chopped. Add chicken, eggs, and salt; pulse, scraping down sides of food processor as necessary, until mixture is the consistency of thick pancake batter. Transfer mixture to a medium bowl; fold in flour and mayonnaise until fully combined.

2 Line a large plate with paper towels; set aside. Pour oil to a depth of ¼ inch in a large frying pan; heat over medium. Working in batches of 3, scoop batter by generous ⅓ cupfuls, and add to pan, gently shaping into 3½-inch rounds (about ½ inch thick). Fry until golden brown on both sides and cooked through, 3 to 4 minutes per side. Transfer cooked burgers to paper towel–lined plate to briefly drain. Sprinkle with salt to taste while still hot.

3 **Assemble the burgers:** Stir together mayonnaise, basil, honey, and sriracha until fully combined. Slather bottoms and tops of buns with mayonnaise mixture. Divide burgers among buns; dress with lettuce leaves, cucumber slices, and onion slices. —LEAH KOENIG

WINE Flavorful California rosé: Rodney Strong Rosé of Pinot Noir

SUPER-CRISPY FRIED CHICKEN SANDWICHES

Seasoning boneless, skinless chicken thighs with a classic Southern fried chicken spice blend and dill pickle brine makes for the juiciest, crunchiest fried chicken sandwiches. Choose dill pickles without much sugar, which can burn during cooking.

ACTIVE 30 MIN; TOTAL 2 HR 30 MIN; MAKES 12 SANDWICHES

2 (16-oz.) jars dill pickle chips, ½ cup brine reserved and about 60 pickle chips reserved, divided

2 Tbsp. kosher salt, divided

2 tsp. paprika

1 Tbsp. plus 1 tsp. black pepper, divided

½ tsp. cayenne pepper, or more to taste

½ tsp. garlic powder

½ tsp. onion powder

12 boneless, skinless chicken thighs (about 3 lb.)

1 cup buttermilk or well-stirred plain whole-milk yogurt

1 large egg

4 cups all-purpose flour (about 17 oz.)

¼ cup cornstarch

Peanut oil, for frying

1 cup mayonnaise

12 hamburger buns

6 cups shredded iceberg lettuce

12 ripe beefsteak tomato slices (optional)

1 Stir together ½ cup pickle brine, 1 tablespoon salt, paprika, 1 teaspoon black pepper, cayenne pepper, garlic powder, and onion powder in a small bowl. Place chicken thighs in a gallon-size resealable plastic bag; pour in pickle brine mixture. Seal bag, and massage until chicken is evenly coated with brine mixture. Place in refrigerator; let marinate at least 2 hours or up to 8 hours.

2 Whisk together buttermilk, ½ cup water, and egg in a large bowl. Remove chicken from brine; discard brine. Add chicken to buttermilk mixture. Whisk together flour, cornstarch, remaining 1 tablespoon salt and 1 tablespoon black pepper in a shallow dish. Set aside.

3 Preheat oven to 200°F. Pour oil to a depth of ½ inch in a 12-inch cast-iron skillet; heat oil over medium to 350°F.

4 Working in batches, remove 3 or 4 chicken thighs from buttermilk mixture, and place in flour mixture. Cover chicken with flour mixture, pressing to adhere. Lift from flour mixture, and gently shake off excess. Carefully place chicken in hot oil, taking care not to overcrowd skillet. Cook, adjusting heat as needed to maintain oil temperature of 350°F and turning every 1 to 2 minutes using tongs, until a thermometer inserted in thickest portion of thigh registers 165°F and breading is golden brown and very crispy, 6 to 8 minutes per batch. Remove chicken from skillet, and place on a wire rack set inside a rimmed baking sheet. Place in preheated oven to keep warm while repeating frying process with remaining chicken.

5 Spread 1 heaping tablespoon mayonnaise onto cut sides of each bun. Arrange 5 or 6 pickle chips on each bun bottom; top with 1 fried chicken thigh, ½ cup shredded lettuce, and, if desired, 1 tomato slice. Drizzle with sauce, and cover with bun tops. —MARY-FRANCES HECK

EXTRA-SPICY BUFFALO Melt ½ cup unsalted butter in a small saucepan over low. Whisk in ½ teaspoon kosher salt, ½ teaspoon freshly ground black pepper, and ¼ teaspoon cayenne pepper. Whisk in ¾ cup Texas-style hot sauce (such as Texas Pete) until creamy.

BUTTERMILK-BLUE CHEESE Whisk together ½ cup buttermilk, ½ cup mayonnaise, ¼ cup sour cream, ¼ cup crumbled blue cheese, 2 tablespoons chopped fresh chives, ½ teaspoon kosher salt, and ¼ teaspoon black pepper until blended.

MAKE AHEAD Chicken can be marinated in refrigerator up to 8 hours.

WINE Chillable, light-bodied red: Willamette Valley Vineyards Whole Cluster Pinot Noir

BLACKENED FISH SANDWICHES
WITH HORSERADISH TARTAR SAUCE

Fresh fillets of haddock are coated with smoky paprika, garlic powder, oregano, and thyme before they get a quick sear to develop a delicious crust. They are then sandwiched between toasted brioche buns smeared with a strong, tangy tartar sauce laced with refreshingly piquant horseradish. If your fish fillets are thicker than ¾ inch, butterfly them by carefully cutting through the center of the fillet (parallel to the work surface), leaving ½ inch of the meat attached at the side so it can be opened like a book.

TOTAL 20 MIN; SERVES 4

TARTAR SAUCE

- ¼ cup mayonnaise
- ¼ cup sour cream
- 3 Tbsp. minced shallot (from 1 medium shallot)
- 2 Tbsp. minced fresh flat-leaf parsley
- 1½ Tbsp. drained prepared horseradish
- 1½ Tbsp. fresh lemon juice
- 1½ Tbsp. minced cornichons (about 4 small cornichons)
- 1 Tbsp. drained capers, chopped
- ¼ tsp. kosher salt
- ¼ tsp. black pepper

SANDWICHES

- 1 tsp. hot paprika
- 1 tsp. garlic powder
- 1 tsp. minced fresh oregano
- 1 tsp. minced fresh thyme
- 1 tsp. kosher salt
- ½ tsp. black pepper
- 4 (4- to 5-oz.) skinless haddock fillets (about ¾ inch thick)
- ¼ cup plus 2 tsp. unsalted butter, divided
- 4 brioche hamburger buns, split
- 1 Tbsp. canola oil
- Butter lettuce leaves, for serving

1 **Make the tartar sauce:** Whisk together mayonnaise, sour cream, shallot, parsley, horseradish, lemon juice, cornichons, capers, salt, and pepper in a small bowl. Refrigerate until ready to use.

2 **Make the sandwiches:** Stir together paprika, garlic powder, oregano, thyme, salt, and pepper in a small bowl. Sprinkle spice mixture evenly over both sides of fish fillets. Set aside.

3 Heat a large cast-iron skillet over high. Spread 1 teaspoon butter over cut side of each bun half. Place buns, buttered side down, in hot skillet; cook until well toasted and browned, about 1 minute. Transfer to a work surface. Do not wipe skillet clean.

4 Add oil and remaining 2 tablespoons butter to skillet; cook over high until butter is melted. Add fish fillets; cook until blackened on bottoms, about 3 minutes. Flip fillets; cook until blackened on other sides and just cooked through, 2 to 3 minutes. Remove from heat, and transfer fish to a plate.

5 Spread 1 tablespoon tartar sauce over toasted side of each bun half. Arrange fish and lettuce evenly on bottom bun halves. Cover with top bun halves, toasted side down. Serve alongside remaining ½ cup tartar sauce at the table.
—JUSTIN CHAPPLE

WINE Lightly spicy Rhône-style white: Tablas Creek Vineyard Côtes de Tablas Blanc

GRILLED CHEESE WITH CORN AND CALABRIAN CHILE

Nancy Silverton's L.A. restaurant Pizzeria Mozza celebrates unfussy, straightforward, focused food that uses fresh California produce. This upgraded grilled cheese by the 1990 Best New Chef alum is filled with a charred sweet corn-studded blend of nutty English cheddar, sharp caciocavallo, and just enough mayonnaise to bind it all together. Thick slices of sourdough get a beautifully buttery, golden crust in a cast-iron skillet, while Calabrian chile sneaks in with just the right amount of heat. Satisfyingly rich, sharp, and indulgent, this cheese filling is a knockout on burgers, or even as a hot dip with crackers and crudités.

ACTIVE 20 MIN; TOTAL 25 MIN; SERVES 6

1 cup fresh corn kernels

3 oz. English-style cheddar cheese (such as Keen's), shredded (about ¾ cup)

½ cup mayonnaise

1 oz. caciocavallo cheese or provolone cheese, shredded (about ¼ cup)

¼ cup finely chopped shallot

¼ cup finely chopped scallions

1 medium-size jarred Calabrian chile, stemmed and finely chopped (about 2 tsp.)

1 tsp. kosher salt

½ tsp. finely chopped garlic

6 Tbsp. unsalted butter (3 oz.), softened

12 (⅓-inch-thick) sourdough bread slices

1 Heat a large cast-iron skillet over medium-high until smoking. Add corn kernels, and cook, stirring occasionally, until tender and charred in spots, about 3 minutes. Transfer corn to a large bowl, and let cool 10 minutes. Wipe out skillet, and set aside.

2 Add cheddar, mayonnaise, caciocavallo, shallot, scallions, chile, salt, and garlic to corn; stir to combine. Spread butter on one side of each bread slice. Place 6 bread slices, buttered sides down, on a piece of parchment paper, and top evenly with cheese mixture (about ⅓ cup each); spread cheese mixture in an even layer. Top with remaining bread slices, buttered sides up.

3 Heat cast-iron skillet over medium. Working in batches, cook sandwiches until golden brown and toasted, 3 to 4 minutes per side. Serve immediately.
—NANCY SILVERTON

MAKE AHEAD Cheese filling mixture can be made up to 3 days in advance, covered, and stored in refrigerator.

WINE Ripe Southern Italian red: Tormaresca Torcicoda Primitivo

QUESADIZZAS

SPRING ONION AND SALAMI SHEET-PAN PIZZA

When making sheet-pan pizza, bring the dough to room temp before shaping. This ensures the gluten is relaxed and the dough doesn't shrink from the pan edges.

ACTIVE 20 MIN; TOTAL 45 MIN; SERVES 8

¼ cup extra virgin olive oil, plus more for drizzling

2 (1-lb.) fresh prepared multigrain or plain pizza dough balls, at room temperature

1 cup jarred pizza sauce (such as Rao's)

10 oz. preshredded mozzarella cheese (about 2½ cups)

4 oz. salami, soppressata, or spicy Italian sausage

1 small spring onion or fennel bulb, thinly sliced (about 1¾ cups)

2 oz. Parmesan or Pecorino Romano cheese, grated (about ½ cup)

½ tsp. fennel seeds, crushed

Flaky sea salt

Fresh baby greens or herb leaves (such as flat-leaf parsley or basil)

1 Preheat oven to 500°F with oven rack in lower third of oven. Grease an 18×13-inch rimmed baking sheet with ¼ cup oil; place 1 dough ball on 1 side. Using your hands, gently stretch outward until it covers half of the baking sheet. (If dough springs back, let it rest 10 minutes before stretching again.) Repeat procedure with remaining dough ball on opposite side of baking sheet. Press seam together in middle to seal, creating 1 large sheet of dough. Spoon pizza sauce over dough; sprinkle with mozzarella, and top with salami, spring onion, Parmesan, and fennel seeds.

2 Bake until crisp and brown on bottom and edges, about 25 minutes. Remove from oven, and sprinkle with salt. Top with greens; drizzle lightly with additional oil. —SARAH COPELAND

WINE Lively, dark-fruited southern Italian red: Cantele Salice Salentino Riserva

QUESADIZZAS

This mash-up of a quesadilla and pizza gets a spicy kick from jalapeño-laced pepper Jack cheese and garlicky Portuguese linguiça.

TOTAL 25 MIN; SERVES 2 TO 4

1 Tbsp. canola oil

4 flour tortillas, divided

6 Tbsp. jarred marinara sauce, divided

6 oz. pepper Jack cheese, shredded (about 1½ cups), divided

½ cup thinly sliced linguiça or Spanish chorizo (about 2 oz.)

Grated Parmesan cheese, dried oregano, and crushed red pepper, for serving

1 Preheat broiler with oven rack 8 inches from heat. Heat a cast-iron griddle over two burners on stovetop over medium; brush with oil. Place 2 tortillas in a single layer on hot griddle. Spread 2 tablespoons marinara sauce on each tortilla. Scatter ½ cup pepper Jack cheese over marinara on each; top with remaining 2 tortillas. Cook until crisp and lightly browned on bottoms, about 3 minutes. Flip quesadizzas. Spread remaining 2 tablespoons marinara sauce evenly over quesadizzas, and sprinkle evenly with remaining ½ cup pepper Jack cheese. Arrange linguiça slices evenly over quesadizzas.

2 Transfer quesadizzas to a rimmed baking sheet. Broil until cheese is melted and linguiça is slightly curled, 1 to 2 minutes.

3 Slice quesadizzas into wedges. Serve with Parmesan, oregano, and crushed red pepper. —JUSTIN CHAPPLE

BEER Mexican-style craft lager: Oskar Blues Brewery Beerito

ZUCCHINI, CORN, AND SHRIMP FLATBREAD

Store-bought naan flatbreads get toasty on the grill, layered with mascarpone cheese, sweet shrimp, juicy corn, and tender ribbons of fresh zucchini.

ACTIVE 30 MIN; TOTAL 40 MIN; SERVES 4

1 (8-oz.) container mascarpone cheese

1 garlic clove, grated with a Microplane grater (¼ tsp.)

2 tsp. kosher salt, divided

3 medium (8-oz.) zucchini, sliced lengthwise into ⅛-inch-thick planks

2 (8-oz.) ears fresh yellow corn, husks removed

¼ cup extra virgin olive oil, divided

½ tsp. black pepper, divided, plus more for serving

1 lb. unpeeled raw medium shrimp (thawed if frozen)

4 (3-oz.) naan flatbreads (such as Stonefire)

½ tsp. smoked paprika

Torn fresh basil, for garnish

1 Stir together mascarpone, garlic, and ½ teaspoon salt in a medium bowl; set aside. Toss together zucchini, corn, 1 tablespoon oil, ¼ teaspoon pepper, and 1 teaspoon salt in a large bowl.

2 Peel shrimp, and devein. Using a paring knife, gently cut along back of shrimp, cutting three-fourths of the way through, until you reach the tail. Toss together butterflied shrimp, 1 tablespoon oil, remaining ½ teaspoon salt and ¼ teaspoon pepper in a medium bowl. Brush both sides of flatbreads evenly with remaining 2 tablespoons oil.

3 Preheat grill to high (450°F to 500°F). Place corn on oiled grates; grill, uncovered, until corn is bright yellow and evenly charred, about 10 minutes, turning occasionally. Add zucchini, shrimp, and flatbreads during final 5 minutes of corn grilling time; grill, uncovered, until shrimp are just pink on each side, about 1 minute and 30 seconds per side; zucchini is charred and just tender, 1 to 2 minutes per side; and flatbreads are lightly toasted on bottoms, 1 to 2 minutes. Transfer corn to a cutting board, and transfer zucchini, shrimp, and flatbreads to a baking sheet. Cut corn kernels from cobs; discard cobs.

4 Reduce grill temperature to medium (350°F to 400°F). Stir corn kernels into mascarpone mixture in medium bowl until combined. Spread about ¼ cup corn-mascarpone mixture over grilled side of each flatbread. Top evenly with zucchini and shrimp. Sprinkle evenly with smoked paprika. Grill flatbreads, covered, until bottoms are lightly toasted, 2 to 3 minutes. Garnish with basil and additional pepper. Cut into planks, and serve. —ANNA THEOKTISTO

MAKE AHEAD Prepared shrimp and vegetables may be grilled up to 1 day ahead and kept covered and chilled before assembling and grilling flatbreads.

WINE Keplinger Eldorado Sierra Foothills White Rhône Blend

SIDES

Sometimes the epitome of a fuss-free meal is a piece of meat, poultry, or fish, simply seasoned and grilled, roasted, or cooked in a skillet on the stovetop, paired with a side that's more interesting than spring mix tossed with bottled dressing or some steamed vegetables. These recipes are for those times.

ROASTED BROCCOLI
WITH PICKLED PEPPER
VINAIGRETTE (P. 223)

GARLIC-AND-HERB MASHED POTATOES

These mashed potatoes are a speedy, nearly effortless dish thanks to a flavor-packed special ingredient: a garlic-and-herb-flecked spreadable cheese (such as Boursin). For a colorful twist, use purple Peruvian potatoes instead of Yukon Golds to make purple mashed potatoes.

ACTIVE 20 MIN; TOTAL 40 MIN; SERVES 8 TO 10

4 lb. Yukon Gold potatoes or purple potatoes, peeled and cut into 2-inch chunks

12 cups water

1 Tbsp. kosher salt, plus more to taste

2 cups garlic-and-herb spreadable cheese (from 3 [5.2-oz.] pkg.), at room temperature

1½ cups whole milk, warmed

Cracked black pepper and unsalted butter, for garnish

1 Place potatoes in a large pot. Add 12 cups water; bring to a boil over high. Add salt, and reduce heat to medium; simmer until tender, 20 to 25 minutes. Drain, shaking off any excess water.

2 Pass potatoes through a ricer back into pot. Add spreadable cheese and milk; fold until smooth. Season to taste with salt. Garnish with black pepper and butter. —JUSTIN CHAPPLE

MINI KABOB POTATOES

A crispy exterior with a soft, fluffy center makes these quick-cooking fried potatoes a fun addition to a kabob feast. At Mini Kabob in Los Angeles, these popular potatoes are served alongside skewers such as beef shish kabob, a delectable eggplant dip, toum, and parsley and onion salad.

TOTAL 30 MIN; SERVES 4 TO 6

Neutral cooking oil, for frying

2 lb. medium-size russet potatoes (about 4 medium potatoes), peeled

1½ tsp. kosher salt, divided, plus more to taste

¾ tsp. black pepper, divided, plus more to taste

¾ tsp. Aleppo pepper, divided, plus more to taste

Ketchup or hummus, for dipping

1 Pour oil to a depth of 1½ inches into a large Dutch oven; heat over medium-high to 375°F.

2 Using a mandoline with crinkle-cut blade, cut potatoes crosswise into ¼-inch-thick slices. Working in 3 batches, add potato slices to hot oil; fry, stirring occasionally, until golden brown and lightly crisped, 4 to 6 minutes. Using a spider strainer, transfer fried potatoes to a large heatproof bowl lined with a paper towel. Gently toss once in bowl. Remove and discard paper towel. Sprinkle potatoes with ½ teaspoon salt, ¼ teaspoon black pepper, and ¼ teaspoon Aleppo pepper; toss to evenly coat.

3 Repeat frying process with remaining potatoes, salt, black pepper, and Aleppo pepper. Oil temperature will drop to about 350°F while frying potatoes; let oil reheat to 375°F between batches. Season with additional salt, black pepper, and Aleppo pepper to taste. Serve immediately. —OVAKIM AND ALVARD MARTIROSYAN

MINI KABOB POTATOES

BRUSSELS SPROUTS WITH SHRIMP SAUCE

Born in a food stall in 2005, Xi'an Famous Foods is now a small empire in New York, with 13 locations serving Western Chinese dishes to legions of hungry fans. Jason Wang, who runs the business with his father, David Shi, shared this family recipe for Brussels sprouts with shrimp sauce, in which salty, briny, umami-rich dried shrimp rehydrate in hot chicken broth before cooking down into a savory glaze, yielding a quick, deeply savory side dish. Toasting the garlic and sautéing the Brussels sprouts before simmering them in the glaze adds flavor and color while cooking the sprouts to a nutty, tender texture without getting soggy.

ACTIVE 20 MIN; TOTAL 55 MIN; SERVES 2 TO 4

20 **dried large shrimp (about ¼ oz.)**

½ **cup hot chicken broth or hot water**

¼ **cup vegetable oil**

6 **medium garlic cloves, chopped**

1 **lb. Brussels sprouts, trimmed and halved, larger ones cut into quarters**

½ **chicken bouillon cube**

Kosher salt, to taste

1 Place shrimp in a small bowl, and add broth. Let stand until shrimp are slightly softened and rehydrated, about 40 minutes.

2 Heat vegetable oil in a large nonstick skillet over medium-low. Add garlic, and cook, stirring often, until fragrant and softened, about 3 minutes.

3 Increase heat to medium-high, and add Brussels sprouts, cut sides down, in an even layer. Cook, undisturbed, until charred and golden brown on cut sides, 4 to 5 minutes. Stir and flip sprouts, and cook, stirring occasionally, until outer leaves are softened and turn bright green and garlic is toasted, 2 to 3 minutes. Add soaked shrimp mixture and chicken bouillon cube, breaking up bouillon with a spoon or spatula. Simmer, stirring often, until sprouts are crisp-tender and shrimp sauce loosely glazes them, 3 to 4 minutes. Remove from heat, and season with salt to taste. —JASON WANG

WINE Minerally, almost salty white: Tenuta di Fessina Erse Etna Bianco

NOTE Dried shrimp are available at Asian markets or online. Choose shrimp with a pinkish hue for the freshest taste.

STIR-FRIED GARLICKY SNOW PEA SHOOTS

This recipe from cookbook author Grace Young is a delicious example of a "clear" stir-fry that uses very few ingredients, focusing on a pure translation of simple flavors. Sweet, tender snow pea shoots shine through mellow garlic, while white pepper perfumes the dish with its mild heat and fragrant floral notes. If using a skillet, cook the pea shoots in two batches to avoid crowding the pan.

TOTAL 10 MIN; SERVES 6 TO 8

- 1 lb. fresh snow pea shoots (about 14 packed cups) or spinach
- ½ tsp. kosher salt
- ¼ tsp. granulated sugar
- ⅛ tsp. ground white pepper
- 2 Tbsp. peanut oil or vegetable oil
- 4 medium garlic cloves, smashed
- 1 tsp. thinly sliced unseeded red jalapeño

1 Wash pea shoots in several changes of cold water; dry greens thoroughly by hand or in a salad spinner. Stir together salt, sugar, and white pepper in a small bowl; set aside.

2 Heat a 14-inch flat-bottomed wok or 12-inch skillet over high until a drop of water evaporates within 1 to 2 seconds of contact. Swirl in oil. Add garlic and jalapeño; cook, making quick scooping motions with a metal spatula, constantly tossing and tumbling (stir-frying) mixture until it is fragrant, about 10 seconds. Add pea shoots; cook, stir-frying constantly, until pea shoots just begin to wilt, about 30 seconds. Sprinkle with salt mixture; cook, stir-frying constantly, until pea shoots are just wilted but still bright green and stems are crisp-tender, 2 to 3 minutes. —GRACE YOUNG

NOTE Find snow pea shoots at Chinese grocery stores and farmers markets.

BRAISED GREENS WITH CRISPY GARLIC AND MISO BUTTER

Hearty autumn greens take on new life when braised in a miso butter–laced broth. These richly flavored greens make a versatile side dish for everything from turkey and fish to sweet potatoes and squash.

ACTIVE 25 MIN; TOTAL 45 MIN; SERVES 8 TO 10

- ½ cup unsalted butter (4 oz.)
- 2 Tbsp. extra virgin olive oil
- ¼ cup white miso
- 6 medium garlic cloves, thinly sliced
- 1 (3-inch) piece fresh ginger, peeled, cut into ⅛-inch-thick slices, and gently smashed
- 3 cups lower-sodium vegetable broth
- 2 lb. curly kale (about 4 bunches), stemmed and torn (about 32 loosely packed cups)
- 2 lb. collard greens, stemmed and torn (about 32 loosely packed cups)
- 1 Tbsp. rice wine vinegar
- 1 tsp. kosher salt

1 Heat butter and oil in a large pot over medium until butter is melted. Add miso; cook, stirring often, until miso begins to bubble, about 2 minutes. Add garlic and ginger; cook, stirring occasionally, until garlic and miso are lightly browned and ginger softens, 4 to 5 minutes. Remove garlic from pot; set aside.

2 Add broth to pot; bring to a boil over high. Stir in kale and collards in large handfuls, letting each handful wilt slightly before adding more. Cover and reduce heat to low; simmer until greens are tender but not mushy, 18 to 24 minutes. Stir in vinegar and salt. Using tongs, transfer greens to a shallow serving dish; discard ginger. Ladle broth over greens. Sprinkle with crispy garlic, and serve. —JUSTIN CHAPPLE

MAKE AHEAD Greens can be cooked up to 3 days ahead and stored in an airtight container in refrigerator.

STIR-FRIED GARLICKY SNOW PEA SHOOTS

DRY-FRIED SICHUAN-STYLE GREEN BEANS WITH SHRIMP

Instead of leaning on a sauce, "dry" stir-fries like this recipe use a small amount of liquid (in this case, fish sauce), relying on heat and movement in the wok to intensify each ingredient's flavors. To ensure that the beans blister, dry them thoroughly with a kitchen towel before cooking. Pickled sushi ginger adds mild, well-balanced sweetness and a hint of spice.

TOTAL 20 MIN; SERVES 4

- 4 oz. peeled and deveined raw large shrimp (about 6 shrimp)
- 2 Tbsp. peanut oil or vegetable oil, divided
- 12 oz. green beans, trimmed and cut into 2-inch pieces (about 3 cups)
- ¼ tsp. kosher salt
- 1 Tbsp. minced garlic
- ¼ cup thinly sliced scallions
- 1 Tbsp. fish sauce
- 1 Tbsp. yellow pickled ginger, minced
- ¼ tsp. granulated sugar

1 Pat shrimp dry using paper towels. Chop shrimp into ½-inch pieces; set aside.

2 Heat a 14-inch flat-bottomed wok or 12-inch skillet over high until a drop of water evaporates within 1 to 2 seconds of contact. Swirl in 1 tablespoon oil. Add beans, and sprinkle with salt; reduce heat to medium-low so that beans are barely sizzling. Cook, making quick scooping motions with a metal spatula, constantly tossing and tumbling (stir-frying) the beans until they just begin to blister and brown in spots and are almost tender, 3 to 6 minutes. Transfer beans to a plate.

3 Increase heat under wok to high, and swirl in remaining 1 tablespoon oil. Add garlic; cook, stir-frying constantly, until fragrant, about 10 seconds. Add chopped shrimp, and break up any clumps using a metal spatula; cook, stir-frying constantly, until shrimp just take on an orange-pink hue, about 1 minute. Return beans to wok, and add scallions, fish sauce, pickled ginger, and sugar; cook, stir-frying constantly, until shrimp are just cooked through and beans are tender, 30 seconds to 1 minute. —GRACE YOUNG

WINE Fresh, light-bodied white: Domaine de l'Ecu Muscadet Classic

NOTE Find yellow (undyed) pickled sushi ginger in the international foods aisle at supermarkets or at Chinese or Japanese grocery stores, or order organic pickled sushi ginger from gingerpeople.com.

ROASTED BROCCOLI
WITH PICKLED PEPPER VINAIGRETTE

PHOTO P. 215

Tossing broccoli pieces with oil, salt, and pimentón (Spanish paprika), then roasting them on a preheated baking sheet in a super-hot oven coaxes out the vegetable's sweet side as the florets crisp and the stems turn meaty and tender. A punchy pickled pepper vinaigrette and shavings of Parmesan cheese transform the roasted broccoli into a satisfying and substantial side dish, delicious spooned over steamed whole grains, or served alongside a juicy steak.

ACTIVE 15 MIN; TOTAL 35 MIN; SERVES 4

1½ lb. fresh broccoli, trimmed and cut into long florets (about 8 cups)

¼ cup olive oil, divided

1½ tsp. kosher salt, divided

¾ tsp. sweet pimentón or paprika

3 Tbsp. chopped pickled peppers (from ⅓ cup sliced Refrigerator Pickled Peppers [recipe follows])

2 Tbsp. pickled pepper brine (from Refrigerator Pickled Peppers [recipe follows])

1 Tbsp. finely chopped shallot

1 tsp. Dijon mustard

1 large garlic clove, grated on a Microplane grater (about ½ tsp.)

Shaved Parmesan cheese, for garnish

1 Place a rimmed baking sheet on middle oven rack. Preheat oven to 450°F. (Do not remove baking sheet while oven heats.)

2 Toss together broccoli, 2 tablespoons oil, 1 teaspoon salt, and pimentón in a large bowl until combined. Carefully remove hot baking sheet from preheated oven; spread broccoli in an even layer on baking sheet. Roast in preheated oven until broccoli is crisp-tender and browned on edges, 15 to 18 minutes, stirring once halfway through cook time. Remove from oven; return broccoli to large bowl.

3 While broccoli roasts, whisk together pickled peppers, pickled pepper brine, shallot, mustard, garlic, and remaining ½ teaspoon salt in a small bowl until combined. Gradually add remaining 2 tablespoons oil to mixture, whisking constantly until combined. Set aside at room temperature until ready to use.

4 Add vinaigrette to broccoli in bowl; toss to combine. Arrange on a serving platter, and garnish with cheese. —MOLLY STEVENS

WINE Herbal Austrian white: Domäne Wachau Grüner Veltliner Federspiel Terrassen

NOTE Sweet pimentón is available at specialty spice shops or online at burlapandbarrel.com.

REFRIGERATOR PICKLED PEPPERS

ACTIVE 15 MIN; TOTAL 1 HR 15 MIN, PLUS 2 DAYS CHILLING; MAKES 1 PINT

2 cups stemmed, seeded, and thinly sliced (into rounds) fresh hot and/or sweet peppers

⅔ cup white wine vinegar or apple cider vinegar

⅔ cup water

¼ cup granulated sugar

1 Tbsp. kosher salt

Pack peppers into a sterilized pint jar (see Note). Bring vinegar, ⅔ cup water, sugar, and salt to a boil in a small pot over high; boil, stirring constantly, until sugar and salt dissolve, about 3 minutes. Pour hot brine over peppers in jar, filling jar to top. Let cool to room temperature, about 1 hour. Seal jar, and refrigerate 2 days before using. —MOLLY STEVENS

MAKE AHEAD Pickled peppers can be refrigerated in jars up to 3 months.

NOTE Submerge heatproof jar in boiling water for 10 minutes or run through the dishwasher on the hottest setting to sterilize.

GRILLED CORN WITH COTIJA AND QUICOS

Hot off the grill, charred sweet corn gets slathered in tangy lime mayonnaise and topped with extra-large crunchy quicos, or corn nuts, in San Francisco–based chef Traci Des Jardins' version of elote. For a plated version, cut the kernels from the cobs and toss with lime mayo and quicos, then scoop and serve.

ACTIVE 20 MIN; TOTAL 30 MIN; SERVES 8

- 1 large pasteurized egg yolk
- 1 tsp. fresh lime juice, plus lime wedges, for serving
- ½ tsp. kosher salt, plus more to taste
- ½ cup grapeseed oil, plus more for grill grates
- 2 tsp. water, if needed

  Black pepper, to taste

  Piment d'Espelette, cayenne pepper, or paprika, to taste
- 8 medium ears fresh corn, husks pulled back, silk removed
- 1 oz. Cotija cheese, grated on a Microplane (about ½ cup)
- ½ cup crushed quicos or corn nuts (about 1 oz.)

1 Preheat grill to high (450°F to 500°F). Whisk together egg yolk, lime juice, and salt in a medium bowl. Whisking constantly, gradually drizzle in oil until mixture is smooth and thick. Whisk in up to 2 teaspoons water, ½ teaspoon at a time, to loosen mixture, if needed. Season to taste with salt, black pepper, and piment d'Espelette. Set aside.

2 Place corn on oiled grill grates, positioning husks over edge of grill to prevent burning. Grill, uncovered, turning occasionally, until corn is tender and slightly charred, 6 to 8 minutes.

3 Brush hot corn with lime mayonnaise (about 1 tablespoon per ear). Sprinkle with cheese, quicos, and piment d'Espelette, to taste. Serve with lime wedges.

—TRACI DES JARDINS

MAKE AHEAD Mayonnaise can be stored in an airtight container in refrigerator up to 3 days.

NOTE Quicos (giant corn nuts) may be purchased on amazon.com.

ROASTED SQUASH WEDGES
WITH COLLARD-PEANUT PESTO

Blanching and shocking the collards preserves their vibrant color in the pesto and removes the greens' slight bitter edge in this dish from James Beard Award–winning vegan chef Bryant Terry. Use best-quality peanuts; their toasty, nutty flavor is the foundation of the creamy pesto.

ACTIVE 25 MIN; TOTAL 30 MIN; SERVES 6

2 medium acorn squash, stemmed, halved lengthwise, seeded, and sliced crosswise into 1-inch-thick half-moons (see Note)

½ cup plus 2 Tbsp. olive oil, divided

4 tsp. kosher salt, divided

½ tsp. black pepper, divided

2 cups loosely packed, chopped and stemmed collard greens

⅓ cup unsalted roasted peanuts

3 Tbsp. white miso (such as Miso Master Organic Mellow White)

¼ tsp. lemon zest plus 3½ tsp. fresh lemon juice, divided

1 tsp. minced garlic

Flaky sea salt, to taste

1 Preheat oven to 450°F with oven rack in lowest position. Toss together squash, 2 tablespoons oil, ½ teaspoon kosher salt, and ¼ teaspoon pepper on a rimmed baking sheet. Spread in a single layer. Roast in preheated oven on lowest rack until squash is tender and browned, 26 to 30 minutes, flipping squash after 18 minutes.

2 Meanwhile, bring 8 cups water to a boil in a medium saucepan over high, and fill a bowl with ice water. Stir 1 tablespoon kosher salt into the boiling water. Add collard greens; cook until tender and bright green, about 2 minutes. Transfer collard greens to ice water; let cool 2 minutes. Drain and pat greens completely dry; set aside.

3 Cook peanuts in a small skillet over medium, stirring often, until fragrant, 4 to 5 minutes. Set aside; let cool 5 minutes.

4 Place greens, peanuts, miso, lemon juice, and garlic in a food processor; pulse until a chunky paste forms, about 10 times. With food processor running, gradually stream in remaining ½ cup oil until well combined, about 20 seconds. Add remaining ½ teaspoon kosher salt and remaining ¼ teaspoon pepper; pulse to incorporate, about 3 times. Spoon into a small serving bowl.

5 Arrange roasted squash on a serving platter; sprinkle with lemon zest, and garnish with flaky sea salt. Serve with pesto. —BRYANT TERRY

MAKE AHEAD Pour a thin layer of olive oil over the pesto, cover, and refrigerate up to 1 week.

WINE Earthy, nutty aged white: Lopez de Heredia Viña Gravonia Crianza Blanco

NOTE Substitute any winter squash, such as butternut or delicata.

BRAISED RED CABBAGE WITH APPLES AND BACON

F&W editor Melanie Hansche really disliked sauerkraut growing up, but sweeter, milder rotkohl she could get on board with. This sweet-and-sour, traditional Bavarian braised red cabbage is always served with goose, duck, or pork. To make it, the cabbage is gently braised with tart apple, smoky bacon, orange zest, and spices. Remove any thick, white ribs when shredding the cabbage so the dish cooks evenly.

TOTAL 45 MIN; SERVES 4 TO 6

2 Tbsp. olive oil

1 medium-size red onion, finely chopped (about 1 cup)

4 oz. speck or bacon, finely chopped

2 garlic cloves, finely chopped

1 small head red cabbage (about 2 lb.), quartered, cored, thick white ribs removed, and finely shredded (about 6 cups)

2 Tbsp. light brown sugar

2 small Granny Smith apples, peeled, cored, and grated on large holes of a box grater (about 1½ cups)

¼ cup (2 oz.) dry red wine or water

¼ cup red wine vinegar

2 tsp. finely grated orange zest

½ tsp. caraway seeds

1 (about 3-inch) cinnamon stick

5 juniper berries

Fine sea salt, to taste

Black pepper, to taste

1 Heat oil in a large, heavy-bottomed saucepan over medium-high. Add onion and speck, and cook, stirring occasionally, until onion is softened and speck is rendered and starting to become crisp, 6 to 8 minutes. Add garlic, and cook, stirring constantly, until fragrant, about 1 minute.

2 Add cabbage to onion mixture, and cook, stirring occasionally, until cabbage is slightly softened and wilted, about 3 minutes. Add brown sugar, and cook, stirring often, until mixture starts to caramelize, about 2 minutes. Add apples, wine, vinegar, orange zest, caraway seeds, cinnamon stick, and juniper berries; stir to combine. Reduce heat to low; cover and simmer, stirring occasionally, until cabbage is softened, 20 to 25 minutes. Season with salt and pepper to taste. Serve warm. —MELANIE HANSCHE

MAKE AHEAD Cabbage can be made up to 1 day ahead and stored in an airtight container in refrigerator. Reheat in a saucepan over low just before serving.

BUTTERY SAUTÉED MUSHROOMS WITH FRESH HERBS

Covering the mushrooms for the first few minutes of cooking helps them release their liquid and brown more quickly. Once uncovered, the liquid evaporates, and the mushrooms begin to brown. The result (which is extra umami-rich thanks to the addition of coconut aminos) is a succulent, versatile batch of mushrooms that can be served as a side dish; they could also be spooned over steak, or stirred into hot pasta for an easy dinner.

TOTAL 25 MIN; SERVES 4

3 Tbsp. unsalted butter, divided

2 Tbsp. extra virgin olive oil

1¼ lb. mixed fresh mushrooms (such as oyster, hen-of-the-woods, beech, cremini, and shiitake), cut or torn into bite-size pieces (about 5½ cups)

½ tsp. kosher salt, plus more to taste

3 garlic cloves, gently smashed

2 fresh thyme sprigs

1 fresh rosemary sprig

3 Tbsp. (1½ oz.) dry white wine

1 Tbsp. coconut aminos or soy sauce

1 Tbsp. fresh lemon juice

Black pepper, to taste

Heat 2 tablespoons butter and oil in a large skillet over medium until butter melts. Stir in mushrooms and salt; cover and cook, undisturbed, until mushrooms release their liquid, about 4 minutes. Uncover and add garlic, thyme, and rosemary. Cook, stirring occasionally, until liquid is evaporated and mushrooms are browned and tender, about 6 minutes. Stir in wine; cook, stirring occasionally, until evaporated, about 1 minute. Stir in coconut aminos and lemon juice; cook, stirring occasionally, until almost evaporated, about 1 minute. Stir in remaining 1 tablespoon butter; cook until butter is melted and mushrooms are glossy, about 1 minute. Remove from heat. Season with salt and pepper to taste.
—JUSTIN CHAPPLE

WINE Earthy, focused Rhône white: Lionel Faury Saint Joseph Blanc

CLASSIC SLAW

Your barbecue needs this cool and creamy classic coleslaw from pitmaster and F&W Best New Chef 2021 Matt Horn.

TOTAL 20 MIN; SERVES 12

1½ cups mayonnaise

⅓ cup apple cider vinegar

3 Tbsp. honey

2 Tbsp. yellow mustard

2 tsp. kosher salt, plus more to taste

1 tsp. dried dill

½ tsp. black pepper, plus more to taste

8 cups finely shredded green cabbage (from 1 small [3-lb.] head cabbage)

4 cups finely shredded red cabbage (from 1 small [3-lb.] head cabbage)

5 medium scallions, thinly sliced (about 1 cup)

Whisk together mayonnaise, vinegar, honey, mustard, salt, dill, and pepper in a large bowl until well combined. Add green cabbage, red cabbage, and scallions; toss to coat. Add additional salt and pepper to taste. Serve immediately.
—MATT HORN

MAKE AHEAD Slaw can be stored in an airtight container in refrigerator up to 4 days.

BEET-CARROT SLAW WITH GARLICKY LABNEH

This sweet, tart, and creamy jewel-tone slaw is filled with freshly shredded beets and carrots and tangy labneh. Make fast work of shredding carrots and beets using a food processor fitted with a grating attachment. Separating the grated vegetables helps keep their rich colors from mixing and muddling. Use rainbow carrots for more color, or swap out the red beets for Chioggia and their pink-and-white swirls.

ACTIVE 15 MIN; TOTAL 20 MIN; SERVES 6

1 cup labneh or plain full-fat Greek yogurt

1 small garlic clove, grated

4 medium carrots

1 large red beet, peeled and quartered

¼ cup extra virgin olive oil

1 Tbsp. lemon zest plus 3 Tbsp. fresh lemon juice (from 2 lemons), divided

1 Tbsp. Champagne vinegar

2 tsp. honey

1 tsp. kosher salt

¼ tsp. black pepper

¼ cup salted roasted pistachios, chopped

¼ cup fresh mint leaves

1 tsp. toasted coriander seeds, crushed

1 Stir together labneh and garlic in a small bowl until combined. Cover and refrigerate until ready to serve.

2 Grate carrots in a food processor fitted with the grating attachment; transfer to a bowl. Grate beet, and transfer to a separate bowl.

3 Whisk together oil, lemon juice, vinegar, honey, salt, and pepper in a small bowl until combined. Drizzle half of the vinaigrette (about ¼ cup) over grated carrots; stir to combine. Let stand 5 minutes.

4 Spread labneh mixture on a serving platter. Top with carrot mixture and grated beets; drizzle with remaining vinaigrette. Sprinkle with pistachios, mint, coriander seeds, and lemon zest. —ANNA THEOKTISTO

MAKE AHEAD Garlicky labneh can be made up to 3 days in advance.

SUMMER SQUASH WITH POBLANO, QUESO FRESCO, AND EPAZOTE

Epazote is a leafy herb with a pungent, bright flavor, with notes of citrus, mint, and oregano. It lends a savory depth to the summer squash, and pairs particularly well with dairy. Leaving the queso fresco in larger chunks allows it to soften slightly, but not completely melt into the dish.

ACTIVE 20 MIN; TOTAL 35 MIN; SERVES 6 TO 8

2 medium-size fresh poblano chiles

5 Tbsp. extra virgin olive oil, divided

1 small red onion, cut into 1-inch wedges and separated into petals

2 medium garlic cloves, thinly sliced

1 (2½-oz.) bunch fresh epazote, leaves separated from stems and stems tied together

1¼ lb. summer squash, cut into 1½-inch pieces (about 5 cups)

1½ tsp. kosher salt, plus more to taste

6 squash blossoms, stems and stamen removed and discarded, blossoms torn into large pieces

5 oz. queso fresco, broken into large pieces (about 1 cup)

1 Tbsp. red wine vinegar

1 Preheat broiler with oven rack in middle of oven. Place poblanos on a baking sheet, and broil, turning occasionally, until blackened all over, 10 to 15 minutes. Transfer poblanos to a medium bowl, and cover tightly with plastic wrap. Let steam 15 minutes. Peel and discard skin from poblanos. Remove and discard stems and seeds. Cut poblanos into 2×½-inch strips, and set aside.

2 Heat 3 tablespoons oil in a large skillet over medium-low. Add onion, garlic, and tied epazote stems; cook, stirring often, until onion is just starting to soften, about 4 minutes. Remove and discard epazote stems. Add squash and salt; increase heat to medium. Cover and cook, stirring occasionally, until squash is just tender, 8 to 10 minutes.

3 Stir in poblano strips, squash blossom pieces, and ¼ cup loosely packed epazote leaves. (Reserve remaining epazote leaves for another use.) Sprinkle with queso fresco. Cover and cook over medium until cheese is just beginning to soften, about 1 minute.

4 Transfer mixture to a serving platter. Drizzle with red wine vinegar and remaining 2 tablespoons oil. Season with salt to taste. Serve immediately. —TRACI DES JARDINS

WINE Herbal, tart New Zealand Sauvignon Blanc: Dog Point Vineyard

NOTE Epazote can be purchased from Latin markets.

PEANUT AND WATERMELON CHAAT

Every chaat has a little bit of sweetness, a little bit of tartness, a little heat, and a little crunch. That's what makes them so fun to eat. This chaat combines the fleeting succulent sweetness of watermelon with the hearty crunch and saltiness of peanuts. "It's a very Southern combination that I thought should work," says chef Vishwesh Bhatt. "And it did." Eating watermelon with a sprinkle of salt and a dash of hot sauce is popular in chef Bhatt's hometown of Oxford, Mississippi. This sweet-savory chaat recipe marries that inspiration with a sprinkle of chaat masala, a tangy spice blend often used as a seasoning for fruit in India.

TOTAL 10 MIN; SERVES 2 TO 4

- 2 tsp. canola oil
- 1 cup lightly salted roasted peanuts
- 1 (4-inch) curry sprig
- 2 tsp. chaat masala, divided
- 1 cup chopped seedless watermelon (about 5½ oz.)
- ½ cup thinly sliced cucumber (from 1 small cucumber)
- ¼ cup finely chopped red onion (from 1 small onion)
- ¼ cup thinly sliced radishes (from 3 medium radishes)
- 1 medium-size serrano chile, seeded and finely chopped (about 1½ Tbsp.)
- ½ tsp. kosher salt
- ½ tsp. cayenne pepper
- 2 Tbsp. fresh lime juice (from 1 medium lime)
- 2 Tbsp. chopped fresh mint
- 2 Tbsp. chopped fresh basil
- 2 Tbsp. chopped fresh cilantro
- 2 Tbsp. cane syrup or sorghum

1 Heat oil in a large skillet over medium-high until shimmering. Add peanuts, curry sprig, and 1 teaspoon chaat masala. Cook, tossing constantly, until well coated and fragrant, about 30 seconds. Set aside to let cool until ready to use.

2 Combine watermelon, cucumber, onion, radishes, serrano, salt, and cayenne in a large bowl, and toss well. Add peanut mixture, lime juice, mint, basil, cilantro, cane syrup, and remaining 1 teaspoon chaat masala. Remove and discard curry sprig. Toss gently and serve. —VISHWESH BHATT

NOTE Chaat masala is available online at spicewallabrand.com.

GRILLED OKRA, CORN, AND TOMATO SALAD

This next-level summer salad turns heads with its punchy dressing spiked with charred jalapeño and herbs and a palate-perking topping of crunchy toasted coriander and cumin seeds.

ACTIVE 35 MIN; TOTAL 40 MIN; SERVES 6

DRESSING

- 2 jalapeños
- ½ cup chopped fresh cilantro
- 7 Tbsp. fresh lime juice (from about 5 limes)
- ⅓ cup peanut oil
- ¼ cup fresh basil leaves
- 1 tsp. granulated sugar
- 1¼ tsp. kosher salt, or to taste

SALAD

- 1 lb. small okra, halved lengthwise
- 3 Tbsp. canola oil
- ½ tsp. kosher salt, plus more to taste
- ⅛ tsp. black pepper, plus more to taste
- 3 ears sweet yellow corn, shucked
- 1 lb. mixed heirloom cherry and grape tomatoes, halved
- ½ (15-oz.) English cucumber, thinly sliced
- 1 small (8-oz.) sweet onion, thinly sliced from root to tip
- 2 tsp. coriander seeds, toasted and crushed
- 2 tsp. cumin seeds, toasted and crushed
- Chopped fresh cilantro
- Toasted sesame seeds (optional)

1 **Make the dressing:** Preheat grill to high (450°F to 500°F). Grill jalapeños on oiled grates, uncovered, turning often, until skins are charred, about 8 minutes. Place chiles in a small resealable plastic bag and seal, or place in a small bowl and cover with plastic wrap. Let stand until cool enough to handle. Peel and discard blistered skins; remove stems and seeds. Process jalapeños, cilantro, lime juice, peanut oil, basil, and sugar in a blender until smooth, about 45 seconds. Season with salt. Set aside.

2 **Make the salad:** Toss together okra, canola oil, salt, and pepper in a medium bowl. Grill okra on oiled grates over high, uncovered, turning once or twice, until okra is slightly blistered and just softened, about 5 minutes. Place okra in a large bowl, and set aside.

3 Grill corn on oiled grates over high, uncovered, turning often, until evenly charred, about 15 minutes. Let cool 10 minutes; cut kernels off cobs, and add to okra in bowl; stir in tomatoes, cucumber, onion, coriander seeds, and cumin seeds.

4 Garnish salad with additional cilantro and sesame seeds, if using. Serve with dressing on the side. —VISHWESH BHAAT

TOMATO AND PLUM SALAD WITH CHRYSANTHEMUM GREENS AND MADRAS CURRY VINAIGRETTE

Chef Melissa Perello's summery tomato salad features chrysanthemum greens. They can be found at Asian markets, but you can also substitute adult arugula. The beautiful yellow-tinted vinaigrette relies on fresh ginger, honey, and curry powder for a balanced but bright flavor.

ACTIVE 15 MIN; TOTAL 30 MIN; SERVES 6

VINAIGRETTE

- ½ cup apple cider vinegar
- 1 small shallot (about ½ oz.), thinly sliced
- 1 Tbsp. fresh lemon juice (from 1 lemon)
- 1 Tbsp. finely chopped peeled fresh ginger
- 2¾ tsp. madras curry powder
- 2¼ tsp. honey
- 1 cup extra virgin olive oil
- 1¼ tsp. kosher salt

SALAD

- 1 lb. assorted heirloom tomatoes, cut into wedges (about 3 cups)
- 1 lb. ripe plums and/or pluots, cut into wedges
- 1 tsp. kosher salt
- ¼ tsp. black pepper
- 1 Tbsp. extra virgin olive oil
- 2 cups packed chrysanthemum greens (also called cresta di gallo or shungiku) (about 2 oz.) or wild arugula
- 1 cup labneh or plain whole-milk Greek yogurt
- ¼ tsp. Aleppo pepper or marash chile flakes
- Pinch of flaky sea salt

1 **Make the vinaigrette:** Combine vinegar, shallot, lemon juice, ginger, curry powder, and honey in a blender. Let stand 15 minutes for curry powder to bloom. Process on high speed until smooth, about 1 minute. With blender running on low speed, slowly drizzle in olive oil until emulsified. Season with salt, and set aside.

2 **Make the salad:** Place tomatoes and plums in a large bowl. Season with kosher salt and black pepper; drizzle with olive oil. Set aside. Toss greens with 2 tablespoons vinaigrette in a medium bowl.

3 To serve, spread labneh on a platter; arrange tomatoes, plums, and greens on labneh. Drizzle with desired amount of remaining vinaigrette, and sprinkle with Aleppo pepper and flaky sea salt. —MELISSA PERELLO

MAKE AHEAD Vinaigrette can be made up to 1 week ahead. Store in an airtight container in refrigerator until ready to use.

TORN ESCAROLE SALAD
WITH WARM BACON VINAIGRETTE

Lightly spicy croutons tossed in chile-sesame oil before toasting, smoky bacon, and crumbled blue cheese add rich, savory dimension to this quick, dinnerworthy salad. A dollop of apple butter adds a natural sweetness to the dressing, but honey can be used in its place.

TOTAL 30 MIN; SERVES 6 TO 8

- **6 cups torn crusty Italian bread**
- **⅓ cup hot chile-sesame oil (such as S&B La-Yu Chili Oil) or olive oil**
- **¾ tsp. kosher salt, divided**
- **4 thick-cut applewood-smoked bacon slices, cut into ½-inch pieces**
- **¼ cup finely chopped shallot**
- **3 Tbsp. olive oil**
- **2 Tbsp. apple butter or 2 tsp. honey**
- **1½ Tbsp. red wine vinegar**
- **1½ tsp. Dijon mustard**
- **6 cups torn escarole**
- **2 small Honeycrisp apples, cut into matchsticks**
- **4 oz. mild blue cheese (such as Gorgonzola dolce), crumbled (about 1 cup)**

1 Preheat oven to 400°F. Toss together bread, chile-sesame oil, and ½ teaspoon salt on a rimmed baking sheet; spread in an even layer. Bake, stirring occasionally, until golden brown and crisp, about 20 minutes.

2 Meanwhile, cook bacon in a large skillet over medium, stirring occasionally, until crisp, 10 to 12 minutes. Transfer bacon to a plate lined with paper towels, reserving 3 tablespoons drippings in skillet. Add shallot to skillet; cook over low, scraping any browned bits from bottom of skillet, until shallot is softened, about 2 minutes. Remove from heat; whisk in olive oil, apple butter, vinegar, Dijon, and remaining ¼ teaspoon salt.

3 Toss together escarole, apples, cheese, and bacon in a large bowl. Add shallot dressing; toss to coat. Transfer to a large platter; sprinkle with croutons.

—LIZ MERVOSH

MAKE AHEAD Croutons can be made a day ahead and stored in an airtight container at room temperature.

BAJA-STYLE
CAESAR SALAD

BAJA-STYLE CAESAR SALAD

Both egg yolks and Dijon mustard help this creamy dressing emulsify easily so it coats each leaf of crunchy romaine. Cotija añejo is an aged cheese with a pecorino-like texture that grates into fluffy crumbles.

TOTAL 15 MIN; SERVES 4

3 medium garlic cloves, finely chopped

4 oil-packed anchovy fillets (such as Ortiz), finely chopped

1 large pasteurized egg yolk

1 Tbsp. Dijon mustard

1 tsp. black pepper

½ tsp. kosher salt

2 Tbsp. fresh lime juice

1 Tbsp. Worcestershire sauce

¾ cup grapeseed oil

1 oz. high-quality aged Cotija cheese, finely grated (about ⅔ cup), divided

4 medium romaine lettuce hearts, halved lengthwise

1 oz. fried pork rinds, coarsely broken (about 2 cups)

1 Whisk together garlic, anchovies, egg yolk, Dijon, pepper, and salt in a medium bowl. Whisk in lime juice and Worcestershire. Whisking constantly, gradually stream in oil until all oil is incorporated and dressing is thick and creamy. Whisk in 2 tablespoons grated Cotija.

2 Divide lettuce heart halves evenly among 4 plates, and top each with ¼ cup dressing, ½ cup fried pork rinds, and 2 tablespoons grated Cotija.
—CLAUDETTE ZEPEDA

MAKE AHEAD Dressing can be made up to 3 days ahead and stored in refrigerator. If needed, thin with a few teaspoons of water before serving.

WINE Natural California white blend: Donkey & Goat Eliza

HAZELNUT, FENNEL, AND GREEN APPLE SALAD

Tucked in among the tender lettuce leaves, sweet-tart apple, fragrant fennel, and toasty hazelnuts add a refreshing crunch to this fall salad.

ACTIVE 20 MIN; TOTAL 40 MIN; SERVES 8

½ cup hazelnuts

3 Tbsp. Champagne vinegar

1 tsp. Dijon mustard

1 tsp. honey

¾ tsp. kosher salt

¼ tsp. black pepper

6 Tbsp. roasted hazelnut oil

1 medium Granny Smith apple (about 8 oz.)

1 large fennel bulb with stalks (about 13 oz.)

1 head Boston lettuce (5 to 6 oz.), separated into leaves

2 oz. Parmigiano-Reggiano cheese, grated (about 1 cup)

1 Preheat oven to 300°F. Line a baking sheet with parchment paper. Spread hazelnuts in an even layer on prepared baking sheet. Bake in preheated oven until very fragrant, about 25 minutes, stirring once after 15 minutes. Let nuts cool slightly, about 5 minutes. Place on a kitchen towel, and rub off skins. Coarsely chop nuts; set aside.

2 Whisk together vinegar, mustard, honey, salt, and pepper in a medium bowl. Gradually whisk in oil in a slow, steady stream until emulsified.

3 Core apple, and cut into quarters. Shave apple quarters into ⅛-inch-thick slices using a mandoline; place in a large bowl. Trim fennel stalks from bulb; coarsely chop fronds to equal 2 tablespoons; discard stalks. Cut bulb into quarters; remove and discard core. Shave bulb into ⅛-inch-thick slices using a mandoline. Add shaved fennel bulb and chopped fronds to apple in bowl.

4 Drizzle fennel mixture with 6 tablespoons dressing; toss to coat. Arrange lettuce on a platter. Top with fennel mixture, cheese, nuts, and remaining dressing.
—ANN TAYLOR PITTMAN

SUMMER TOMATO SALAD WITH JICAMA AND AVOCADO

San Francisco–based chef Traci Des Jardins' take on a classic, produce-forward summer salad features juicy tomatoes, crunchy cucumbers, and lightly sweet slices of jicama. The simple lime dressing gets a hit of fresh, herbal brightness from plenty of cilantro leaves.

TOTAL 15 MIN; SERVES 6 TO 8

- 1 lb. heirloom tomatoes, cut into bite-size pieces (about 3 cups)
- 1½ cups sliced English cucumbers
- ½ cup thinly sliced red onion, rinsed under cold water
- ½ cup matchstick-cut jicama
- ⅓ cup thinly sliced radishes
- 1 medium avocado, cut crosswise into ⅓-inch-thick slices
- ¼ cup extra virgin olive oil
- 3 Tbsp. fresh lime juice
- 1½ tsp. kosher salt
- ¼ cup loosely packed fresh cilantro leaves
- Flaky sea salt, for finishing

Arrange tomatoes, cucumbers, red onion, jicama, radishes, and avocado on a serving platter. Whisk together olive oil, lime juice, and kosher salt; drizzle dressing over vegetables. Sprinkle with cilantro leaves, and season to taste with flaky sea salt. —TRACI DES JARDINS

NOTE Shop for jicama roots that are dry and firm to the touch.

HEIRLOOM TOMATO SALAD
WITH PICKLED RAMP VINAIGRETTE

PHOTO P. 30

This simple salad from chef Suzanne Tracht of L.A.'s JAR is all about perfect, in-season produce like oniony ramps and juicy heirloom tomatoes. It sits well and makes a great potluck or barbecue side salad.

TOTAL 15 MIN; SERVES 6

- ¼ cup extra virgin olive oil
- 2 Tbsp. rice vinegar
- 2 Tbsp. pickled ramp brine plus 1 cup chopped pickled ramps (such as Blackberry Farm), divided
- 2½ tsp. kosher salt, divided
- ½ tsp. black pepper, divided
- 3 lb. heirloom tomatoes, sliced
- 15 cherry tomatoes (about ½ lb.), halved
- 2 medium sweet Maui onions (about 1 lb.), cut into ½-inch rings
- ½ cup fresh leafy herbs (such as basil, tarragon, parsley, and chervil)

1 Whisk together olive oil, rice vinegar, pickled ramp brine, 1½ teaspoons salt, and ¼ teaspoon pepper in a small bowl. Set aside.

2 Layer heirloom tomatoes, cherry tomatoes, onion slices, and herb leaves on a serving platter. Sprinkle with remaining 1 teaspoon salt and remaining ¼ teaspoon pepper.

3 Scatter chopped pickled ramps over salad, and drizzle with pickled ramp vinaigrette. —SUZANNE TRACHT

NOTE Order pickled ramps from blackberryfarmshop.com, or substitute pickled onions.

DESSERTS

Keeping things simple—whether for a weeknight meal or a weekend dinner party—doesn't preclude dessert. These pies, cakes, crisps, crumbles, fruit desserts, and frozen delights are a fuss-free way to cap off any meal, anytime.

SALTED CARAMEL S'MORES (P. 254)

BOURBON-PECAN-APPLE PIE
WITH CINNAMON WHIPPED CREAM

Chef and cookbook author Alexander Smalls spikes his sticky-sweet pecan pie with just enough bourbon to add a kick of flavor that accents the sweet chunks of apple. Fuji apples are perfect for this pie; they bake up soft but retain their texture. Braeburn and Honeycrisp also work well.

ACTIVE 15 MIN; TOTAL 1 HR 25 MIN, PLUS 3 HR COOLING; SERVES 6 TO 8

- 1 (9-inch) refrigerated pie dough
- 4 large eggs
- 1 cup light corn syrup
- ¾ cup granulated sugar
- ¼ cup unsalted butter, melted
- 2 Tbsp. (1 oz.) bourbon
- 1 tsp. vanilla extract
- ½ tsp. grated lemon zest
- ¼ tsp. plus a pinch of ground cinnamon, divided, plus more for garnish
- ⅛ tsp. ground nutmeg
- 1½ cups pecan halves
- 1 cup chopped (about ½-inch pieces) peeled Fuji apple
- 1 cup heavy cream

1 Preheat oven to 350°F. Fit piecrust in a 9-inch pie plate; crimp edges as desired. Refrigerate 15 minutes.

2 Whisk together eggs, corn syrup, sugar, butter, bourbon, vanilla, lemon zest, ¼ teaspoon cinnamon, and nutmeg in a large bowl until well combined. Stir in pecans and apple. Pour into chilled piecrust.

3 Bake in preheated oven until filling is mostly set but jiggles slightly, 55 minutes to 1 hour. Transfer pie to a wire rack; let cool completely, about 3 hours.

4 Beat heavy cream and remaining pinch of cinnamon with an electric mixer fitted with the whisk attachment on medium-high speed until soft peaks form, about 1 minute. Slice pie; dollop slices with whipped cream, and garnish with additional cinnamon. —ALEXANDER SMALLS

STRAWBERRY-RHUBARB CORNMEAL SKILLET CAKE

Juicy strawberries and tart rhubarb stud the golden brown top of this simple skillet cake. The mix of all-purpose flour and fine cornmeal gives this dessert a pound-cake-like density, while goat cheese and buttermilk keep the crumb nicely tender and moist. A dollop of rosemary-infused whipped cream ties the sweet and savory flavors together.

ACTIVE 25 MIN; TOTAL 1 HR 35 MIN, PLUS 2 HR REFRIGERATION; SERVES 8

ROSEMARY WHIPPED CREAM

- 1 cup heavy cream
- 1 tsp. vanilla bean paste
- 3 (5-inch) fresh rosemary sprigs
- 1 Tbsp. powdered sugar

STRAWBERRY-RHUBARB CAKE

- 1 cup all-purpose flour, sifted (about 4¼ oz.)
- ½ cup fine yellow cornmeal (about 2⅞ oz.)
- ½ tsp. kosher salt
- ¾ cup plus 1 Tbsp. unsalted butter, at room temperature, divided (6½ oz.)
- 1½ cups granulated sugar
- 3 large eggs, at room temperature
- 1½ oz. goat cheese, at room temperature (about 3 Tbsp.)
- ⅓ cup buttermilk, at room temperature
- 2 tsp. vanilla bean paste
- 1 cup halved fresh strawberries
- ¾ cup diagonally sliced fresh rhubarb (½-inch pieces) (from about 3 oz. rhubarb stalks)
- 2 Tbsp. turbinado sugar

1 **Make the rosemary whipped cream:** Combine heavy cream and vanilla bean paste in a small bowl. Rub rosemary sprigs between hands to release their oils, and add to bowl; stir mixture until combined. Cover with plastic wrap; refrigerate at least 2 hours or up to 4 hours. Pour mixture through a fine wire-mesh strainer into a large bowl; discard solids. Beat cream mixture with an electric mixer on medium-high speed until soft peaks form, about 2 minutes. Sprinkle with powdered sugar; beat on medium-high speed until stiff peaks form, about 45 seconds. Cover rosemary whipped cream with plastic wrap; refrigerate until ready to use, up to 12 hours.

2 **Make the strawberry-rhubarb cake:** Place a 10-inch cast-iron skillet in oven, and preheat oven to 350°F. Let skillet preheat about 10 minutes.

3 Meanwhile, whisk together flour, cornmeal, and salt in a small bowl until combined; set aside. Place ¾ cup butter in bowl of a stand mixer fitted with the whisk attachment; beat on high speed, stopping occasionally to scrape down sides of bowl, until pale and fluffy, about 2 minutes. Gradually add granulated sugar, beating on high speed and stopping occasionally to scrape down sides of bowl, until mixture is light and fluffy, about 4 minutes. Add eggs, 1 at a time, beating well after each addition. With mixer running on low speed, crumble in goat cheese; beat until just combined, about 30 seconds. Gradually add flour mixture, beating until just combined, about 1 minute. Add buttermilk and vanilla bean paste, beating until just combined, about 1 minute.

4 Carefully remove hot skillet from oven, and add remaining 1 tablespoon butter. Swirl skillet until butter is melted. Carefully pour in cake batter; smooth top if needed. Arrange strawberries and rhubarb in an even layer on batter; sprinkle with turbinado sugar.

5 Bake in preheated oven until a wooden pick inserted into center of cake comes out clean, 55 minutes to 1 hour. Let cool slightly on a wire rack, about 15 minutes. Serve cake warm with a dollop of rosemary whipped cream. —JOCELYN DELK ADAMS

MAKE AHEAD Rosemary whipped cream can be made up to 12 hours in advance and refrigerated in an airtight container.

SUMMER FRUIT COBBLER
WITH VANILLA-MASCARPONE BISCUITS

Let the farmers market be your guide when it comes to this cobbler—any mixture of fresh summer stone fruits and berries can be cooked down to make the perfectly sweet-tart, jammy filling. Aim for 2½ pounds (about 10 cups) of fruit total, using any combination of the following: blackberries, blueberries, or raspberries; Bing or Rainier cherries (stem and pit them first); stone fruit (pitted and sliced into ¾-inch wedges; you can leave the skin on plums and apricots but should peel peaches and nectarines). Tender vanilla-mascarpone biscuits have a shortcake-like texture and a delightfully crunchy top from the turbinado sugar. They're also highly customizable: You can swap the mascarpone in the biscuit topping for crème fraîche or sour cream if that's what you have, and trade the semolina for fine cornmeal for a more crumbly texture.

ACTIVE 25 MIN; TOTAL 1 HR 55 MIN; SERVES 6 TO 8

2½ lb. prepared fresh or thawed frozen fruit (about 10 cups)

1¾ cups granulated sugar, divided

1⅓ cups all-purpose flour, divided (about 5¾ oz.)

3 Tbsp. aged sherry vinegar or white balsamic vinegar

2 tsp. grated lemon zest plus 1 Tbsp. fresh lemon juice

1½ tsp. kosher salt, divided

1 (8-oz.) container mascarpone cheese, crème fraîche, or sour cream

¼ cup unsalted butter, melted and cooled

6 Tbsp. heavy cream, divided

1 Tbsp. vanilla bean paste or 1 vanilla bean, seeds scraped

½ cup fine semolina flour or fine cornmeal (about 2¾ oz.)

2½ tsp. baking powder

2 Tbsp. turbinado sugar

Vanilla ice cream, for serving

1 Preheat oven to 375°F. Toss together fruit, 1½ cups granulated sugar, ⅓ cup all-purpose flour, vinegar, lemon zest and juice, and ¾ teaspoon salt in a large bowl. Transfer fruit mixture to a 3-quart baking dish (such as a 13×9-inch dish), and spread in an even layer. Set aside.

2 Whisk together mascarpone, butter, ¼ cup cream, and vanilla bean paste in a medium bowl until mostly smooth; set aside. Whisk together semolina flour, baking powder, remaining 1 cup all-purpose flour, remaining ¼ cup granulated sugar, and remaining ¾ teaspoon salt in a large bowl. Add mascarpone mixture to flour mixture; stir with a fork until a shaggy dough forms.

3 Using a 2¼-inch scoop, divide dough into 9 mounds (about ¼ cup each), and arrange on top of fruit filling. Brush dough mounds with remaining 2 tablespoons cream; sprinkle with turbinado sugar.

4 Bake in preheated oven until biscuits are golden brown and cobbler is bubbly and thickened in center, 1 hour to 1 hour and 10 minutes. Let cool on a wire rack 30 minutes. Serve warm with vanilla ice cream. —PAIGE GRANDJEAN

RED, HOT, AND COOL STRAWBERRIES

The chile-induced heat in this dish doesn't kick in until the last moment, creating a gentle afterburn that is cooled by sweet strawberries and a smooth bed of tangy cream. Look for chiles de árbol at your local Latin grocer.

ACTIVE 25 MIN; TOTAL 50 MIN; SERVES 4

1 chile de árbol or similar chile, stemmed and seeded

7 oz. strawberries, hulled and chopped into ½-inch pieces

¼ cup superfine sugar

1 Tbsp. fresh lemon juice

⅔ cup plain whole-milk Greek yogurt

⅔ cup cream cheese, softened

Fresh mint leaves, for garnish

1 Heat a small skillet over high; add chile, and cook, tossing occasionally, until toasted and a nutty aroma is released, 3 to 5 minutes. Remove from skillet, and crush in a mortar and pestle.

2 Stir together crushed chile, strawberries, sugar, and lemon juice in a heavy-bottomed saucepan. Bring to a boil over high, and cook, stirring occasionally, until thickened and syrupy, about 15 minutes. (Strawberries should mostly keep their shape; if they start collapsing, remove from heat sooner.) Remove from heat, and let strawberry mixture cool completely, about 25 minutes.

3 While strawberry mixture cools, whisk together yogurt and cream cheese in a medium bowl until smooth. Cover and chill until ready to serve.

4 Divide yogurt mixture among 4 bowls, and top evenly with strawberry mixture. Garnish with mint leaves, and serve. —CAROLINE EDEN

WINE-POACHED STRAWBERRIES AND APRICOTS

Semi-dry Riesling, which is refreshing and not too sweet, is the secret to this impressive, balanced dessert. Dried apricots lend a gentle bitterness while the strawberries add sweetness and impart the rosiest color. Does unsweetened whipped cream make you nervous? Trust us—the boozy berries provide all the sweetness this dessert needs.

ACTIVE 10 MIN; TOTAL 45 MIN; SERVES 8

1 (750-ml) bottle semi-dry Riesling

⅓ cup granulated sugar, or more to taste

1 fresh tarragon sprig

½ cup dried apricots (preferably California) (about 4 oz.)

1 lb. fresh strawberries, hulled (halved lengthwise if large)

Unsweetened whipped cream, for serving

Fresh tarragon leaves, for garnish

1 Fill a large bowl with ice and water; place a large heatproof bowl on top. Stir together wine, sugar, and tarragon sprig in a large saucepan; bring to a boil over medium. Add apricots, and cook 2 minutes. Add strawberries; reduce heat to medium-low, and cook until fruit just softens, about 3 minutes. Transfer fruit mixture to bowl set over ice-water bath, and let stand until cool, about 45 minutes.

2 Serve fruit and wine mixture in glasses topped with unsweetened whipped cream and garnished with tarragon leaves. —JUSTIN CHAPPLE

SALTED CARAMEL S'MORES

PHOTO P. 245

Homemade graham crackers add a deeper, almost caramel-like flavor to these next-level s'mores from Walla Walla, Washington–based chef, adventurer, and whitewater rafting guide Andrae Bopp. Filled with the classic combo of marshmallow and chocolate squares, they get a drizzle of salted caramel for a rich and gooey bite. Bopp opts for drama and uses his kitchen torch to char the marshmallows; your oven's broiler or a campfire will work just as well.

ACTIVE 20 MIN; TOTAL 55 MIN; SERVES 12

- 1 cup unsalted butter, softened (8 oz.)
- ½ cup packed light brown sugar
- 2 Tbsp. unsulphured molasses
- 2 Tbsp. honey
- 1¾ cups whole wheat pastry flour (about 7⅞ oz.)
- ¾ cup all-purpose flour (about 3¼ oz.), plus more for work surface
- 2 tsp. ground cinnamon
- 1 tsp. kosher salt
- 12 (½-oz.) semisweet chocolate squares
- 12 marshmallows
- 1 cup salted caramel sauce

1 Preheat oven to 325°F with oven racks in upper third and lower third of oven. Combine butter, brown sugar, molasses, and honey in a stand mixer fitted with the paddle attachment; beat on medium-high speed until fluffy, 3 to 4 minutes. Add whole wheat pastry flour, all-purpose flour, cinnamon, and salt; beat on low speed until just combined, about 1 minute, stopping to scrape down sides of bowl as needed.

2 Roll dough out on a floured work surface to about ¼-inch thickness. Prick all over using a fork. Cut into 24 (2½-inch) squares, rerolling scraps as needed. Carefully arrange dough squares on 2 baking sheets lined with parchment paper.

3 Bake in preheated oven until cracker edges turn brown, 15 to 20 minutes, rotating baking sheets between top and bottom racks halfway through bake time. Let cool completely on baking sheets, about 20 minutes.

4 Preheat oven to broil with oven rack 6 inches from heat source. Place 12 graham crackers on a large baking sheet; top each cracker with 1 chocolate square and 1 marshmallow. Broil in preheated oven until marshmallows are browned, 1 to 2 minutes. (Alternatively, toast marshmallows over a campfire or with a kitchen torch until browned.) Drizzle evenly with caramel sauce, and top with remaining 12 graham crackers. —ANDRAE BOPP

MAKE AHEAD Graham crackers can be made up to 2 days ahead and stored in an airtight container at room temperature.

OLIVE OIL ICE CREAM

One of Portland, Oregon–based ice cream shop Salt & Straw's classic flavors, this Olive Oil Ice Cream is a perfect beginner batch to whip up. The combination of olive oil and whole milk in this ice cream results in a perfectly creamy and silky texture, no eggs or tempering required. You can even play with different nut oils (like hazelnut or walnut) in place of olive oil—just avoid those that are solid at room temperature, like coconut oil. Use the best oil you can as it will intensely flavor the ice cream, even with only ¼ cup per batch.

ACTIVE 20 MIN; TOTAL 12 HR 55 MIN; SERVES 8

½ cup granulated sugar

2 Tbsp. nonfat powdered milk

¼ tsp. xanthan gum

1⅓ cups whole milk

2 Tbsp. light corn syrup

1⅓ cups heavy cream

¼ cup grassy extra virgin olive oil (such as Red Ridge Farm Durant Arbequina), plus more for garnish

½ tsp. kosher salt

Flaky sea salt (such as Maldon)

1 Stir together sugar, powdered milk, and xanthan gum in a small bowl. Whisk together milk and corn syrup in a medium saucepan. Add sugar mixture, and whisk until smooth. Heat mixture over medium, whisking often, until sugar has fully dissolved, 3 to 4 minutes. (Do not simmer.) Remove from heat, and whisk in cream. Cover and chill at least 6 hours. For even better texture and flavor, chill mixture up to 24 hours. Base can be stored in an airtight container in freezer up to 3 months; thaw completely before using.

2 Whisk together chilled base, olive oil, and kosher salt until well combined. (There will still be little droplets of oil on the surface.) Pour mixture into freezer bowl of a 1½-quart electric ice cream maker, and proceed according to manufacturer's directions until ice cream has the texture of soft-serve, about 35 minutes. (Instructions and times may vary.)

3 Quickly transfer ice cream to a freezer-safe container; press parchment paper directly onto surface. Cover container, and freeze until firm, at least 6 hours. Ice cream can be stored in freezer up to 3 months. To serve, garnish with additional olive oil and flaky sea salt. —FOOD & WINE

MAKE AHEAD Ice cream can be stored in freezer up to 3 months.

NOTE Xanthan gum can be found by the specialty flours or near the baking powder in grocery stores.

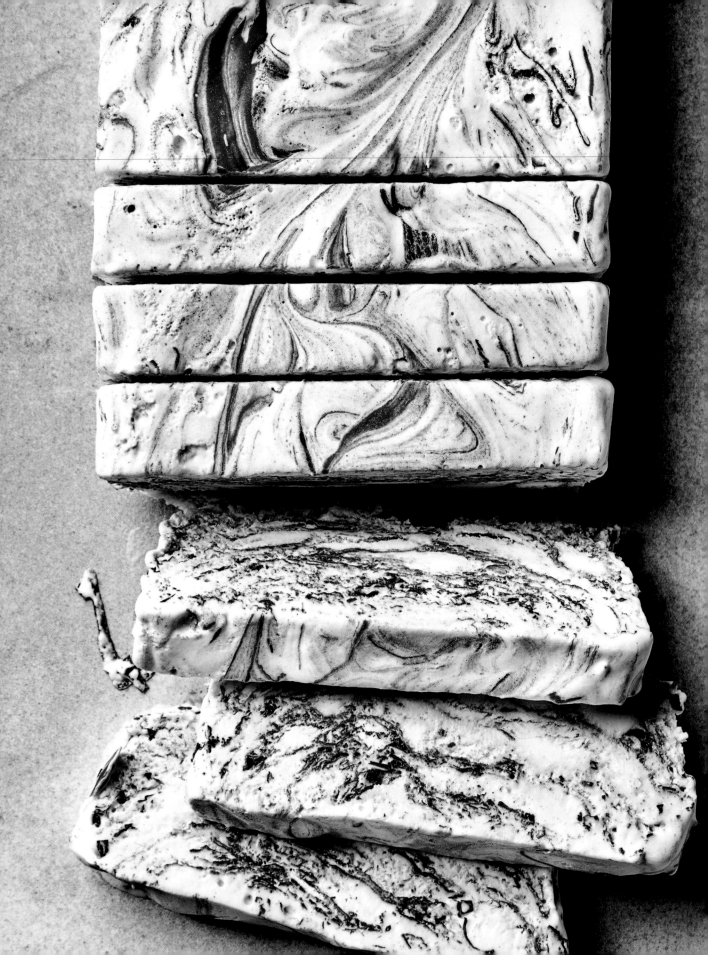

MINT STRACCIATELLA SEMIFREDDO

Fistfuls of fresh mint are steeped in the custard base of this semifreddo; a slow simmer releases the herb's oils into the base without leeching any color. The key to extracting the most mint flavor is to bruise the mint beforehand; chopping herbs ruptures only the plant cells that the knife touches. Instead, bruise herbs with a rolling pin or a wooden spoon to rupture more of the cell walls and free the flavorful oils. To make the dreamy swirls in this dessert, gently fold the chocolate into the custard-cream mixture, stirring just once or twice. (The mixture will continue to combine when it's poured into the pan before freezing.)

ACTIVE 30 MIN; TOTAL 8 HR 30 MIN; SERVES 8

- 1 cup heavy cream
- 1 (4-oz.) semisweet chocolate baking bar, chopped
- 2 tsp. coconut oil
- 4 large eggs
- 1 cup granulated sugar
- 2 bunches fresh mint (1 oz. total), bruised
- 1 tsp. vanilla extract
- ¼ tsp. fine sea salt

1 Line a 9×5-inch loaf pan with plastic wrap, leaving a 4-inch overhang on all sides. Beat heavy cream with an electric mixer fitted with a whisk attachment on medium-high speed until medium peaks form, about 1 minute and 30 seconds. Cover and chill until ready to use.

2 Bring 1 inch of water to a simmer in a medium pot over medium. Place chocolate and coconut oil in a medium heatproof bowl; place bowl over simmering water. Cook, stirring often, until mixture is melted and combined, about 4 minutes. Remove bowl, and cool chocolate mixture 15 minutes.

3 Meanwhile, whisk together eggs, sugar, mint, vanilla, and salt in another medium heatproof bowl; place bowl over simmering water. Cook, whisking constantly, until mixture reaches 165°F, about 18 minutes. Pour mixture through a fine wire-mesh strainer into bowl of a stand mixer fitted with a whisk attachment, pressing on solids to extract all liquid; discard solids. Beat on high speed until thick, fluffy, and room temperature, 6 to 8 minutes.

4 Fold half of whipped cream into egg mixture. Fold in remaining whipped cream until just incorporated. Drizzle chocolate mixture over top, and gently fold into egg mixture, 2 to 3 times, to create a swirl. Pour mixture into prepared pan, and fold overhanging plastic wrap over top. Freeze at least 8 hours or up to 2 days. To serve, invert onto a plate, remove plastic wrap, and cut into slices.

—PAIGE GRANDJEAN AND LIZ MERVOSH

CHOCOLATE-RASPBERRY ICEBOX CAKE

This Chocolate-Raspberry Icebox Cake is the answer to summer days when you want to serve a beautiful cake but it's too hot to turn on the oven. It's creamy, it's dreamy, and it's so simple to make. Crushed cookies, fresh raspberries, and layers of tart raspberry sorbet and vanilla ice cream transform into a gorgeous marbled layer cake in about 15 minutes—no frosting required. The raspberries sink into the milky, sweet layers of ice cream, adding a tart flavor and pops of color to the cake, and crunchy chocolate cookie crumble layers are the perfect sweet and salty counterpoint, adding satisfying texture and a hint of bittersweet flavor. Finally, after a deep chill in the freezer, the cake is topped with whipped cream and more raspberries. The finished cake slices beautifully, revealing deep pink, creamy white, and rich dark-chocolate cookie swirls. Bonus: The recipe doubles easily, if you're making cake for a crowd—or if you just want more for yourself. Leave your ice cream at room temperature for about 10 minutes to soften before using.

TOTAL 15 MIN, PLUS 4 HR FREEZING; SERVES 8

Cooking spray

2 pt. vanilla ice cream, softened

1 pt. raspberry sorbet, softened

9 oz. chocolate wafer cookies, crushed (about 2½ cups)

2 cups fresh raspberries (about 9 oz.), plus more for garnish

1 cup heavy cream

3 Tbsp. powdered sugar

1 Lightly coat a 9×5-inch loaf pan with cooking spray. Line with parchment paper, making sure all sides are fully covered and leaving a 2-inch overhang on all sides.

2 Fold softened ice cream and sorbet together in a large bowl until sorbet is just streaked through ice cream but not quite swirled, 2 to 3 folds.

3 Sprinkle ½ cup crushed cookies into bottom of prepared loaf pan. Spread 1½ cups ice cream mixture over crushed cookies. Scatter ½ cup fresh raspberries over top, gently pressing into ice cream mixture. Repeat layers 3 times, ending with remaining ½ cup crushed cookies.

4 Wrap loaf pan tightly with plastic wrap, and freeze until cake is firm, at least 4 hours or up to 24 hours.

5 Remove ice cream cake from freezer; unwrap and let stand at room temperature 5 minutes. Meanwhile, whisk together cream and powdered sugar in a medium bowl until stiff peaks form, about 2 minutes.

6 Lift ice cream cake out of loaf pan using parchment paper overhang as handles, and invert onto a large plate or platter. Dollop whipped cream over top of cake. Garnish with additional fresh raspberries. Slice and serve. —ANNA THEOKTISTO

MAKE AHEAD Cake can be frozen up to 3 weeks. Top with whipped cream just before serving.

NOTE This recipe easily doubles to serve 16. Make the cake in a 9-inch square pan, and double the ingredients.

RECIPE INDEX

Page numbers in **bold** indicate photographs.

**PORK LOIN WITH TONNATO SAUCE
AND SUMMER SALAD (P. 54)**

CROSTINI WITH GRILLED SWEET
ONIONS AND BLUE CHEESE (P. 15)

PHOTO CREDITS

ANTONIS ACHILLEOS 29, 213

CEDRIC ANGELES 119, 147, 232

JOHNNY AUTRY 245

CAITLIN BENSEL 27, 105, 239

JENNIFER CAUSEY 21, 22, 89, 190

TARA DONNE 209

GREG DUPREE Cover, 33, 36, 39, 48, 56, 59, 60, 64, 67, 72, 75, 79, 90, 125, 131, 161, 169, 173, 176, 180, 187, 193, 205, 210, 215, 218, 240, 256, 263

JOHN KERNICK 86, 183

EVA KOLENKO 202

HEAMI LEE 126

DAVID MALOSH 101, 108, 111, 197

KELLY MARSHALL 246

AUBRIE PICK 224, 243, 266

VICTOR PROTASIO 1, 7, 11, 12, 17, 30, 40, 44, 47, 55, 68, 71, 76, 80, 85, 93, 94, 97, 102, 115, 116, 120, 123, 132, 135, 136, 139, 151, 152, 155, 157, 158, 162, 165, 166, 179, 185, 194, 198, 201, 206, 221, 229, 235, 236, 249, 250, 259

OLA O. SMIT 253

JULIA STOTZ 217

CHRISTOPHER TESTANI 51, 144

JUSTIN WALKER 63

ERIC WOLFINGER 5, 43

MEASUREMENT GUIDE

BASIC MEASUREMENTS

GALLON	QUART	PINT	CUP	OUNCE	TBSP	TSP	DROPS
1 gal	4 qt	8 pt	16 c	128 fl oz			
½ gal	2 qt	4 pt	8 c	64 fl oz			
¼ gal	1 qt	2 pt	4 c	32 fl oz			
	½ qt	1 pt	2 c	16 fl oz			
	¼ qt	½ pt	1 c	8 fl oz	16 Tbsp		
			⅞ c	7 fl oz	14 Tbsp		
			¾ c	6 fl oz	12 Tbsp		
			⅔ c	5⅓ fl oz	10⅔ Tbsp		
			⅝ c	5 fl oz	10 Tbsp		
			½ c	4 fl oz	8 Tbsp		
			⅜ c	3 fl oz	6 Tbsp		
			⅓ c	2⅔ fl oz	5⅓ Tbsp	16 tsp	
			¼ c	2 fl oz	4 Tbsp	12 tsp	
			⅛ c	1 fl oz	2 Tbsp	6 tsp	
				½ fl oz	1 Tbsp	3 tsp	
					½ Tbsp	1½ tsp	
						1 tsp	60 drops
						½ tsp	30 drops

US TO METRIC CONVERSIONS

The conversions shown here are approximations. For more precise conversions, use the formulas to the right.

VOLUME			WEIGHT			TEMPERATURE			CONVERSION FORMULAS
1 tsp	=	5 mL	1 oz	=	28 g	475°F	=	246°C	tsp × 4.929 = mL
1 Tbsp	=	15 mL	¼ lb (4 oz)	=	113 g	450°F	=	232°C	Tbsp × 14.787 = mL
1 fl oz	=	30 mL	½ lb (8 oz)	=	227 g	425°F	=	218°C	fl oz × 29.574 = mL
¼ c	=	59 mL	¾ lb (12 oz)	=	340 g	400°F	=	204°C	c × 236.588 = mL
½ c	=	118 mL	1 lb (16 oz)	=	½ kg	375°F	=	191°C	pt × 0.473 = L
¾ c	=	177 mL				350°F	=	177°C	qt × 0.946 = L
1 c	=	237 mL	**LENGTH**			325°F	=	163°C	oz × 28.35 = g
1 pt	=	½ L	1 in	=	2.5 cm	300°F	=	149°C	lb × 0.453 = kg
1 qt	=	1 L	5 in	=	12.7 cm	275°F	=	135°C	in × 2.54 = cm
1 gal	=	4.4 L	9 in	=	23 cm	250°F	=	121°C	(°F − 32) × 0.556 = °C

More books from
FOOD&WINE

Holiday

Celebrate the joy of the season with this collection of more than 300 recipes that will become holiday favorites at gatherings large and small. Whether hosting a festive holiday party, preparing a cozy family brunch, or baking tempting cookies for platters, you'll find trusted recipes to share.

One Pot Meals

Getting a delicious dinner on the table is a snap when the whole thing comes together in just one pot, slow cooker, skillet, or sheet pan. Including hearty soups and stews, vegetarian entrees, breakfast favorites, and decadent desserts, this is a must-have collection for busy cooks.

Pasta

This book features pasta and noodle dishes from around the world. From weeknight dinners to handmade pastas and special Sunday suppers, you'll find the perfect pasta dish for every occasion. It includes basic sauce recipes, step-by-step techniques, and chef secrets. It's a must-have for every home cook.